The Year's Work in Medievalism

Edited by Gwendolyn A. Morgan

XX and XXI
2005 and 2006

Wipf & Stock Publishers
Eugene, Oregon

The Year's Work in Medievalism
Series Editor, Gwendolyn Morgan

The Year's Work in Medievalism, volumes XX and XXI, is based upon but not restricted to the proceedings of the International Conference on Medievalism for those years, organized by the Director of Conferences of for the International Society for the Study of Medievalism, Gwendolyn Morgan, and conference hosts, for 2005 Karl Fugelso of Towson University, and for 2006 Clare Simmons of the Ohio State University. *The Year's Work in Medievalism* also publishes bibliographies, book reviews, and announcements of conferences and other events.

The 2005 and 2006 volumes are indexed in *The Modern Language Association International Bibliography.*

Copyright © *Studies in Medievalism* 2007

ISBN 978-4982-5046-7

First published in 2006 by Wipf and Stock Publishers
199 West 8th Ave., Suite 3
Eugene, OR 97401
http://www.wipfandstock.com/Publish.htm
for *Studies in Medievalism*

The Year's Work in Medievalism is an imprint of *Studies in Medievalism*. For the series, generally, write Gwendolyn Morgan, Editor, *The Year's Work in Medievalism,* Department of English, Montana State University, Bozeman, MT 59717.

Introduction

Gwendolyn A. Morgan

This double issue of *The Year's Work in Medievalism* owes its format to several factors, the most important being that holding the already delayed 2005 volume by only a few months allowed me to produce two strongly themed collections rather than two eclectic mixtures of essays. However, since essays from 2005 and 2006 are found in both volumes, it seemed logical to make them a single issue and thereby avoid any confusion in publication dates. The result, then, is that the first volume included herein contains essays focusing on medievalism as a means of exploring of sexuality and gender issues, while the second contains those examining the contrast between the medieval past and the nineteenth- and twentieth-century presents, not as nostalgia for a bygone age but as a remedy for the current and a plan for the future. As always, the contributions for these volumes are based upon, but not limited to, papers presented at the International Conference on Medievalism and sessions sponsored by the International Society for the Study of Medievalism at other conferences, primarily those at Kalamazoo, Michigan and Leeds, England.

Re-inventing Medieval Sexuality

The first issue in the present collection (volume XX) considers how contemporary fiction re-imagines medieval sexuality as a means of addressing today's unresolved issues associated with gender and sexual preference. Taking on the most traditional of feminist complaints—inequality in the workplace—Katya Skow notes the preponderance of recent German novels positing successful women entrepreneurs in the Middle Ages, an age notorious for its *lack* of feminine professional power. Ultimately, she links their popularity to the persistence of the problem in Germany's workforce, an issue, she asserts, which the media and politicians are loathe to address. This attitude is reflected in the pervasive motif of cross-gendering and identity-switching necessary for the protagonists of such fiction to achieve their professional goals, along with the forced choice, at one level or another, between career and the traditional feminine role of wife and mother. On the one hand, the sub-genre's popularity indicates that women recognize their disadvantages and seek recognition of and restitution for them. On the other, the fact that the successful protagonist must either eschew love, give up her career once she marries, or continue her business under—or behind—her husband's aegis indicates that the "powerfrauen" of such novels, like contemporary German women, have yet to be fully empowered.

Kara Cahill's essay generalizes the issue of power imbalance between the genders as it is addressed in Leslie Steven's appropriation of the *droit de seigneur* tradition in her play *The Lovers*. Cahill examines how "historical" and "psychoanalytical" explanations of the assumed medieval practice intertwine with popular (mis)conceptions, especially as regards the play's reception in its short 1956 Broadway run. Stevens' drama moves beyond the traditional conflict inherent in the *droit*—that between lord and husband for possession of the female—to focus on the opposing desires within the female herself. She imbues Douane, her protagonist, with a strong libido and a will to transgress boundaries, as well as a sense of her own contradictory desires. These allow Douane to remove herself from male control, symbolized by her suicide and the subsequent deaths of both males in their feud for her body, but the utter annihilation in the ending, along with the fact that it is possession of the woman's empty physical shell which underlies it, indicates that the female can only exercise control over her sexuality in a negative manner. The play's almost universal rejection at that time, Cahill concludes, resulted from the unreadiness of American society to admit that female sexuality and social roles were at odds. Only a quarter of a century after the first feminist movement can Stevens' bald demand that the disjunction between expectation and reality for women find acceptance.

Peter Christensen's survey of recent novels centering on Gilles de Rais moves the focus from heterosexual feminine to queer sexuality. As is the usual practice in historical fiction, the various authors recast Gilles to further their own social agendas. The novels range in vision from traditional condemnation of Gilles as depraved monster to assertions that his reputation results from political conspiracy. Their stances on his sexuality are equally diverse. Some authors center on his homosexuality, others on his pedophilia; some condemn one or both, others exhibit quasi-acceptance of them. Christensen suggests they do so as part of the greater contemporary debate over the rights of both marginalized groups. Implicit in all, however, is the sense that the surge of contemporary interest in Gilles rises, at least in part, from his association with Joan of Arc, herself recently resurrected as, among other things, a poster girl for lesbian rights but within the context of her own age necessarily a virgin and hence asexual.

Indeed, the centrality of virginity to the medieval female saint is a major issue addressed by Anita Hembold in her examination of Tobias Wolff's "In the Garden of the American Martyrs," which appropriates medieval sexuality for the purpose of moving beyond it. Hembold observes that Wolff's story is, in fact, an adaptation of the medieval genre of the female saint's life, which in the original form placed inordinate emphasis on the saint's virginity or chastity, both as virtue and as focus of conflict in her struggle to retain it. Wolff's tale adapts each stage in the formula not, however, to a sexual crisis but to a professional, as the protagonist moves from recognizing her own cowardice and lack of integrity as a history professor, through the various attempts to satisfy both outside expectations and her own conscience, and ultimately to the willing sacrifice of her professional life to inner conviction. Nonetheless, the story is not merely the adaptation of a spiritual journey; it is a criticism of the soullessness of contemporary academe. Moreover, it emphasizes its connection to the medieval conventions of the saint's life by introducing a subplot focusing on chastity. An old friend responsible for the protagonist's sham interview at a prestigious college continually relates details of her extramarital affairs. The same friend is everything the protagonist is no longer: without integrity or compassion, professionally parasitic, and spiritually barren. In this apparently unimportant subplot, the author's equation of sexual promiscuity to the immorality of American business practices is unmistakable.

The final essay in *Year's Work in Medievalism: 2005*, Cory Rushton's discussion of miscegenation in medieval and modern fantasy, bridges, I hope successfully, to the following issue. Beginning with the medieval romance *Sir Gowther*, Rushton examines the progress of the hero from half-demon to saint, noting that the difference between Gowther's case and other medieval tales results from the motivation of the sexual encounter resulting in his conception. His formerly barren mother prays to conceive—no matter how. Without any sense of bending to divine will, she in essence curses herself and her son. It is Gowther's recognition of his own free will, and his subsequent submission to correction and penance imposed by the Church, which set him on the path of redemption and ultimately sainthood. In other words, the poet uses his tale as a metaphor for the essential human choice between good and evil, and the salvation which results from the correct decision. The same metaphor, and very much to the same end, according to Rushton, appears in Tolkien's fiction. The children of human-elf unions are beneficial, strengthening humankind and forging alliances which help rid the world of demonic threat. On the other hand, Orcs represent a similar but unholy union (whether the corruption of Elf by human or wizard, or the offspring of demon and human), and the Uruk-hai a conscious usurpation of God's power to create life in cross-breeding Orcs and Men. As Rushton's examination illustrates, such unions, when made in accordance with divine will, produce positive effects; those in rebellion against it create an inherently evil travesty of a cross-breed. In Terry Pratchett's Discworld series, Rushton finds the logical conclusion of the miscegenation of Tolkien's fantasy, in which the choice between good and evil literally becomes one between life and death. The protagonist, Susan, is Death's granddaughter and, from him, has inherited unusual powers. Her choice, much against Death's wishes, is to use them to assist humanity in its development. The essential theme of *Sir Gowther* remains. What makes the modern tales different is that they concentrate not on the individual salvation but upon the future redemption of the human race.

The Once and Future Middle Ages
Frequently, we interpret the retreat into the medieval in protest of the present as mere nostalgia. However, *The Year's Work in Medievalism: 2006* (XXI)

presents essays that deliberately contradict this, examining how authors and film-makers employ the Middle Ages not as retreat but as stepping stone to the future, recalling their moral code to revitalize that of the artist's own age. In other words, the redemptive nature of miscegenation in Rushton's analysis of modern fantasy moves to a philosophical plane.

Karen Borresen Walsh's contribution examines how film-makers adapt references to the medieval past to ensure the salvation of the future in translating J.K. Rowling's Harry Potter series to the big screen. Indeed, while the films take their cue from Rowling's books, which exude references to the period, they also do much more. Evoking two disparate visions of the period—the barbaric and romantic Middle Ages, to borrow Eco's terms—and pitting them against each other, they not only underscore the inhumanity and destructive nature of the Dark Wizard and Muggle worlds, they also indicate that the good wizard society teeters on the brink of collapse from its own outmoded traditions, true in form but not in spirit to the idealized past. It is, says Walsh, up to Harry to revitalize the best of the romantic Middle Ages beyond mere tradition and combine it with the best of Muggle culture to ensure a humane, productive, and peaceful future for both races. Walsh elucidates how this is carried out, not with dialogue or scenes lifted directly from Rowling's texts, but by artistically manipulating various cinematic techniques (lighting, scenery, sound-track, camera angle, and so forth), in concert with foregrounding what appeared as insignificant details in the books and, indeed, inventing entirely new scenes to make the point. More than merely comparing, the Potter series filmmakers condemn both visions of the past as inadequate for the future.

Delving even deeper into popular culture, Michael Cramer's essay explores the development of the Society for Creative Anachronism during the 1960's and '70's as a protest against the violence and inhumanity of modern American culture by returning to an age in which, according to the popular imagination, "just war was possible" and morality won out over evil. Nonetheless, as Cramer points out, many early SCA members deliberately contradicted the idea that the movement was a retreat into nostalgia by being deliberately *un*-time-bound in their costumes, role-playing, and ideologies, making reference to the classical as well as the medieval period, combining tunics and swords with jeans and engineer boots to assert themselves as ultimately contemporary. In a sense, their melding of past and present illustrates T.S. Eliot's thesis that we are a sum of all that has come before us, individually and communally, and that Time Future is indeed contained in Time Present and Time Past. Thus, the SCA resurrection of a popular notion of medieval honor and justice blends it with their own sense of humaneness to create a stronger ideology for the future.

With Young-Min Han's analysis of *The Mill on the Floss*, we return to more conventional literary analysis, but not to critical consensus. As Han suggests, at first glance Eliot appears to be criticizing her own time by comparing it unfavorably with the medieval past, through the legend of St. Ogg, and is thus in line with other manifestations of nineteenth-century nostalgia. However, as Han points out, Eliot departs from Victorian medievalism by positing that the individual "sympathy" and humaneness which sufficed for communal salvation in the Middle Ages were not longer enough in her own age, which had become too distanced from nature in a too-long history of "man's inhumanity to man." Instead, the community as a whole must embrace that same faculty of sympathy, achieved through a recollection of childhood *caritas* in Nature (a sensibility obviously born of her Romantic predecessors), in place of a *particular* individual (the medieval saint), in order to rehabilitate contemporary society. Saints, consequently, no longer can exist—neither Maggie nor Mrs. Tulliver's gentle heart can set an example for nor overcome the cruelty of a community so far gone—and everyday individuals acting in concert with each other must take their place.

The collection ends with Karl Fugelso's playful examination of contemporary theories of time, not as a continuum but as a dimension, allowing a kind of time travel which would permit medieval masters to be influenced by much later artists, using William Blake's illustrations of Dante's *Divine Comedy* as a focus. The early illustrations and illuminations exhibit uncanny likenesses to Blake's work, explained neither by Blake's reference to art he could never have known nor by any continuing tradition carried down to him by intervening artistic schools. While Fugelso concludes that such apparent "reverse time continuum" influences are definitely NOT the result of a time warp, he does conclude that they are instead the products of universal rules in art which transcend time, in a sense proving the generality of contemporary theory where he disproves the particular. In adhering to such universal rules, in their re-discovery and re-application, the future can indeed reach new artistic heights.

The constant, then, among the essays of the 2005 and 2006 issues of *The Year's Work in Medievalism* contained herein is that the medieval past is not merely our heritage but our future. We have, on some level, moved past Eco's contention that we return to the Middle Ages as to our childhood, with the purpose of explaining our problems and justifying our ideologies. We advocate not a return but a re-discovery and adaptation, recognizing the weaknesses of that era along with its strengths and demanding that we, like Harry Potter, combine them with our own if we our to survive our own inhumanity. And, if the implications of Karl Fugelso's essay are correct, this is what was meant to be all along, for the universal laws governing the human condition are not bound by time but always out there, like Tolkien's great cycle of stories, to be tapped into at any time, whenever we need them to explain, understand, remedy, or revitalize.

MONTANA STATE UNIVERSITY

Volume XX
2005

Medieval 'Powerfrauen' in Popular German Literature

Katya Skow

Iny Lorenz's *Die Goldhändlerin* and Ines Thorn's *Die Pelzhändlerin* share an ending—that would be the grammatical suffix "in"—with a growing list of historical novels. In German, "in" can be appended to agent nouns to form elegantly the feminine counter-part. As in English master becomes mistress and poet becomes poetess, so in German "Lehrer"—or teacher—becomes "Lehrerin"—or female teacher, and "Pelzhändler"—fur dealer—becomes "Pelzhändlerin"—woman, or female fur dealer. Here are some, but not all, of the recent titles I have come across: *Die Totenwäscherin* (The Female Corpse Washer), *Die Zuckerbäckerin* (The Female Confectioner), *Die Wagenlenkerin* (The Female Charioteer), *Die Philosophin* (The Female Philosopher), *Die Salzbaronin* (The Salt Baroness), *Die Glasbläserin* (The Female Glass Blower), and possibly the strangest, *"Die Kastratin"*, which as many of you will surmise means the female eunich. As we gather from the above list, the prevalence of female job titles as book titles in German popular fiction occurs too frequently to be coincidental. A quick glance in a bookstore finds these books temptingly grouped together; likewise, the German Amazon website links the titles so that if you click on one, the others are displayed as suggestions. Both the sheer number of the titles, and the way they are grouped by bookstores online and off, signal an acknowledged trend that should be examined.

The settings for the novels I just listed span history from Ancient Greece through post-reunification Germany. The medieval component includes *Die Safranhändlerin* (Female Saffron Dealer), *Die Kastellanin* (The Female Keeper of the Castle), *Die Rechenkünstlerin* (The Female Mathematician), *Die Raubritterin* (The Female Robber Knight), and, of course, the two that are the subject of this paper—*Die Goldhändlerin* and *Die Pelzhändlerin*.

These books are by no means "bodice rippers." They present themselves as respectable and informative historical novels. Cleo McNelly Kearns remarks on the popularity of this genre in her study "Dubious pleasures: Dorothy Dunnet and the historical novel," commenting that "only historical novels, after all, offer [...] slightly gender-determined, comfortable, rather middle-brow pleasures" (36). The reader of such a novel expects to be educated as well as entertained, is familiar with "good" literature, and is looking for some lighter reading with the veneer of respectability. The covers of these novels highlight this aspect of genteel respectability, often depicting scenes from paintings. My copy of *Die Safranhändlerin,* for example, has the Salome portion of Titian's *Salome* (c.1550), and *Die Rechenkünstlerin* sports a painting by the Renaissance painter Colantonio called "San Gerolamo and the lion."

The novels are full of period ambiance and tantalizing facts, giving the impression of painstaking research and an aura of credibility. The plots, although not exactly formulaic, are certainly predictable, and in general they are less compelling than the atmosphere.

Not only do most of these novels feature townspeople or peasants, the protagonists are all women. Gone is the "nostalgie de la cour," described by Kearns as "a form in which royal blood, aristocratic manners, and the shenanigans of kings and queens take precedence over the cultivation of sheep and cabbages or even, for the most part, the solid laudable accumulations of investment capital" (37). The novels that are the subject of this paper are solidly rooted in the lower and middle classes. Kearns's observation that "no one wants to fantasize herself powerless and a peasant, or plump and middle class, even if ever so beautiful and good" (37), no longer seems to pertain. One would think her logic beyond dispute, but the recent titles of historical fiction—at least in Germany—indicate otherwise. People now prefer to read about more mundane aspects of life and fantasize about their historical counterparts. The improbable natures of the plots are offset by tantalizing facts about middle-class life in late-medieval German cities.

The Middle Ages enjoy incredible popularity as a setting for contemporary literature and film. Mysteries and novels set in medieval Europe are multiplying exponentially, and films such as *The Name of the Rose* (1986) and *Braveheart* (1995) were commercially successful, to say the least. In his article on the postmodern historical novel, Ansgar Nünning comments on the recent popularity of historical fiction (my translation):

> In a time in which the borders between reality and fiction are becoming more and more blurred by the growing influence of the media, great significance is allocated to the representation of history in narrative, and the conventional idea of the relationship between literature and historiography has lost its validity. The contemporary historical novel is suddenly back in trend (36).[1]

In a study on historical detective novels, Uwe Baumann mentions the large number of visitors at historical exhibits and the high sales of history books as well, leading to a general reawakening of the historical novel since the beginning of the eighties. The eighties and early nineties saw a surge in historical research on medieval *Alltag* and medieval women. Books like Carlo Ginzburg's 1976 *Il formaggio e il vermi* (English translation, *The Cheese and the Worms*, Baltimore: Johns Hopkins, 1980) and Steven Ozment's 1986 *Magdalena and Balthazar* (New Haven: Yale UP) drew attention to the life of farmers and burghers, respectively. Scholars such as Barbara Hanawalt, Merry Wiesner, Susan Mosher Stuard, and Natalie Zemon Davis focused research on the medieval women who had, until then, been nameless.[2] Instead of Eleanor of Aquitane and her four kings, they researched women in trade, women in cities, and women as wives and mothers. The subjects of these studies did not live in castles or palaces, but rather in hovels, in smelly townhouses, or in brothels.

The trend in historical fiction that is the subject of this paper is clearly an offshoot of this recent focus in historical research. Medieval who-done-its no longer attempt to uncover the murderer of the little princes in the tower. Their new protagonists reflect modern research and the previously silent are given voices as Marcella, the Safron Dealer, or Sybille, the Furrier, their professions reflecting the knowledge that women were active in trades. Likewise, medieval novels no longer dwell on royalty, and Isabella d'Este has made way for Ratsfrau Alheyd. If, along the way, the female protagonists become too empowered or manage to pull off coups that are unlikely given the time frame, it is all in the name of progress…or is it?

Both Lorentz's *Die Goldhändlerin* and Thorn's *Die Pelzhändlerin* are set in the fifteenth century and posit a somewhat unlikely breaking of the medieval "ordo," the code that regulated social and gender hierarchies. In the former, a girl masquerades as a boy, becoming very successful in a masculine business. The latter has as its primary transgression against the "ordo" one of social hierarchy. A young woman born into a low social caste assumes the identity of a wealthy member of the newly powerful burgher class. Not only does she successfully navigate her jump into prosperity, she also becomes a successful business woman, thus making another assault on the medieval order of things.

Lorentz's 2004 *Goldhändlerin* centers on breaking the medieval gender order. Lea, a young Jewish girl, is tempted by circumstance to take on the identity of her brother. Only as a man can she carry on the family business of banking after her father and elder brother die. She masquerades quite successfully as a male and becomes a well-known and respected banker. She avoids discovery for years, only to be betrayed by the jealousy of her own family. Although her true sex is never revealed outside her home, and thus does not cause any public outrage, her acting as a man causes much consternation within the family and truly reflects a breaking of the code. Lea's success provides another launching point for the plot—the treatment of Jews in late-medieval Germany. In addition to hiding her sex, Lea, as a Jew, must be careful not to flaunt or even reveal her wealth for fear of persecution. Her wealth and success as a Jew also go against the perceived order of things, at least from a Christian perspective.

The main premise of this story, the gender/identity switch, is made believable. The protagonist is unusually tall for a woman. As she matures, she employs the usual tactics of binding her breasts and speaking in a low voice. Several scenes describe the difficulties of keeping her gender secret while living with others in close quarters. Nonetheless, potential problems are explained away, and the plot progresses unhindered. The gender switch is prefaced by descriptions of the status quo that illustrate the necessity for it. Towards the beginning of the novel, Lea, the hero/ine, is put in her place by her much younger brother, and "because she was only a girl, she had to obey him" (10).[3] In addition "her father ignored her questions or scolded her because it wasn't fitting for a girl to show the desire for knowledge" (11).[4] Even her appearance is criticized. She is too tall, and her nose is "too long for a girl" (14).[5] Later, she is complimented by a respected doctor on her ability in medicine. She has just saved her younger brother's life by successfully setting a complicated break in his leg. The doctor states, that "if a girl were allowed to become a doctor, [he] would train her immediately" (81).[6] Thus, when Lea's father and elder brother die, it has already been made clear to her that the only way she can rescue the family's fortunes is to assume her brother's identity. Neither society at large, nor the closer confines of her Jewish community, is ready to conduct business with a girl.

Once the necessity of her action has been established, the plot twists and turns as Lea wanders through late fifteenth-century Germany investing her money—often with uncharacteristic rashness (for a girl, that is)—and reaping her profits. At one point, she is able to help the Duke of Burgundy, later Emperor Maximillian I, solve his money problems in return for some lucrative wine monopolies. In another episode, Lea meets Columbus and is given credit for convincing Isabella of Spain to finance his venture. There is, of course, a love interest—a man modern enough to recognize and respect her abilities as a woman. At the end of the novel they are united, and Lea quite literally puts her skirts back on and marries her Orlando. Interestingly enough, one of the last scenes in the book shows her highly pregnant and busily running her new family's not inconsiderable shipping business.

Thorn's 2005 *Pelzhändlerin* is also the story of a successful identity switch. The young daughter of a washerwoman assumes without detection the identity of the daughter of the rich fur dealer who employs her mother. The daughter dies while away at a convent school, and her father has a heart attack upon hearing the news. Luisa, who had always borne a striking resemblance to the daughter of the house, quietly becomes Sybille. Because she is quick and smart, she is able to carry off the coup. The new Sybille becomes wildly successful as a furrier, waking the envy of her male counterparts. Since she has transgressed against both the medieval social and gender orders, she lives in a mixture of guilt for what she's done and fear of discovery.

Even before Luisa becomes Sybille, she has ideas above her station. She loses her good position as a washerwoman in a local household because of her "Hochmut," or pride (23). She was caught trying on her mistress's dress in front of a mirror of "highly polished metal" (a tasty bit of medieval realia).[7] Luisa's explanation for her transgression is that she wanted to see if the dress looked better on her than on her mistress (24), belying her subconscious quarrel with the unbending order of the medieval world. She realizes that "she was a washerwoman, and not made for frills and trinkets" (24).[8] Even Luisa's mother has problems with the medieval hierarchy. She wants Luisa to have an easier and better life than she, and it is she who instigates the switch.

Once Luisa has performed the identity swap, she notices that she is measured by her deeds, and "not by her origins, not by her birth, perhaps not even by the fact that she wants to be someone else." "What is important is what I make of it" she says (39).[9] She soon realizes that her illegitimate birth and poor origins do not make her less deserving (40). As Sybille, however, she learns that, by assuming a higher station in life, she must sacrifice some of her independence as a woman. She notes that the kitchen is the "only room in which the woman has the say" (49).[10] When she has to appear before the furriers' guild to claim her inheritance, she is belittled and mocked because she is a woman (56). The Guild Master adds, "Thinking is nothing for woman. Buy yourself a few new dresses and a few trinkets" (61).[11] Later, when Sybille starts to make changes in the shop, her husband cautions her not to act like a man and reminds her that her place is in the kitchen (80).

Sybille nonetheless persists in running her business, adding to her transgression of aiming above her station that of assuming the man's role in both home and business. Although her identity switch remains a secret, she engenders the wrath of two consecutive husbands, the vast majority of the guild of furriers, and most of the rest of the town. While she is trying to win a place in the town hierarchy, she comes up with the concept of name brands (196), manufactures the first "muff" (202), and becomes the first paid German interior designer. The love interest in this novel is an enlightened doctor, much influenced by the culture and ideas of the Italian Renaissance. This conveniently explains his liberal views regarding professional women.

In her study on medievalism in modern culture, Angela Jane Weisl notes how "medieval images are used to construct new conflicts as old ones, reclaiming a past to incite the present to certain reductionist modes of thought and behavior." The novels I have just described, as well as many of the other similarly-titled texts listed above, all share an image—that of a powerful woman who shapes her own existence—and a theme—women upsetting the medieval status quo. Whether it is as a robber knight, saffron dealer, or fur dealer, the title figure in these novels takes control of her circumstances to an unusual, if not an improbable, degree. If, as Weisl points out, this modern image of the role of women in medieval times reflects a new conflict, then what is the conflict? Women in modern Germany are an integral part of that country's workforce and their role is no longer questioned, at least openly. Women are involved in government to a greater degree than even in the United States. A significant percentage of Germany's parliament is female, for example, and the new chancellor is a woman. What possible conflict could the prevalence of these historical novels be signaling?

It is true that women are accepted members of business, academia, and government in Germany, but how has this been achieved? How seamlessly are women able to merge their professional and private lives? And what about the strictures placed on women who want both a profession and a family? I suspect that these are the modern conflicts that are subtly, or perhaps not so subtly, presented in these novels. In *Die Goldhändlerin*, Lea wears women's clothing when she is home, and after she marries, she wears them when working—which she does from home—as well. Once she gives up on the cross-dressing, Lea no longer represents the family business in public. Obviously, she wants to be both successful in business and a woman, not one or the other. Because of her forward-thinking husband, combining the two is not a problem, as long as it stays within the home's four walls.

In contrast, in *Die Pelzhändlerin*, Sybille is unable to combine her profession with her love life. Although her lover is modern in that respect, the medieval guild system requires that she marry a master furrier in order to keep her business. Unfortunately, her lover is a doctor, not a furrier, and she is unwilling to sacrifice her career. When Sybille does not find happiness in trying to combine the two, she finally comes to the conclusion that love is more important. It is not until she gives up all pretensions to material gain and literally takes to the road with a hand cart that she is united with her man.

In *Die Goldhändlerin*, Lea is ultimately able to have both a family and a career because she remains behind the scenes and works from home. The irreconcilable dichotomy between the two is much starker in *Die Pelzhändlerin*. Sybille cannot have both because she is not willing to work behind the scenes. Since a compromise is not possible, she must choose. The message that combining career and family is impossible and that, in the general scheme of things, the latter should win out—even if you do invent the concept of name-brand marketing—is transparent.

That the protagonists in the two works are somewhat anachronistic and improbable does not matter, for they are only meant to signal a lack in our society. As the German authors exiled by the Third Reich and authors of the more recent GDR used the medium of the historical novel to reflect contemporary issues, so too do these authors. As Weisl maintains: "The contemporary presence of medievalism has the surprising result of questioning the assumption that between now and the Middle Ages lies an 'unpassable abyss,' a divide of time, distance, and often language"(3). The message that today's women confront many of the same difficulties faced by women in the fifteenth century is not popular, and the idea that combining love and/or family and career successfully is rare and not necessarily to be emulated, is not how most women in contemporary Germany want to think of themselves. This brings us back to the titles of the novels, which name the profession of the female protagonist. Although, at first glance, the titles promise empowerment, perhaps they do just the opposite. Perhaps the emphasis on the profession at the expense of the individual in the titles is actually meant to bring things back into perspective, and to silence the women to whom they have just given voice.

THE CITADEL

NOTES

[1] The translations into English that appear in the main body of the text are my own. The original German is given in the endnote. In this case, the original German is as follows: "In einer Zeit, in der die Grenzen zwischen Realität und Fiktion allein durch den wachsenden Einfluß der Medien immer mehr verschwimmen, in der Narrativität wieder eine große Bedeutung für die Darstellung von Geschichte zugemessen wird und in der herkömmliche Vortellungen vom Verhältnis zwischen Literatur und Historiographie ihre Gültigkeit verloren haben, liegt der zeitgenössische historische Roman plötzlich wieder ganz im Trend."

[2] A selection of scholarly works about women and *Alltag* includes: Merry Wiesner, *Women and Gender in Early Modern Europe* (Cambridge: Cambridge UP, 1993), Beatrice Gottlieb, *The Family in the Western World from the Black Death to the Industrial Age* (New York and Oxford: Oxford UP, 1993), *Women in Reformation and Counter-Reformation Europe. Private and Public Worlds*, ed. Sherrin Marshall (Bloomington and Indianapolis: Indiana UP, 1989), *Sisters and Workers in the Middle Ages*, eds. Judith M. Bennett, Elizabeth A. Clark, Jean F. O'Barr, B. Anne Vilen, and Sarah Westphal-Wihl (Chicago and London: U of Chicago P, 1989), *Women and Work in Preindustrial Europe*, ed. Barbara Hanawalt (Bloomington: Indiana UP, 1986).

[3] "und weil sie nur ein Mädchen war, hatte sie ihm zu gehorchen" (10).

[4] "Wenn sie etwas wissen wollte, überhörte der Vater zumeist ihre Fragen oder tadelte sie sogar, weil es sich nicht gehörte, dass ein Mädchen Wissbegier zeigte" (11).

[5] "die für ein Mädchen jedoch etwas zu lang war" (14).

[6] "Wenn ein Mädchen Wundärztin werden dürfte, würde ich dich auf der Stelle ausbilden" (81).

[7] "vor dem Spiegel aus poliertem Metal" (23).

[8] "Sie war eine Wäscherin und nicht gemacht für Putz und Tand" (24).

[9] "Nicht an [ihrer] Herkunft, nicht an [ihrer] Geburt, vielleicht nicht einmal daran, dass ich eine andere sein möchte. Wichtig ist, was ich daraus mache" (39).

[10] "Der einzige Raum, in dem die Frau das Sagen hatte" (49).

[11] "Nachdenken ist nicht Sache der Weiber. Kauf die lieber ein paar neue Kleider, ein bisschen Tand dazu" (61).

WORKS CITED

Baumann, Uwe. "Die historischen Kriminalromane von Paul Doherty" *Unterhaltungsliteratur der achtziger und neunziger Jahre*, eds. Dieter Petzold and Eberhard Späth, *Erlanger Forschungen. Reihe A. Geisteswissenschafter. Band 81.* Erlangen: Universitätsbund Erlangen-Nürnberg, 1998): 7-27.

Durst-Benning, Petra. *Die Glasbläserin.* München: Econ Ullstein List Verlag, 2000.

_____. *Die Salzbaronin.* München: Econ Ullstein List Verlag, 2000.

_____. *Die Zuckerbäckerin.* Düsseldorf und München: Econ & List Verlag, 1997.

Glaesener, Helga. *Die Rechenkünstlerin.* München: Paul List Verlag, 1998.

_____. *Die Safranhändlerin.* München: Paul List Verlag, 1997.

Hegewisch, Helga. *Die Totenwäscherin.* München: Econ Ullstein List Verlag, 2000.

Kearns, Cleo McNelly. "Dubious pleasures: Dorothy Dunnet and the Historical Novel" *Critical Quarterly* 32.1 (1990): 36-48.

Köster-Lösche, Kari. *Die Raubritterin.* München: Econ Ullstein Verlag, 2000.

_____. *Die Wagenlenkerin.* München: Econ Ullstein Verlag, 2000.

Lorentz, Iny. *Die Goldhändlerin.* München: Knaur Taschenbuch, 2004.

_____. *Die Kastellanin.* München: Knaur, 2005).

_____. *Die Kastratin.* München: Knaur, 2003.

Prange, Peter. *Die Philosophin.* München: Knaur, 2004.

Thorn, Ines. *Die Pelzhändlerin.* Reinbek: Rowohlt Verlag, 2005.

Weisel, Angela Jane. The Persistence of Medievalism: Narrative Adventures in Contemporary Culture (New York: Palgrave Macmillan, 2003).

Around 1956:The *Droit de Seigneur* on Broadway

Kara Cahill

Leslie Stevens's play *The Lovers,* which had a brief four-day run on Broadway at the Martin Beck Theater in 1956, recaptures the Romanticism of the Middle Ages through a dramatic lens, depicting the *droit de seigneur* as a *bona fide* tradition and law, unquestioned by society, both the laymen and clergy. The cultural layering of sexual violence in some Romantic works offers a particularly important lens for insight into medieval and modern attitudes. Violence in such a society is viewed as sexually pleasurable, and the culture condones physical and emotional abuse of women as normative behavior. However, the word "rape" connotes a multiplicity of linguistic meanings in a broad semantic field. As Hélène Cixous suggests, "[l]anguage conceals an invincible adversary because it is the language of men and their grammar. We mustn't leave them a single place that's any more theirs alone than we are"[1] (257). It is notable that medieval culture fails to offer a single term that designates forced intercourse; instead, it relies on metaphor and lexematic exchanges that do not clearly signify of a sexual assault. The terms *droit de cuissage, droit du seigneur,* and *jus primae noctis* are utilized interchangeably in the descriptions of this act throughout the literature and legal documentation of the last several centuries. Furthermore, a review of the chivalric code introduces the concomitant element of force.

During the middle and latter twelfth century, the rubric of chivalry denotes effort, power, force, heroism, strength, bravura, and manliness. Tracing the history of early written accounts of forced intercourse, the romances of this era, such as Chrétien de Troyes' *Le Conte du Graal, Le Chevalier de la Charette,* and *Eric and Enide,* employ the word *esforcer* for the concept of rape, and its use implied that rape was systemic in feudal hegemony.[2] The Latin word *rapere,* which appears in several medieval texts, means an appropriation, or theft, or abduction, the carrying off by force. The Latin *raptus,* when considered in conjunction with abduction, shifts meaning towards sexuality: that of abduction by violence for the purposes of forced intercourse. Kathryn Gravdahl argues, "Never would a [medieval] woman dare say with her own mouth what she desires so much [as rape]; but it pleases her greatly when someone takes her against her will, regardless of how it comes about. A maiden *suddenly ravished* has great joy, no matter what she says."[3] By the fourteenth century, the word "ravishment" began to appear, signifying a state of being carried away emotionally. Beyond this psychological troping lies the sexual trope: a state of rapture or extreme sexual pleasure or joy. In reality, sexual violence [rape] rarely produces sexual pleasure or joy. However, medieval discourse often assumes that whatever is attractive begs to be ravished: carried off, seized, or raped. The ideas of a woman's attractiveness and a man's desire to rape are conflated in ravishment. Such a transformation is inflected by a shift in gender coding. *Ravrir,* the Old French word derived from the Latin *rapier,* if taken literally, meant that it was the male who ravished the female. When the term is employed in the realm of the figurative, it is the female who is ravishing, who causes the male to be carried away, and who is responsible for any ensuing sexual acts[4]. Thus, a woman's natural beauty causes her to be victimized. When "rape" and "ravishment" are blended linguistically within the Romantic troping of ravishment, the literal meaning of sexual violence and the responsibility for it are blurred.

The *jus primae noctis*[5] remains a locus in which women can re-examine their position within the framework of society, both ancient and modern. Throughout history, rape has been treated as pardonable both by the secular authorities and by the Roman Catholic Church, a view that completely ignores the woman who has been raped and silences her response. I argue, Leslie Stevens' *The Lovers* actively promotes the continuation of a rape culture in contemporary society through the use of the *droit de cuissage.* Politics, economics, and gender all factor into power relationships of the Middle Ages. In the dialectic of the master and the peasant maid as presented in this drama, the tyranny of power and the use of sexuality as an emblem for the procurement and retention of social power and status drive the title character, Chrysagon, forward. Moreover, the male-centered camera gaze alters the perception of the action in the minds of the audience and is coded to exclude the feminine viewpoint.

Perhaps the appeal of the *jus primae noctis,* or *droit de seigneur* as it is often called, for contemporary audiences is that it reinforces the idea that there is no such thing as a "normal" life, for behind the closed doors of an individual's private life lurks the violent and bizarre, suppressed sexuality gone rampant, the mayhem, and the various peculiarities that encompass a modern life. And, quite possibly, modernocentrism really is not so different from the medieval, after all. Society has been attempting to regulate sexuality since the beginning of recorded history. Sexual regulation was a primary focus of early canon law and remains a large part of the public sphere today. Society has, as its primary goal, the desire to place limitations on the individual, to decrease rights and entitlements, supposedly for the greater good of all inhabitants. History, religion, and our community are all circles that shape individual lives, and we have the power to re-shape our lives, to act upon the narrative frames in which we exist. The battle for freedom—of thought, action, and sexual expression—is a battle each individual must wage against reigning authorities, be they church, state, or other entities. Such battles become quality defenses, akin to works of art. To extend the boundaries of the metaphorical frontier, to expand the possibilities of one's life, and to achieve an expansion of the self, one must push outwards against the unknown.

Startlingly unique to this play is the positive light which is shed upon the practice with regards to the female perspective; although a woman's viewpoint is rare within the body of literature and historical records relating to the *droit de seigneur*, Stevens portrays the peasant bride heroine, Douane, as being receptive to the advances of the overlord Chrysagon. However, the positive aspects are tempered by the limited range of choice that Douane is given by her position within the class structure. The expectation of violence was the cultural norm, and as such, it was inevitable that she would suffer sexual violence from the imposition of the *droit*; therefore she tacitly acquiesces to the culture of rape, accepts the inevitability of her violation, and attempts to look for something positive in the character of Chrysagon.

The three-act play, set in the twelfth-century countryside near Flanders, opens with a pregnant young peasant woman from the Beauvaix family, Clothilde, seeking last rites for her deceased brother, Marc, and his wife, Douane, from a passing cleric, Grigoris. Grigoris initially refuses, referring the matter to the local friars, Sextus and Xegan. A second man has also died, the seigneural Lord Chrysagon; both men mortally wounded each other. The fight occurred over Chrysagon's reluctance to release Beauvaix's bride, Douane, after exacting his due privilege on the wedding night. Chrysagon's failure to return the bride to her husband caused a revolt among the serfs of the village. The bride, who had mixed emotions, torn between love for her husband and her fascination with the powerful lord, has killed herself as a final release from her dilemma. Beauvaix and Lord Chrysagon battle for possession of her body, which results in the triple fatality. However, the local friars have denied religious burial for all of them, as they died in apparent sin. At the close of the play, after Grigoris has heard the details of the *jus primae noctis* debacle, he defies his superiors within the Church to perform the burial rites.

The Lovers recasts the barbarity of the *droit de seigneur* to separate the present and the past while capitalizing on its universal interest, and I contend that Stevens' reconstruction of the social and religious context of the thirteenth-century in this drama is linked with anthropologists' views of primitive people and Sigmund Freud's notion of the Oedipal complex in relation to the taboo of virginity, which is particularly evident in the staging.

Stevens sets the stage for the introduction of the *droit du seigneur* in Act I[6] through an encounter between the Lord Chrysagon and Douane by the river. She is bathing whilst being observed by the Lord. This scene establishes the character of the Lord as an honorable gentleman; although he is a voyeur, the physical restraint he exhibits by not compromising her virginity on the spot reveals his respect for the laws and customs of the land.

Chrysagon: A virgin bride. I respect your wedding. I won't touch you. You may dress yourself and go. I-I was happy looking at you. (Act I, p. 22)

Chrysagon describes his encounter with the future bride to his brothers, Draco and Herstal De La Crux, who rise up in disbelief that he did not ravish the girl at that time, instead, awaiting his legal opportunity just after the wedding. It is during this scene that the legal concept of the *jus primae noctis* is first introduced:

> Chrysagon: She belongs to the village. We're here to protect the village! She is not one of your she-goats, Draco. She's clean. I'll take a woman—I'll take a virgin—but I won't take her the night before her wedding!
> Herstal: I was only trying to help.
> Draco: You want her?
> Chrysagon: Keep quiet.
> Draco: You can knock me through the wall. I'm only saying if you want her, you can have her.
> Chrysagon: Draco—
> Herstal: Sit down, Draco.
> Draco: Wait a minute! It's wrong tonight—I'm talking about tomorrow! Tomorrow! The wedding is tomorrow! *Le droit de seigneur*—the right of the first night!
> Herstal: *Jus primae Noctis*. It's true.
> Chrysagon: I know it.
> Herstal: You're Seigneur du Chatel
> Draco: You have the right.
> Chrysagon: To take the virginity of brides? The "right"?
> Herstal: The Barons enforce it—the Knights Ulterlec—the Sascheverals.
> Chrysagon: My Lord Escavalon?
> Draco: Yes!
> Chrysagon: Why not my father?
> Herstal: He must have—when he was young.
> Draco: Yes!
> Chrysagon: Call Austrict.
> Herstal: Draco—
> Draco: Blaise--!
> Herstal: Get him yourself!
> Chrysagon: Herstal—I want this woman. If Austrict agrees it is my right—by my honor—I'll take her! (Act I, p. 31-2)

After this honorable start, however, Chrysagon abuses his authority as the seigneur, for while the *jus primae noctis* gives him the authority to take the virginity of a newly wedded woman within his district, he cannot command the peasant bride to become his lover, even if only for one night. Had Chrysagon not seen Douane unclothed by the river, it quite conceivable that he would not, as a general custom, have invoked the *droit,* as his father was reputed to have done with some degree of regularity. But Chrysagon and his brothers seek ecclesiastical counsel from their brother, Austrict, who serves as the district church official, on the validity of the claim to the *droit*. The Catholic Church in *The Lovers* does not condone the action but rather turns a blind eye, preferring to distance the institution from the practice. However, the legal precedent has already been set and the *droit* is, therefore, recognized by the community at large as a lawful practice. Stevens reiterates the social acceptance of the *droit* in the dialogue between Probus, the peasant father of bridegroom Marc Beauvaix, and his fellow peasant contemporary Saul:

Probus: He [Chrysagon] is looking at her.
Saul: Do you think he wants her?
Probus: Yes
Saul: But not one of our women—He is a man of honor.
Probus: He has the right. To take a bride.
Saul: Probus--!
Probus: Yes—"*Le Droit de seigneur.*" (Act II, p. 38.)

Saul reacts in disbelief that Chrysagon would invoke the *droit,* sure that the Lord's sense of morality would prevent the imposition of his legal right. The *droit* was, in Saul's mind, an antiquated and barbaric custom; its historicity was problematic.

Analysis of the history of the *droit* will provide the contextual basis for Stevens's play. Alain Boureau's 1998 *The Lord's First Night* examines the *droit* from within a historical and literary reception paradigm, defining it as a myth surviving from barbarian times. Boureau argues: "The medieval antecedents of seigneurial domination have lost their relevance; the *droit du seigneur* is no longer a valid accusation in law" (15). He further states: "It has nonetheless gained a new pertinence in common discourse by recalling something primordial; perhaps the medieval custom, whether it ever existed or not, serves to transcribe extremely ancient nuptial rites related in varying degree to the taboo of virginity."[7] This concept had been explored earlier by sociologists and anthropologists.

Westermark's 1921 *The History of Human Marriage*, subtitled "A Criticism of the Hypothesis of Promiscuity: *Jus Primae Noctus,*" considers the notion of individual marriage as opposed to an ancient communal marriage concept. Through analysis of case histories, he determines that the exclusive possession of a wife could be lawfully gained, specifically if an acknowledgement of communal rights were made by the parties involved: "A recognition of this is the *jus primae noctis* accorded to a priest, king, chief, or nobleman, who is then looked upon as representative of the community after the ancient right was taken away from its male members in general" (166). In tracing the origins of the concept, Westermark finds two primary sources of documentary proof, the first, a fine (*merchet / marchet*) paid by a vassal to an overlord upon his marriage, which Westermark asserts has been "mis-interpreted" as a pecuniary reprieve from the lord's right to sleep with the bride on the wedding night. The second proof comes in the form of a fee paid to an ecclesiastical official for the right to sleep with his new bride, as otherwise, the groom was to uphold the Church's enforced policy of chastity for three days, a concept derived from Biblical references to Tobias and Sarah. Westermark remarks, "the tradition of such a right has to do not so much with a mere privilege exacted by a ruler, but with a custom rooted in some popular idea similar to those found in some parts of the world in connection with the defloration of brides or maidens" (179-80). He notes that, "Among certain peoples it is said to be the custom for a father to deflower his daughter" (190). Fear was the dominant reason given by grooms for their reluctance to engage in intercourse with virgin brides; since defloration was considered a dangerous action, many grooms preferred someone else perform the ritual. Westermark's conclusion is that the *jus primae noctis* right of a priest or lord ultimately springs from "hope of benefits resulting from intercourse with a holy or superior person or from the sexual appetite of the man who has the right; it is always the consequence of his own personal qualities or authority and cannot, therefore, be regarded as the relic of an ancient communal right" (196).

In contrast to Westermark's statement, no such religious benefit is alluded to in *The Lovers*. Chrysagon's interest in the imposition of the *droit* in his seigneury appears to be motivated purely by a desire for sexual dominance over Douane. Stevens clearly portrays his strong sexual interest in the river scene and again in his initial dialogue with Douane subsequent to his capture of her after the wedding:

Chrysagon: I want to say, "Douane, you are free to go or stay." But I am afraid you'll go and so "My Lord" orders you to keep still—
Douane: My lord.
Chrysagon: Those are the only words you know. Douane—look at me. I don't move a muscle. I brought you here to take you—and I don't touch you. I thought I would grab your hair and bend you back—I thought of crushing you down to the ground—like fighting. I should have taken you to the tower—or to the hunting house out in the forest—But I had to come here. I want the ground under us as God made it and I want you to be with me as you are. Don't say, "My Lord." Don't say it.
Douane: I wasn't going to.
Chrysagon: I can't stop giving orders. Douane—what can I tell you? I don't know soft ways. I know how to ride and—fight. Douane—what happened to me?
Douane: I don't know.

Chrysagon: When I saw you swimming there in the sunlight I wanted you
the way a stallion wants a mare... (Act II, p. 46)

In equating his desire to animal instinct, Chrysagon attempts to convince
Douane that his interest in her is only "natural" and, therefore, she should not
try to resist him. There is no religious benefit to be reaped from their sexual
intercourse.

Stevens does, however, suggest the "hope of benefits" from the *droit* in
non-religious terms, evident in the dialogue between Douane's father, Probus,
and another, un-named, peasant:

Probus: The younger men have heard of the right of the first night but
they have never seen it. The elders remember the old ways—holy seeds
buried in the fields—the sacred oak—virgin sacrifice—It hurts us to see
the girl torn from her husband—even for these few hours—
Peasant: Yes!
Probus: --but it is a short time out of the years to come and life will go on
in peace. (Act II, p. 41)

For the sake of peace and tranquility, the sacrifice of the bride to the *droit* is
tacitly accepted, and the entire community benefits from the absence of hostility
and fighting; therefore, *The Lovers* exemplifies Westermark's hypothesis that the
droit can be viewed as a communal rite. Nonetheless, such a position fails to
account for the feminine viewpoint and resulting fear of defloration.

The concept of phobia has been extensively explored in the writings
of Sigmund Freud, who investigates *jus primae noctis* as a manifestation of
woman's sexual dependence in his 1918 article "The Taboo of Virginity."[8] Freud
notes a gap in sociologists' and anthropologists' thinking, suggesting they fail
to differentiate between the physical aspects of the loss of virginity and the
psychological investment in a woman's first sexual act. In his 1913 *Totem and
Taboo*, Freud asserts that primitives and neurotics exhibit the tension inherent
to a nuclear family and that communal cultures preceded the construction
of a monogamous family. In an attempt to comprehend the fascination and
horror of a woman's first sexual act, Freud offers four possibilities: initially,
he offers a parallel between the male's emotional/religious fear of blood with
the prohibition of murder and the avoidance of any contact with menstruating
women. While this may provide a partial explanation for hesitation to deflower,
Freud finds it is not comprehensive; therefore, he suggests additionally that
the fear of first sexual contact can be compared to neurotic tendencies. Freud
identifies still another possibility, that being a generalized taboo against females,
which illuminates the differences between the genders and demonstrates the
danger inherent in sexuality, especially the soporific effects. Thus, a groom
would be relieved of the duties of the first sexual contact and remain free from
a special bond or dependence that might offend his masculinity. Fourth, Freud

considers all of the above as acting in concert together, noting the trauma of the first sexual encounter for the female—both the physical pain and possible emotional disappointment. Moreover, he asserts that the female libido is fixated on a father figure. The Oedipal complex thus offers an explanation for the existence of the *droit de seigneur*, where the lord fulfils the role of the father.

Douane, perhaps unconsciously, views Chrysagon in an Oedipal role. Her interest in him supports Crawley's assertion that fear of defloration would be mitigated by a father figure, such as the seigneurial Lord. In the play's second act, Douane voices her fascination with the Lord shortly after she is taken captive:

> Douane: My Lord—I won't try to run away. You know I saw you the way you saw me. I felt the pupils of my eyes open—and I thought about you when my mind wandered. I should be the happiest girl alive to have a man—a man with so much honor in him—take me beside the moonlight river and growl at me the way you do…(Act II p. 47)

While perhaps not realizing the Oedipal implications of such a union, Douane nevertheless is at first able to rationalize her own desires for the man who is not her legally wedded spouse. She knows her desires are a sacrilege in the eyes of the Church and that, if she gives in to her attraction and his ardent pursuit, she will face the scorn not only of the Church, but of her husband, family, and community. Douane alludes to the assistance of village female elders in ascertaining the period of optimal fertility for her wedding day, implying that others recognize her capacity to bear a child from the *droit* union, signifying again the idea that the community accepts the legality of such a union. However, she also wants to be faithful to her spouse and to bear his child, and thus rebuffs Chrysagon's advances, but Stevens's stage notes are explicit: "[Chrysagon] [t]akes her to him. They are very still and slow. The quality of radiance—a sense of force, implacable beyond belief—hovers around them increased to incandescence" (48). Thus, Douane is unable to resist the implacable force. She simply gives in to her erotic (or Oedipal) desires for the Lord, the powerful father figure. The theatrical staging of this moment would be critical in terms of dominance and submission.

As we return to the historical analysis of the *jus primae noctis*, we find Boureau suggesting that "Freud's conclusion approaches Westermark's because in both cases the lord in the *jus primae noctis* serves as an institutional interpreter of a universal mode of psychic organization, marked in one case by a horror of virginal blood and in the other by the female's desire for the father and the male's fear of the initial bond" (27). Boureau's interpretation of Freud is that a *psychism* remains profoundly immutable, so it can never totally coincide with any one stage in the evolutionary process of an institution, and that the tendencies produced with the *jus primae noctis* are always at play, even if they operate on different levels within the constraints of the family in the nineteenth century. Thus, it remains impossible to verify the validity of either position in the equation, for the family cannot accurately express the tensions inherent within any more than the participants in a *droit de seigneur* are capable of full cognition of their roles. Since the ethnographic and psychological interpretations remain outside the realm of verifiable criticism and essentially within the state of the unconscious, the concept of the *droit de seigneur* serves as a continuing metaphor for the sexuality of the Other. Douane becomes subservient to her primordial desires and to the dialectic of the master. Since both she and Chrysagon share a mutual desire, the domination becomes merely symbolic. Douane does resist Chrysagon at first, but her reluctance is subsumed by her sexual curiosity and desires. Her subsequent suicide suggests that her unhappiness is due to her conflicting desires for Chrysagon and her husband, Marc. Stevens portrays Douane as wanting both men: the playwright supplies a stimulating sexual fantasy. However, while Chrysagon and Douane share a mutual desire, he punishes them for acting upon it, perhaps to reify a 1950s sense of morality and conformity to accepted social norms.

Concomitant with the primary action, a second story-line runs through the Stevens play which involves the traveling monk, Brother Grigoris, and the two local Friars, Sextus and Xegan, who debate whether a final blessing and burial in consecrated ground can be offered for Chrysagon, Douane, and her husband, Marc Beauvaix. The Friars have decided against any such blessing, yet Grigoris wishes to hear a recitation of the events surrounding the deaths before making his decision. The power of the liturgy is mighty, and the Catholic Church's positions on the sacrament of marriage, the sin of suicide, and the blasphemy of adultery are foremost in the minds of Sextus and Xegan. The contextual framework of the Catholic Church shapes the thought processes and action of the friars in *The Lovers.*

The position of Sextus and Xegan is illuminated by Alain Boreau. In an attempt to connect the *droit* with the Church, wherein the monks were "raising the specter of lay barbarity by accusing lay lords of practicing" the *droit*, Boureau comments that, "[u]nregulated power—denounced or claimed, imagined or represented—engenders threats to the individual and to what he or she holds most dear. Thus, the individual must draw the consequences, negotiate local rules (payments or subjection), or take refuge in the Church or the state" (118). This entails a decentralization of power that is in play, for each community or state must set its own customs and traditions and define for itself the limitations of personal power and rights within its jurisdiction.

A triangular power structure is evident within the Stevens play, among Lord Chrysagon, the Catholic Church, and the peasant subjects. Sextus and

Xegan, as the local representatives of the Church, hold the power to give or withhold the blessing and burial. However, the traveling monk Grigoris tempers the local official's power, as he can also provide such a blessing. The representatives of the Church possess the capacity for ecclesiastical tyranny. Sextus and Xegan are poised to exert such a force by their adamant refusal to consider the commoner woman Clothilde's pleas for a review of the facts surrounding the deaths. Their power is made clear in a conversation at the beginning of the First Act:

> Grigoris: But, how did all this power of darkness gather?
>
> Sextus: Out of its primal source as always, Brother Monk. These three had cinders in their flesh and the fallen angels fanned them with their wings. Lust, Grigoris, Brother—wicked, worldly, deadliest of the seven sins. Be glad these vestment walls—white and black—keep it out. (Act I, p. 11-12.)

Yet Grigoris is not convinced of the Church's safety, his reply anticipating the contemporary crisis facing the U.S. Catholic Church regarding sexual abuse: "Do they keep it out or in?" (Act I, p. 12). Grigoris serves as the voice of impartiality, of neutrality and reason. Since he is not accountable to this particular community, he is able to consider the circumstances surrounding the deaths without consequence to himself from the inhabitants of the village. While he remains a part of the Church as a whole, he is outside the local jurisdiction and is not a participant within the political power scheme of the region. He therefore remains able to make a non-partisan decision about the blessing and burial.

In an aside, Clothilde reveals that Chrysagon has the *droit* for a single night—but no more,[9] thereby, setting up the ensuing conflict when Chrysagon refuses to release Douane on the morning after the wedding, when Marc is patiently waiting. Patience wears thin as time drags forward, and Marc becomes incensed, seeking approval from the Friars to re-take her by force:

> Sextus: I hear your words—but what do you want of us, Marc?
>
> Marc: De la Crux [Chrysagon] won't let her come back to me. I want to know what to do.
>
> Sextus: We have protested with all our might—and my Lord Austrict frowns at us, my Lord Herstal pours us wine and the Dragon gazes at the ceiling.
>
> Matthew: Is that all?
>
> Sextus: We have sent a written paper describing this abuse to the Abbott of Metz.
>
> Probus: Father Prior, forgive me, but my son wants to know—what are you going to do about it?
>
> Sextus: We have sent a written paper!

Marc: A piece of paper! Two days to get there, a month to read it and they send back a piece of paper agreeing with you.

Sextus: Probus—what does your son want us to do?

Probus: Go to them, Father. Tell them to send back his wife.

Sextus: We have already spoken to them.

Marc: Order them.

Sextus: We don't order the Lord Knights de la Crux.

Marc: Then it will be within the right if I do it?

Sextus: Is there a further question? If not, I will say—

Marc: Father—

Sextus: I will say God bless.

Marc: Father!

Sextus: Probus—

Probus: My son has asked you a question, Father.

Sextus: It is right to obey those whom God has placed above.

Marc: Yesterday you said words over me and I believed you. You said, "Bless this ring—these heads, these hands—" You said, "What God hath joined, let no man put asunder." Now I ask you, Father, is it my right to go and get my wife? (Act II, p. 52-3)

Silence is the only answer Marc receives from the Friar, who seeks to avoid any confrontation with other male authority figures, the Lords, or the Church officials. Perhaps Stevens' conception of the Friars was similar to Boureau's assertion that: "growing cities produced a sizable mass of 'clerics' who received minor orders but were not fully integrated into the Church and who sometimes led a merry life, enjoying exemptions and privileges of a clerical status that set them apart from their fellow-citizens."[10] Sextus then, may have been such a cleric, wishing for preservation of the status-quo in his refusal to answer Marc's queries, which he must have realized would lead to bloodshed and carnage. Austrict, the local Church officiate, however, is fully aware of the impending fight, and is unafraid to challenge Chrysagon in the Third Act:

Chrysagon: She belongs to me.

Austrict: Wait—now wait! I don't care what you say—this is a rebellion! You don't have the right.

Chrysagon: I don't have the right? Austrict, I am the Seigneur du Chatel. The first son de la Crux!

Herstal: Chrysagon—

Chrysagon: A letter. Restlessness!

Austrict: If you keep this woman there will be bloodshed—I warn you.

Chrysagon: This woman belongs to me.

Austrict: No!

Chrysagon: I don't ask, I order.

Austrict: Don't order me. (Act III, p. 58-9)

Although Austrict's position is clear, Chrysagon threatens him with personal harm, and he retreats. The power triangle has shifted, and Chrysagon exerts his might. However, the Church regains the power Austrict lost after the death of the Lord and Marc, in the personage of the Abbott of Metz, Clement, who supports the Friars' decision not to bury the dead on consecrated ground. In a discussion with townsmen Volc Sturmer and Matthew, and with Herstal and Draco De La Crux, brothers of the deceased lord, Clement says:

Clement: This is a grave and grievous matter I have been called to look upon. I have heard the Lord Knights de la Crux and the Friars of the village. I have contemplated the faces of the dead and I have prayed to God in Heaven. And I do now pronounce my finding and my instructions in the name of the Holy Church. It is my solemn judgment that the Lord Knight Chrysagon de la Crux, the woman Douane of Calais and the ploughman, Marc Beauvaix—all three—died in a state of mortal sin.

Matthew: No!

Draco: My brother!

Volc: Silence!

Clement: The deadly sins of lust and anger led to the mortal sins of Suicide and Murder. In order to protect the Christian dead from evil and contamination there will be no burial in this churchyard. It is my order that no servant of the Holy Church shall administer sacred rites to these sinful bodies on pain of excommunication! (Act III, p. 61-2.)

Grigoris, remaining true to his heart and beliefs, nonetheless pronounces a blessing on the dead after the departure of Clement, thereby risking his own position within the Catholic Church for the price of retaining his moral honor and sense of duty acquired after hearing a full account of the events preceding the deaths. Clement voices the position of the medieval Church that adultery was a much more grievous sin than simple fornication, for it was "blasphemy as well as a crime and a sin" (Boureau 168). The Church used its institutional weight to control social mores in the delicate equilibrium among the various cultural practices of marriage, and its constant vigilance increased throughout the Middle Ages as the network of Church parishes grew.[11] The dialogue between Austrict and Chrysagon thus reflects a negotiation attempt to retain the Church's control over the wayward Lord.

Stevens's treatment of the *droit de seigneur* in *The Lovers* showcases the dangers of a vast imbalance in power, as held by Chrysagon, who is unable to restrain himself to the confines of the law and keep Douane for just a single night. Chrysagon's frailty of character is inconsistent with the might implied by his birthright, for, if he had been able to reign in his sexual desires, bloodshed could have been avoided. The barbarism of the custom of the *droit* might be evident to a contemporary spectator, but Stevens softens the anticipated reaction of horror toward the practice by Douane's surprising willingness to go along, by her response to Chrysagon's protestations of love, and, most tellingly, by her failure to respond to Clothilde's inquiry about the union with the Lord, implying that his advances were, indeed, welcomed. Stevens' play was, perhaps, informed by knowledge of Freud's Oedipal complex, possibly by his theories of subconscious sexual desire, thereby further differentiating the medieval time period of the action from the present, where such a relationship between a girl and a father or father figure would be unacceptable to contemporary societal mores. The *droit* would, for all practical purposes, be considered an instance of sexual harassment in today's society. Marie-Victoire Louis has written an extensive treatise on modern-day French harassment laws that arose to address abuses women encountered at their places of employment during the latter half of the nineteenth century; Louis titles the book *Le Droit de Cuissage*, which Boureau takes to be a misnomer.[12]

The Lovers provides a subtle critique of the Cold War, unmasking the horror of tyrannical behavior. Class conflict and the extreme regulation of many aspects of the private life of individuals in the former Communist bloc countries may have figured into Stevens' portrayal of the peasant revolt. Stevens also critiques the Catholic Church for punishing its practitioners for erotic sexual desires, perhaps to tap into the emerging movement for sexual freedom. He provides a new twist on the literary use of the *droit* via a receptive woman, foreshadowing the women's rights movement, which came into pre-eminence in the 1960s and 1970s. The portrayed biological ambiguity of potential parentage arising from the *droit* union also possibly provides a justification for birth control, one of the major issues of contention between the Catholic Church and American women of the 1950s.

A power triangle of the magnitude found in the Middle Ages, between a peasant, a Lord, and the Church, could not exist in the lives of the contemporary readers, which again represents another major difference between past and present—a shift from an institutional level to an individual level which cannot not carry the same signification as the *droit*. Nonetheless, fear or threat of sexual abuse from dominant persons is a cultural constant, simultaneously real and symbolic in all societies.[13] Stevens realizes the possibility of a universal understanding and broad-based interest in the topic, and invokes the *droit du seigneur* for dramatic interest and perhaps to humanize the legend. Perhaps he was expecting *The Lovers* to have the popularity of the plays and operas of his predecessors Voltaire, Beaumarchais, and Mozart, yet critics and spectators were not ready to face Douane's anxiety in 1956.

Critic Richard Watts Jr., in his *New York Post* review of the play's opening, states: "It seems that the lord had taken advantage of his *droit de seigneur*, but it turns out that he had really loved the girl and she had been far from cold to him, and it is clear that the author has equal sympathy for all of them, including the bewildered young bridegroom."[14] Watts broadens the discussion: "I don't deny that it is splendid for him to pity all concerned, but I can't help feeling that his characters fail to be touching and that their plight hardly ever achieves dramatic poignancy."[15] Perhaps the sentiment of character flatness could be alleviated with changes in the staging and actor performance. The play's theme of male dominance finds relevancy for contemporary audiences, as does the correlating notion of Oedipal relationships. The female character's anxiety and divided loyalties are ideas that merit exploration in modern society, and this play subtlety hints at the importance of the feminine perspective, possibly an idea ahead of its time during the 1950s when the women's rights movement was yet a decade or so off.

Critic John McClain considers the play meritorious, yet in his review he finds it "difficult to accept an idea [the *droit de seigneur*] which seems almost ludicrous in terms of what we call modern enlightenment."[16] Brooks Atkinson concurs in his review in *The New York Times*: "To us that [the *droit de seigneur*] may seem like a monstrous betrayal of everything that is human or sacred...."[17] Thus, a typical 1950s response was one of both incredulity and outrage, one which parallels the strong sense of social morality, duty, honor, and order that marked the 1950s in America. Nonetheless, while the *droit* itself may have been preposterous in the 1950s as it is today, the notion that women are sexually constrained by society is still very true, and male domination of and competition for a women's affection remain elements of everyday life in the early twenty-first century. Stevens' treatment of the *droit de seigneur* in *The Lovers* showcases the dangers of a vast imbalance in power. His probable disappointment over the short (four-day) Broadway run was, undoubtedly, tempered by the success of the film version of the story, *The War Lord,* which was produced in 1965, and remains active in the film repertoire today.

UNIVERSITY OF MISSOURI -- COLUMBIA

NOTES

[1] Article originally published in French as "Le Rire de la méduse."
[2] For a broader view of Chrétien de Troyes, see Owen.
[3] Refer to Gravdahl 5; *Ravishing Maidens: Writing Rape in Medieval French Literature and Law.* Gravdahl has also published additional works related to rape and medieval French literature: "Camoflaging Rape: The Rhetoric of Sexual Violence in the Medieval Pastourelle;" "1175: Fables and Parodies;" and *Vilain and Courtois: Transgressive Parody*

in Old French Literature of the Twelfth and Thirteenth Centuries. Another related study of gender and the French literary genre is by Gaunt.

[4] Gravdahl 2-8 gives an extensive discussion of French vocabulary derived from Latin in relation to rape.

[5] Jorg Wettlaufer has compiled an outstanding bibliography on the *jus primae noctis.* Some particularly helpful sources on the *jus primae noctis* include Bordier; Boutrouche, Bullogh; Cenec-Moncaut; De Foras; De Saint-Amand; Howarth,; Michelet; Searle; and Schmidt.

[6] All quotations are taken from the Samuel French publication of the play, which does not reference either scene numbers or line numbers. Thus, citations will include an act number and a page number for reference purposes.

[7] Boureau 15.

[8] Freud 191-208.

[9] Stevens 50.

[10] Boureau 157.

[11] Boreau 173.

[12] Boureau 266. The Louis monograph provides a fascinating view of contemporary French legal usage of the *droit.* However, the topic goes beyond the scope of this paper.

[13] Boureau 229-30.

[14] Watts 302-5.

[15] Watts 303.

[16] McClain 303.

[17] Atkinson 302.

WORKS CITED

Andrew, D. T. "Uncertain Unions: Marriage in England 1660-1753."*Journal of the History of Sexuality* 5 (1994) 2: 308-10.

Atkinson, Brooks. Rev. of *The Lovers. New York Times.* 11 May 1956. Rpt. *New York Theater Critics Reviews.* Microfilm. (1950-7): 302.

Bennett, Judith M. "Medieval Peasant Marriage: An Examination of Marriage License Fines in the Liber Gersumarium." *Papers in Medieval Studies* 2 .Ed. J.A. Raftis. Toronto: 1981.

_____. "The Tie That Binds: Peasant Marriages and Families in Late Medieval England." *Journal of Interdisciplinary History* 15 (1984): 111-29.

Boureau, Alain. *The Lord's First Night: The Myth of the Droit de Cuissage.* Trans. Lydia G. Cochrane. Chicago: U Chicago P, 1998.

Boutruche, Robert. *Seigneurue et féodalite.* Paris: Aubrier-Montaigne, 1968.

Bullough, Vern L. "Jus primae noctis or droit du seigneur." *Journal of Sex Research* 28 (1991): 163-66.

Bullogh, Vern L., and James Brundage, ed. *Sexual Practices and the Medieval Church.*

Buffalo: Prometheus, 1982.

_____. *Handbook of Medieval Sexuality.* New York: Garland, 2000.

Cénac-Moncaut, Justin Eduard Mathieu. "Du droit d'ainesse et du droit du seigneur." *Revue de Toulouse et du midi de la France*. Toulouse, 1870.

Chrétien de Troyes. *Les Romans de Chrétien de Troyes: Edités d'après la Copie de Guiot* Bibl. Nat. Fr. 794.

_____. *Erec et Enide*. Ed. Mario Roques. Paris: Champion, 1973.

_____. *Le Chevalier de la charette*. Ed. Mario Roques. Paris: Champion, 1975.

_____. *Le Chevalier au lion*. Ed. Mario Roques. Paris: Champion, 1975.

_____. *Le Conte du Graal*. Ed. Félix Lecoy. Paris: Champion, 1975.

_____. *Philomena: conte raconté d'après Ovide*. Ed. C. de Boer. (1909). Geneva: Slatkine Reprints, 1974.

Cixous, Hélène. "Le rire de la méduse." *L'Arc* 61 (1975): 39-54.

_____. "The Laugh of Medusa." Trans. Suzanne Horer and Jeanne Socquet. *New French Feminisms*. Ed. Elaine Marks and Isabelle de Courtivron. New York: Schocken, 1981. 257-74.

De Foras, Amedee. *Le Droit du seigneur au Moyen Age: Etude critique et historique*. Paris, 1884.

De Saint-Amand, H. Gaultier. *Les Droits du seigneur*. Paris: Librarie du Temple, 1911.

Freud, Sigmund. "Instincts and their Vicissitudes." *The Complete Psychological Works of Sigmund Freud*. Ed. James Strachey. Vol. 14. London: Hogarth Press, 1966-95. 109-40.

_____. "The Taboo of Virginity." *The Complete Psychological Works of Sigmund Freud*.
Ed. James Strachey. Vol. 11. London: Hogarth Press, 1966-95. 191-208.

_____. "Three Essays on the Theory of Sexuality." *The Complete Psychological Works of Sigmund Freud*. Ed. James Strachey. Vol. 7. London: Hogarth Press, 1966-95. 123-243.

Gaunt, Simon. *Gender and Genre in Medieval French Literature*. Cambridge: Cambridge UP, 1995.

Gravdal, Kathryn. "Camouflaging Rape: The Rhetoric of Sexual Violence in the Medieval *Pastourelle*." *Romance Review* 76 (1985): 361-73.

_____. *Ravishing Maidens: Writing Rape in Medieval French Literature and Law*.
Philadelphia: U Pennsylvania P, 1990.

_____. Vilain and Courtois: Transgressive Parody in Old French Literature of the Twelfth and Thirteenth Centuries. Lincoln: U Nebraska P, 1989.

_____. "1175: Fables and Parodies." *A New History of French Literature*. Ed. Denis Hollier. Cambridge: Harvard UP, 1989. 46-50.

Hanawalt, Barbara A. *The Ties that Bind: Peasant Families in Medieval England*. Oxford: Oxford UP, 1986.

Howarth, W. D. "Droit du Seigneur: Fact or Fantasy?" *Journal of European Studies* 1 (1971): 291-312.

_____. "The Theme of the Droit du Seigneur in the Eighteenth-Century Theater." *French Studies* 15 (1961): 228-40.

Litvack, Frances Eleanor Palermo. *Le Droit du Seigneur in European and American Literature from the Seventeenth through the Twentieth Century*. Birmingham: Summa Publications, 1984.

McClain, John. "Play Marked by Ingenuity." Rev. of *The Lovers*. *Journal American* 11 May 1956. Rpt. *New York Theater Critics Reviews*. Microfilm. (1950-7): 303.

Michelet, Jules. *Origines du droit Français*. Paris: Hachette, 1837.

Mozart, Wolfgang Amadeus. *Le Nozze di Figaro*. Libretto. Lorenzo da Ponte. Vienna, 1786.

Owen, D. D. R. "Theme and Variations: Sexual Aggression in Chrétien de Troyes." *Forum for Modern Language Studies* 21 (1975): 376-85.

Schmidt, Karl. *Jus Primae Noctis:Eine geschichtliche Untersuchung*. Frieburg im Breisgau: Herder, 1881.

Searle, Eleanor. "Freedom and Marriage in Medieval England: An Alternative Hypothesis." *Economic History Review* 29 (1976): 482-6.

_____. "Seigneural Control of Women's Marriage: The Antecedents and Functions of Merchet in England." *Past and Present* 82 (1979): 3-43.

Stevens, Leslie. *The Lovers*. New York: Samuel French, 1956.

Stevenson, Kenneth. *Nuptial Blessing: A Study of Christain Marriage Rites*. New York: Oxford UP, 1983.

Voltaire. *Le droit du seigneur* (play). Geneva, 1763. *War Lord*. Dir. Franklin Schaffner. Perf. Charlton Heston, Richard Boone, Rosemary Forsythe. Universal Pictures, 1965.

Watts, Richard, Jr. "Tragedy of a Medieval Triangle." Rev. of *The War Lord*. *New York Post*. 11 May, 1956. Rpt. *New York Theater Critics Reviews*. Microfilm. (1950-7): 302-5.

Westermark, Edward. *The History of Human Marriage*. 2 Vols. New York: MacMillan, 1891.

Wettlaufer, Jörg. *Erweiterfe Bibliographie "Jus Primae Noctis."* 1999. <www.frbri.de/jus/jugsort.htm>

Really Queer or Just Criminally Insane? Novelists Confront Gilles de Rais

Peter Christensen

In 1992, Gilles de Rais (1404-1440), was retried twice in France, once in Nantes and once in Paris. Although he had been publicly executed in Nantes after an ecclesiastical and civil trial in 1440 and has had one of the foulest reputations of any individual of the Middle Ages, there have been those in the last hundred years who have felt that he was either innocent of some of the heinous crimes of which he was accused, since they were too outrageous for anyone to believe, or that his trial was a mockery of justice which does not allow us to conclude with any certainty that he was actually guilty of any of the crimes. The trial included torture and threat of torture, no bodies were produced (no *habeas corpus*), no clothes or trinkets of the deceased were in evidence, and it is possible that the surviving transcripts of the trials are incomplete with perhaps deliberate censorship of material in Gilles' favor.[1]

Interest in Gilles, mass murderer of pubescent and pre-pubescent children, particularly boys, and former comrade of Joan of Arc turned diabolist, has captured the literary imagination for almost two hundred years, with novels on him appearing as far back as 1834. René de Maulde-La Clavière edited the documents in Latin (the ecclesiastical trial) and Middle French (the civil trial) for inclusion in the first biography of Gilles, that of Eugène Bossard in 1885, but even here certain omissions were made for propriety's sake.[2] Six years later, with the appearance of Gilles as an important character from the past in Joris-Karl Huysmans' *Là-bas*, a decadent novel about Satanism (translated into English in 1924 as *Down There* and retranslated in 2001 as *The Damned*), Gilles as historical figure received the first of several new leases on life.[3] In 2005, Candace Black edited for Creation Books a collection of interesting writings about Gilles, *Dark Star: The Satanic Rites of Gilles de Rais*. Unfortunately, although it includes such interesting selections as Richard Thoma's story "Tragedy in Blue" (1936), this volume suffers from a lack of explanatory and editorial material.

It is now over one hundred years since Salomon Reinach in the decade after *Là-bas* made the first modern attempt to find Gilles innocent, a project which has been continued up to the near present in such books as Jean-Pierre Bayard's *Plaidoyer pour Gilles de Rais* (1992). The interest in Joan of Arc in the 1920s after her canonization (Shaw, Delteil, Dreyer, etc.) coincided with the publication of several books about him. Joan and Gilles form a pair made for artistic contemplation. We have either the saint and the sinner or else two people framed by the Catholic Church in alliance with forces (Burgundian, in Joan's case, and Breton, in Gilles') opposing the Valois Dauphin, later Charles VII.

It was not until 1959 that the first complete translation of the records of both trials into modern French was made, by Pierre Klosowski, in an edition prepared by Georges Bataille called *Le Procès de Gilles de Rais*, with Bataille's lengthy preface, "La Tragédie de Gilles de Rais." Richard Robinson translated this book into English in 1991, seven years after Reginald Hyatte had made his own English translation of the trials as *Laughter for the Devil*. Bataille was more of a philosopher than a historian, yet his view dominated studies of Gilles probably up to the retrials of 1992. Bataille presented Gilles as a homosexual (1991: 31, 32, 34, 42) and pederast, and, as was typical of his style of writing, painted a detailed, lurid picture of Gilles' sexual activities as derived from the witnesses at his trials and his own testimony, which, indeed, is the only written record that we have concerning these activities and crimes.

Given the wealth of responses to Gilles, are there other ways of looking at his sexual activities? Obviously, Bataille wrote too early to be influenced by Michel Foucault and the arguments of the medicalization of deviancy, which locate the invention of homosexuality in the late nineteenth century. Perhaps implicitly Bataille would have been closer to the view of historians writing in the wake of John Boswell, looking for continuities in same-sex feelings across a historical trajectory. As at least sixteen novels about Gilles de Rais have been published since the end of World War II, and at least twelve dramatic pieces since World War I (stage plays, opera, and radio plays), not to mention poetry, stories, and comic book/graphic novel treatments), it seems fair to say that Gilles has captured the hearts of medievalists in general, if not queer medievalists specifically.

One of the most famous novels about Gilles is by gay French novelist and essayist, the celebrated Michel Tournier, who published his *Gilles et Jeanne* in 1983; since then, at least nine other novels have appeared. This famous short novel raises, as do the retrials, the question of whether or not, in addition to Bataille's florid writings and the retrial themselves, new views of same-sex attraction have been significant in promoting interest in Gilles de Rais. Of course, because of his alchemical activities and his association with Joan of Arc, Gilles is also the potential subject for pseudo-historians looking for fanciful conspiracy theories, the people who mix the Cathars, Templars, and the keepers of the Holy Grail. Fortunately, few of the novelists writing on Gilles have gone in this direction, and there has been a stronger tendency to stick close to the testimony of the trials, particularly in the case of Robert Nye's *The Life and Death of My Lord Gilles de Rais* (1990).

In 2003, two books were published which treat Gilles de Rais in literature. The first is the more concentrated study by Val Morgan, *The Legend of Gilles de Rais (1404-1440) in the Writings of Huysnams, Bataille, Planchon, and Tournier*. The second is an immensely detailed study by Michel Meurger, *Gilles de Rais et la littérature*, which concentrates on writers of the nineteenth century. Only the last chapter of Meurger's book (207-28) deals with the twentieth century and the twenty-first, and so his book crosses paths with Morgan's only in their treatments of Huysmans. Further discussion of Gilles in literature can be found in Meurger's earlier essay, "L'Imaginaire de Gilles de Rais: La Bête, l'esthète, et Barbe-Bleue." Meurger especially has read widely in the history of the fifteenth century, and he cites several times Jacques Heers' *Gilles de Rais*, published in 1994, which responds to the recent retrials and is probably today the best historical study of Gilles. Of other post-1992, books on Gilles, the most insightful are Martine Le Coz's *Gilles de Rais: ignoble et chrétien* (1995) and Ernesto Ferrero *Barbablu: Gilles de Rais et il tramonto del Medioevo* (1998).

There are three areas in which queerness may afford a viable look at Gilles. First, we have his attraction to boys, some of whom he characterized as angels or Holy Innocents and placed in his personal choir. Second, there is ambiguity in his relationship with François Prelati, who came from Florence in 1437, five years after Gilles, according to the testimonies of his two servants and accomplices, Etienne Corillaut (Poitou) and Henriet Griart, had already begun the tortures and murders. Prelati seemed to hold Gilles under a psychological spell, leading him in efforts to summon demons and produce gold through alchemy. Third, Gilles was in the campaign against Orléans and Patay with the male-clad, boyish, Joan of Arc and with her at Charles VII's coronation at Rheims. There is no proof, however, that they knew each other personally. The degree of interaction between Gilles and Joan has been downplayed by Jacques Heers, but in the novels of Michel Tournier, Violaine Bérot and Michel Ragon, they have a major interaction.

According to the testimonies of the two servants, Gilles killed boys and girls, sometimes sodomizing them before, during, or after death, and he sometimes ejaculated on them at these times. They were fondled, tortured, and incinerated after death. Gilles sent out his young pages and the old woman Meffraye to lure and capture the children. He had as adult accomplices his cousins Gilles de Sillé and Roger de Bricqueville, but the latter two fled and did not give testimony. Prelati claimed at the trial that he himself did not have anything to do with the murders. Sentenced to imprisonment, he later escaped. The other member of the households of Tiffauges and Machecoul brought to trial was the priest Dom Eustache Blanchet, who also denied involvement in the murders. It is unclear how many children met their end in Gilles' domains, but it may have been about eighty. Given the nature of these accusations, one needs to ask if Gilles was crazy or not, and whether or not he understood Christianity in the conventional sense of the time.

Novelists have capitalized on the lack of documentation of much of Gilles' life. We know very little about his parentless youth under the governance of his grandfather Jean de Craon, an immensely wealthy man who acted as a law unto himself. Married, Gilles appears to have had little contact with his wife after the birth of their child Marie in 1429. The one document in addition to the court records that has been used over and over to understand Gilles is the declaration of his family members that he had squandered the family's huge fortune. However, this document may reflect the avarice of his relations more than the actual situation. Further insight may also be gained by studying the *Le Mystère du siège d'Orléans*[4], which is the long, lavish spectacle that Gilles had performed to commemorate his and Joan of Arc's participation at the siege. Although historical novelists are free to use the past as a backdrop on which to project anachronistic concerns, including anxieties and ideas about sexuality, homosexuality, and queerness, in the specific case of Gilles, those novelists who attempt to connect the dots in his strange life may be able to offer new insights to historians

We will examine the approaches taken towards Gilles's sexuality in the following novels, listed here in order of discussion: Michael Ragon's *Un Amour de Jeanne; roman* (2003); Gilbert Prouteau's *Gilles de Rais, ou le gueule de loup* (1992); Jacquemard-Sénécal's *Le Printemps du loup: Une Jeunesse de Gilles de Rais; roman* (1998); Robert Nye's *The Life and Death of My Lord Gilles de Rais* (1990), and Michel Tournier's *Gilles & Jeannne; récit* (1983). Ragon, Tournier, and Prouteau are widely published authors and intellectuals, Jacquemard-Sénécal is the pseudonym for Yves Jacquemard and Jean Michel Sénécal, a pair of talented and prize-winning author of mysteries and historical novels, and Robert Nye a distinguished English novelist. Whereas the narratives of Ragon and Tournier require only a general knowledge of the events in the lives of Gilles and Joan, Jacquemard-Sénécal's demands more familiarity with the historical period, and both Prouteau's and Nye's novels require one's having read the trial records to be properly evaluated.

Both Ragon and Tournier construct narratives in which Gilles murders little children, but they avoid dealing directly with sex and murder. Ragon never mentions Gilles's sexual activities with children, only child murder. Tournier presents the subject only as rumor, although the smell of burning flesh is noticed by the most intelligent and reliable witness, Eustache Blanchet. Jacquemard-Sénécal shows us Gilles as a same-sex-oriented, troubled teenager at age twelve to thirteen. Although the story is told from a 1440 viewpoint preceding Gilles' execution, the main story line does not advance beyond 1429. In strong contrast, Prouteau offers a sympathetic view of Gilles's sexual relations with boys and denies that he ever sodomized, tortured, or killed them. Of the five novelists, only Nye takes from the trial records the traditional story of Gilles as ghastly sexual deviant and murderer and presents it in a new form, this time, from the point of view of Dom Eustache Blanchet, increasingly aware of what monstrosities are going on.

Michel Ragon's 173-page novel *Un Amour de Jeanne* (2003) is, on the most obvious level, a novel concerned with the possible silence of God, and its existential nature is tied directly to its queerness in approach. *Un Amour de Jeanne* is queer in the sense that Ragon does not put any twentieth-century labels on the strong physical and emotional attractions felt by Gilles; and he gives a prominent place to the blurred lines separating Gilles' attractions for youths in battle, for Jeanne, and for Prelati.

The story is told in short chapters, five of which are devoted to Gilles and told in the first person. The remaining chapters are given in third person voice. Five are labeled "Jeanne," one is labeled "Charles," three are not labeled at all, and one is the Epilogue. The structure of the novel is circular, since Gilles in the first chapter hears of Jeanne's capture. The tale's main part is then the chronological story that takes Jeanne and Gilles, mostly together, through to a point shortly before Jeanne's capture in 1431. However, the two characters are split up at the end of this extended sequence, with Jeanne spending her time in the company of Charles VII and then going out on a raid. Meanwhile, in the chapter before the Epilogue, Gilles returns to his lands, is seduced by François Prelati, starts calling on Lucifer, seeks the blood of children, and finally flees to Machecoul. This chapter takes us to a date later than Jeanne's capture, presumably c. 1440. At the end of this chapter, Gilles remembers Jeanne's statement that someone would betray her, and he amends the statement to 'someone will betray us." The last chapter reads, "Qui a trahi Jeanne? / Ses voix qui se sont tues? / Mais d'où venaient ses voix? ... Qui a trahi Gilles? / Ce démon qui jamais ne lui apparut?" (173) [Who betrayed Jeanne? Her voices, which fell silent? But where did her voices come from? ... Who betrayed Gilles? / This demon that never appeared to him?]. A brief statement reminds us that each protagonist is burned at the stake. Then the Epilogue closes, "Ainsi se consuma dans les flammes et la cendre l'amour impossible entre Jeanne d'Arc et Barbe-Bleue" (173) [Thus the flames and ash consumed the impossible love between Joan of Arc and Bluebeard].

It is only in the last three chapters that one can see that Ragon is juxtaposing Jeanne and Gilles as characters who were betrayed—be it by humans, by supernatural powers, or by their own unwarranted belief in supernatural powers. Jeanne, after the consecration of Charles VII at Rheims, feels that her voices have become silent and that she had no further mission, while Gilles, receiving no communication from Lucifer, despairs. Perhaps Jeanne was betrayed by La Trémoille when she fell into the hands of Jean de Luxembourg near Compiègne. Perhaps Prelati was playing tricks on Gilles. With Prelati in the valley of Crûme, Gilles comes upon a woman who seems to be Jeanne and immediately feels that she must be the real Jeanne. Later, he hears that the King had denounced this imposter, the false Jeanne (163-65). Shortly afterward Gilles falls into the hands of Jean V of Brittany (198). Ragon uses the connections linking the youths, Jeanne, and Prelati to explain in part Gilles' sinking into vice. His story also shows how the Hundred Years' War degraded the populace and how local pillage followed in its wake. Jeanne starts off as a heroine, but we see her doubts and suspect that she has outlived her calling. Were she and Gilles betrayed by men such as La Trémoille and Jean V, by the silence of supernatural powers, or by their belief in the cosmic battle between good and evil? The novel gives no answer to this question.

Gilles is drawn to Jeanne first by her boyishness (37-39, 103). Her boyish body is like those of the youths he tries to sleep with. He is the one who is so devoted to her that he sucks the poison out of her wounds when she is injured. He becomes upset by his attraction for her, which through her wounds is connected to thoughts of blood. Later, at Bourges, Jeanne is introduced to feminine courtly dress through the queen, Marie d'Anjou, Charles's wife. Jeanne had reminded Gilles of boys, and now Prelati reminds him of Jeanne (160) and seduces him. Gilles notices that Prelati was twenty-five years old, the same age as Jeanne if she had lived. Although there was no actual physical resemblance between them, Gilles confused them in his mind (160-61).

In addition to the magnetic attraction that Prelati exerted on Gilles, a further reason for Gilles going over to the side of Prelati was Gilles' feeling that Jeanne must have chosen the weaker side, God's side, in the fight with Lucifer, since she was executed (162). Gilles does call Prelati "mon amant," (164) but there are no sex scenes between them. Furthermore, although we are told briefly about "le sang des sacrifices" ["the blood of sacrifices"], the narrator includes nothing about orgies with their dying and dead bodies (166). Instead, Gilles mentions that François and an alchemist mutilated the bodies after their deaths, mixing blood with crushed minerals (167).

Ragon makes no judgments about Gilles's sexuality. Withholding dates, he is likely to give the impression that Prelati came to Gilles several years before 1439, the year before he died.

We do not see a Gilles who has sexual relations with children but rather a Gilles who is misled into making child sacrifices to demons. Ultimately, Ragon suggests we can only approximate what desires and forces drove Gilles onward. The premise that Prelati and Gilles were lovers makes sense, although there is nothing in the trial records related to this question. The novel is well written and moving. However, given the absence of details about the torture and murders of the children, Ragon does skirt an important issue.

In contrast to the philosophical tenor of Ragon's novel is the polemical denial of Gilles' traditional crimes in Gilbert Prouteau's *Gilles de Rais, ou, La*

Guele du loup (1992). The book is in five parts. First comes Henri Laborit's endorsement of the novel, which aims at vindicating Gilles of any crime. Then follows the Avant-Propos, in which Prouteau tells how, in 1962, he heard from his now deceased friend Maurice Garçon that in 1939 the Congrès National des Avocats had hoped for a retrial of Gilles in Nantes. Prouteau took part in getting the retrial in conjunction with UNESCO in Paris in 1992, as fulfillment of the failed effort fifty-three years before. In Part One of the book, "La Gueule du loup" Prouteau novelistically recreates the world of the villain of the trial, Jehan de Malestroit, the Breton clergyman and ally of the English, who masterminded the framing of Gilles by circulating gossip, suborning witnesses, and promoting torture. In this presentation Malestroit is even more repulsive than Bishop Cauchon in Joan of Arc's trial.

Gilles de Rais, in his prison cell, writes down the true story of his life in the next section, "Les Nuits de la Tour Neuve." He is an alcoholic, and Malestroit has denied him alcohol in order to disorient him. Gilles insists that his famous prodigality was an attempt to show his contempt for the grasping actions of his grandfather, who grabbed whatever land he could get and overtaxed the peasants. He did want to rescue Jeanne at Rouen but failed to do so. Gilles reveals that he did take part in alchemical experiments, and it was the smell from these that was used by his enemies to create the idea that he had killed children and incinerated their bodies. Gilles confesses to having been led astray to the invocation of demons when Prelati joined him. Gilles recognizes that what will shock people the most is his love of boys. He claims that he fondled and ejaculated on them because he loved them. He wanted to initiate them into the delights of sex, and he feels that the boys benefited from the sexual relationships that he had with them. He states that he did not sodomize the boys and had no desire to do so. He believes that pederasty has been misunderstood, and that he is a victim of this prejudice in a hypocritical world which delights in the castration of boys just so that they can sing an octave higher. He did not use castrati in his Choir of the Holy Innocents. Gilles, realizing that no one will listen to him in a frame-up, offers to retire to a monastery for the rest of his life and give up the rest of his property, but he is not given this chance. Interwoven in this section are translations of documents of the trial and other archival documents of the time, including an excerpt from one anonymous chronicle, which presents the view that Gilles had a larger role in Jeanne's campaigns than the other sources have suggested.

The third section, with the ominous Zolaesque title, "J'accuse," which had been used by Graham Greene a few years earlier in a pamphlet about the dark side of Nice, explains in essayistic form many of the points that have been made in the novel. His approach combines a historical perspective with standards of human rights in 1992. Although the trial of Gilles was understandable in a world in which the Catholic Church launched a vicious Crusade against the Cathars and then created the Inquisition, a world in which Jacques de Molay and Jeanne d'Arc were savagely killed, it makes no sense in Prouteau's view not to hold it up to contemporary liberal UNESCO expectations of justice. Prouteau denounces Christianity's demonization of sexuality and declares that, because Gilles loved eight- to twelve-year-old boys, he has gone down in history as a killer of children and host of sacrificial orgies in the spirit of the Marquis de Sade, with whom he has nothing in common. He points out that, according to Gabory (1926), ten pages are missing from the trial records, and that he has tried to offer an understanding of what has been suppressed by Malestroit. We do not see the outcome of the retrial. The book ends with the case for the defense. For Prouteau, Gilles really is queer and he is not criminally insane. He would not be insane to any reader, and in Prouteau's view of sexuality he is not criminal either. It does not seem as if many historians have accepted Prouteau's argument, although his book is far more researched than Jean-Pierre Bayard's *Plaidoyer or Gilles de Rais*, also published in 1992. Jacques Heers, the distinguished historian, did not accept their revisionism and arguments for Gilles' innocence in his book, *Gilles de Rais*, two years later, and I find Heers' case convincing.

Jacquemard-Sénécal in the novel *Le Printemps du loup: Une Jeunesse de Gilles de Rais*, rather than echoing Prouteau's claims of Gilles' innocence, avoids his crimes by dealing only with Gilles' youth. This writing team depicts Gilles as a sexually frustrated teen-ager with a strongly marked sadistic tendency. He will not be able to live out his sexual desires without problems. Gilles is not an attractive figure in this novel, but neither is he wholly without sympathy, since he is also capable of deep emotion in a repressive society. Furthermore, there are bigoted characters around him, including churchmen and a former Crusader, who are more violent and ferociously intolerant. The speculative quality of the novel is underlined by the use of "une jeunesse" in the title; this is one of the possible periods of youth that we can imagine for him, given the lack of historical record.

The action takes place almost entirely from late 1417 to early 1418, during a cold winter about two years after the battle of Agincourt. It is not clear in this mystery where the several different plot strands are heading. One group of sympathetic characters is centered on Hermeline Peau-de-Loup, who unexpectedly encounters Gilles' younger brother René La Suze and René's friend, Thibault de Monsoreau, in the forest near her home in Tufforé in Anjou. Sexually attracted to René, but fearing his possible malice, she sets forth, after her elderly grandmother's death, with her uncle Frère Colin and her brother Ernault to go downriver on the Loire in the direction of Champtocé to lie low. In the course of their journey, they are joined by the boatman, Mathelin, and later by the survivors of a troupe of entertainers, who have been attacked and massacred. The leader of the group is Yvain Marjac, and other members are the thirty-year-old Marianne Boulisse, who is quite attracted to Hermeline, and two teenaged boys, Philippe Breghel and Yoann Broulaine. At a fair in the town of Igrandes, they also add to their group Guillemette, who was Gilles' nurse when he was an infant, and her only son Jeannot, now thirteen like Gilles.

As Gilles, living at Champtocé in Anjou, does not become a main character in this plotline until midway through the novel, the actions of the villains, led by Jehan de Malestroit (who in 1440, as controller of the finances of Brittany, presses for Gilles' trials), are intercut with the story of the above-mentioned characters. One night in a churchyard, Malestroit meets the forty-year-old Perinne Martin, who years later will be known as Meffraye, the woman who lured children into Gilles' clutches. Perinne has had a shady past, at one point being in the service of the notorious Isabeau of Bavaria, helping her to conceal away from court her bastard child named Philippe. Frère Colin eavesdrops on them talking that night, before Meffraye and Malestroit go to the Château de Monsoreau, where they meet Thibaut de Monsoreau and René La Suze, who decide to accompany them toward Chamtocé, where Meffraye claims to have family business.

This business turns out to be her desire to find her cousin, Jauffré Beaugeois of Champagne. They encounter him earlier than expected when he rescues them from the local brigands, "les écorcheurs de Boire." Jauffré leads them to the fortified chapel of Saint-Georges, where they meet up with an anti-Semitic prior, Antioche de Plessis-Macé, who in turn takes them to his friend Olivier le Fol at the crypt of Le Nid du Corbeau. Olivier le Fol is quite demented with hatred for the family of Olivier Clisson, his son-in-law, because Clisson, who had had murdered with the aid of Jean de Craon (Gilles' guardian, his mother's father) his own child, Gaucelm, whose mother was Olivier le Fol's daughter. Not only does this group despise the Craon and Clisson clans, but the Valois as well, through their friendship with Meffraye, who sympathized with Isabeau of Bavaria's hatred of her husband Charles VI. In fact, we learn that it was Olivier and Jauffré who were responsible for the Bal des Ardents of 28 January 1393 and the provocation of Charles VI to madness in the forest near Le Mans on 5 August 1392. They have been biding their time for more mischief since then. Mettraye has wanted to get Malestroit in contact with them to strengthen the Breton opposition to Charles VI.

Gilles comes in contact with both groups of characters. When we meet him as a boy, he gets into a fight with his tutor, Michel de Fontenay, for making a manuscript illumination of a hunt after human prey, featuring a torn-up cadaver of a human body. Fontenay reveals his horror at Gilles' illustration and tries to get Jean de Craon to punish Gilles, but the evil old man scorns him instead.

Then, the traveling players and other characters with Hermeline stop at the castle to perform. At a party there, Gilles is smitten by young Yoann, and, losing control of himself, he humiliates the drunken Fontenay in public by knocking him to the floor and pouring wine down his throat.

The plot thickens when Gilles falls passionately in love with a Jewish ceramicist named Élie, whom he has persuaded his grandfather to lodge in a cave-atelier on the Champtocé estate. One day, Gilles tried to force himself on Élie, fearing that Élie's complete indifference to him may be because he is interested in a local commoner named Macaire, who enters briefly at this point and then runs out. Gilles leaves Élie's atelier, hurling terrible anti-Semitic insults at him. Soon after, he receives a thrill when Élie is burned to death after his workshop is torched. However, Gilles had nothing at all to do with the arson and murder.

Meanwhile, at Champtocé, René has fallen in love with Hermeline, and he kisses her in public, which causes an enraged Jean de Craon to leave the castle with Gilles and to send René away. During this time, Gilles works on a play about Caligula to star Yoann. After a terrible nightmare, Craon agrees to go back with Gilles to Chamtocé. When they arrive there, a massacre has taken place, and the actors have been killed along with Father Tournfeuille, their friend. Frère Colin, dying as a result of wounds sustained in the attack, tells Gilles as best as he can what happened: three unknown, mysterious monks were responsible. Soon afterward, Gilles learns from a partially repentant Jauffré part of the story: Jauffré Beaugois, Prior Antioche, and Olivier le Fol perpetrated the killings. Colin tells him to track down the three men, who are responsible for persecuting infidels, Jews, and artists in the name of a purifying God. In their case, says Colin, "L'ange cache le loup" [a wolf hides in angel's guise] (174). Gilles tells him that he himself will become a wolf. Gilles begins a life of murder by having Jauffré kill Antioche and Olivier. Meffraye predicts to Gilles that he will sell his soul to the Devil in alchemical pursuits. She also reveals that Malestroit sacrificed a child at the foot of the cross for Jeanne le Sage, the benefactor of Gilles' father, Guy de Laval. A decade after, in 1429 just before he meets Joan of Arc, Jauffré tells Gilles that Joan is actually the bastard of Isabeau, the so-called Philippe, who had been deliberately declared dead so that no one would look for her. After the taking of Orléans, René kills Jauffré for murdering his beloved Hermeline.

Gilles' attraction to boys of his own age as a thirteen-year-old has three manifestations in the novel. At his first meeting with Yoann, at the party when René has returned home, we read that one would have to have been quite blind not to be able to see a cursed flame in Gilles' eyes (121). A little later, as the minstrels perform, Gilles eyes are riveted on Yoann (126). Unfortunately, even at this age Gilles associates sadism and sex. When, several months later,

Gilles finally has a private scene with Yoann, his confession of his uncontrollable sadistic feelings prompts a fierce rejection. Gilles tells him of a hunt, but this story reminds Yoann of an occasion when he was a pre-teen and a troubadour wanted to carry him off to the Orient as his beloved. Yoann turned him in and was responsible for his torture and hanging. He says he can never forget this event.

Next, Élie provokes guilt feelings mixed with bizarre fantasies in Gilles. Gilles threatens Élie with destruction for rejecting him (151). Gilles considers Élie an artist, and for him artists and perverts are similar. Gilles whips Élie in their last meeting, while Élie, tied up like Saint Sebastian, is begging for mercy at his knees (149). Gilles tells him that he wants to die of pleasure, and he claims that Élie should have sacrificed to him his virginity on the altar of Eros (149). Later, Gilles boasts about having brought about Élie's death (152), but he is raving, since ultimately we find out that he had nothing to do with it.

Finally, Jeannot, the son of his nurse, actually has sex with Gilles, unlike Élie and Yoann. Gilles first scandalized him with talk of possibly having sex with his four-year-old financée and then tried to provoke Jeannot even further by asking him to hit him. At last, Gilles grabs him after they bathe and tells him that he is going to baptize him. They repeatedly have sex together. A repentant Jeannot tells the priest that he was overcome with pleasure and could not resist Gilles' desire. When he is finally able to do so, Gilles mocks him (132). Yet, we never get to see Gilles with Jeannot directly, only through the eyes of the frightened youth.

The novel had begun with a scene the night before the execution, when Michel, the sixteen-year-old son of the jailor, Gilbert Peau-de-Loup, comes to Gilles' cell because he is not convinced of Gilles' guilt and wants to hear the story from the prisoner's lips. Gilles tells Michel that he has been accused of the vice of sodomy (10) and that witnesses claimed that he ejaculated semen on the stomachs of his victims before, during, and after their deaths (11). Gilles never actually says if the accusations are true or not. The novel then moves into flashback, but the point of view is only a few times that of Gilles. Just before we hear the story, Gilles tells Michel, who wants to learn the truth, that there is no truth. The narrator then tells us, "Personne ne serait aussi attentif [que Michel] pour entendre, du printemps du loup, le secret…"13) ["No one would have been more attentive [than Michel] to hear the secret of the springtime of the wolf"].

When we return to the frame story at the end of the novel, and Gilles talks again with Michel, Gilles admits to no crimes, and the main story, by showing the evil nature of Malestroit, leads us to conclude that Malestroit had framed him to get his estates. Gilles goes to his death looking his enemy Malstroit right in the eye. Apparently, Gilles confessed only so that Malestroit would not get the pleasure of torturing him. Gilles dies heroically, as the last line of the novel reads: "C'etait, de Rais, le dernier triomphe. Michel se réjouit en lisant une folle colère sur le visage de Malestroit, spectateur de ce "Jeu de Martyr" (197), ["It was the last triumph of de Rais. Michel rejoiced in reading a mad anger on the face of Malestroit, spectator of this 'Game of Martyrdom.'"]

Unlike Ragon, Prouteau, and Jacquemard-Sénéscal, Robert Nye draws on the trial records to present a traditional view of Gilles as murderer and pervert. A note in the back of the volume makes it clear that Nye has worked closely from the trial records, their translations in Georges Bataille's volume (1959, rpt. 1965) and the major sources up to 1924. At the heart of Nye's *The Life and Death of My Lord Gilles de Rais* is the slowly dawning realization of the narrator, Dom Eustache Blanchet, that Gilles is a great criminal. The novel is the story as set down by Blanchet in Subiaco, Italy, where he is suffering from leprosy, from 4 July 1456 to 28 December 1457. Blanchet has no sympathy for sexual behavior not endorsed by the Catholic Church, and so Nye's novel offers the most traditional view of the five of Gilles as sexual deviant and killer. The novel falls entirely outside the rehabilitation process that infuses the novels of Prouteau and Jacquemard-Sénécal.

From the moment that he arrives at Tiffauges, finds Gilles is away, and meets Messire Roger de Bricqueville, Giles's cousin, instead, Dom Eustache tries to read signs that he does not understand. The first is the erect penis of the naked Roger. Eustache cannot remember if it was actually offered to him or if it was part of a dream or vision (21). Arriving home, Gilles shows Blanchet his strange braquemard, which had seven scenes engraved on it, some of which seem to refer to Jeanne d'Arc. Another sign is the volume of Suetonius's *Lives of the Caesars*, with its depiction of the sex orgies of Tiberius with little boys.

Soon afterward, the false Jeanne becomes a member of the castle's bizarre ménage. Prelati is predictably one of the most eccentric, but there is also a double of Gilles called Rais le Hérault. Blanchet becomes so troubled by Tiffauges that he flees to the village inn at Mortmagne, where he has one of his terrifying dreams about a secret chamber as white as alabaster, probably to be read retrospectively as the charnel room that he does not want to know about. A traveler tells Blanchet that Gilles kills little children and uses their blood to write a special book. However, Gilles' agents take Blanchet back to Tiffauges on 28 December 1439, Holy Innocents Day, by which time the false Jeanne has fled. An even more sinister figure, Meffraye, the collector of pretty children, now appears.

Still unaware of Gilles' crimes, the frightened Eustache moves back with Gilles and the others to Machecoul in Brittany. Gilles engages Blanchet in theological discussions, patronizes him as "my man," and insists that he himself is a perfect Christian. Then Gilles begins to call Blanchet "God's spy."

Gilles insists that he is the mirror of Jeanne (151) and that he feels much guilt for not trying to save her (158); justifies his alchemical work by comparing it to the transubstantiation during the Mass (133); and asks Blanchet to pray for the souls of various boys, some of whose names are written on pieces of parchment (171).

Blanchet senses that there is some key to Gilles's story in that of Jeanne d'Arc:

> The problem of whether it is morally reprehensible to dwell upon Gilles's story is more interesting than the man. As a matter of opinion, I would say that it might be better to forget him if it were not for Joan of Arc. If all that we had here was an account of a life given up to vile enjoyment of the kind of depravities common to the worst of the Roman emperors, then he would be an object fit only for contempt, or at best pity, and the account should be made in such a manner that he would be soon forgotten, for the good of all. I say that it is because of the great mystery of Gilles' love for Joan that he is worth our study. Is his evil to be explained as a dreadful No of an answer to her goodness? Or, as in some moods he sought over-simply to explain it to me, as an act of revenge against God for allowing her death? Gilles was a spoiled child swayed by pride, and just as a man in church is tempted most easily to imagine orgies on the altar, in the holy of holies, so his expression of rebellion against God by the mere satisfying of fantastic lusts need not too much surprise us. It is in the coincidence of Gilles and Joan that the mystery lies. Only when I imagined their marriage did I start to tell the story. (172-73)

Blanchet wants to place Gilles on a continuum with other sinners, not in special category. He is neither a metaphysical sinner nor a figure of diabolic proportions, but a person carried away by fantasies stemming from his worst self. When Gilles wants to use Blanchet as his confessor, the priest is petrified of what he might learn, and he escapes from the situation by having Gilles confess instead to Dom Olivier, a priest who is obviously dying from something like tuberculosis (163). Soon after Blanchet makes this comment, Gilles commits the sacrilege of interrupting the Pentecostal mass at St. Etienne, and his days are numbered. He relives Jeanne's death and, in the middle of his agitated state, hits Blanchet on the mouth, knocking him against the wall so that he falls from his bench (185). After moving back to Tiffauges in a hurry, Gilles is accused of murder, witchcraft, and sodomy, and arrested.

Reflecting on the accusation of sodomy, Blanchet states:

> Why did I find it so dreadful, this accusation that my master was a sodomite? I suppose because of all sins that one has always seemed to me the act of most deliberate rebellion against the will of God. St. Augustine once defined sin in essence as any thought, word or deed against the law of

God. There is therefore a sense in which by any sin a man prefers to choose some self-gratification in opposition to and in defiance of God's laws. This particular sin, the pursuit of self-gratification against Nature, *contra Naturam*, seems to me Luciferian in its malice, an act of deliberate and calculated wickedness. (214)

For Blanchet, sodomy drags the soul down and constitutes a sin against grace as well as against Nature, and it is no better or worse than murder (214). This is his one major statement about Gilles' sex crimes, and it is interesting that the issue of sex with children is not mentioned, given that in this retrospective narration, Blanchet is writing a philosophical paragraph interrupting the narrative, with knowledge of what was revealed at the trial. As Blanchet is taken off to Nantes as a prisoner, he thinks of Gilles, Prelati, Poitou, and Griart as "a dainty gang of perverts" (218).

Nye goes into much detail of Gilles' two trials; they constitute the last third of the book. Here Michel de Fontenay, priest of Angers, claims that he had heard that Gilles had been found in bed with a page once at about the age of sixteen (238) and that he had also heard that Gilles "liked to practice cruelties upon boys in private" (239). Meffraye reveals that, when she hunted down children, "I was told that the children could be either boys or girls, but that for preference they should have fair hair and be clean-limbed" (241). She maintains that she was never in the room when the impurities or murders were done and did not know of any sacrilege or of the fates of the children (242). Prelati, insisting on his scientific spirit, stated, "I might have given it to Gilles as my opinion, that the offering of boys' members was more efficacious than shedding the blood of cocks or doves. But that is no more than the teaching of Agobard or Avicenna applied to reality" (271). Prelati states that Gilles seemed to be haunted by the ghosts of his victims (273). The confessions of Poitou and Griart are given in much detail, as is Gilles' own confession: "I delighted in strangling little boys even as those boys discovered the very first pleasures and pains of their innocent flesh" (288). He admitted to lusting after their innocence and death (289). In his detailed description of the sexual murders, he says,

Coitus only excited me when I could prick the object of my desire until the blood came. Even then I would reject the usual orifice, in the case of the girls, and spills my seed on their bellies and arses. Stabbing and sodomy were my principal pleasures with these children. (289)

He claims that he thinks he was born with "an innate desire to humiliate and hurt, to wound and even destroy others in order thereby to create a sexual pleasure in myself" and that "I am different only in degree, not kind, from others who have given themselves over to these savage desires" (297).

Blanchet is glad that Gilles has repented and done one good thing in his life when he died. He went first to execution, so that his pages could see that he was really dead and would not be escaping while they were left to be killed because they had no social prestige. Blanchet believes that even Gilles was redeemable, and that he changed for the better at the trial. Blanchet states:

> It is my contention that all Gilles ever did in his life, after a certain date, was as the direct result of Joan's inspiration. Therefore, I say, at some point Gilles was inspired by Joan to confess his sins, to tell the truth, to return again to God. Joan came to him, in some way, at the turning point in his trial. There can be no other explanation for how he changed. (312).

Gilles asked forgiveness as a brother in Christ and begged the parents of the murdered children to pray for him and forgive him (317).

In the Epilogue, Blanchet states that he finally has stopped dreaming that he has to return to the castle where, in some dreams, he imagined the wedding of Gilles and Jeanne. This dream marriage he now considers his attempt to "make sense of the confluence of Good and Evil" (319). His ultimate conclusion: "I have come to realize that the key to evil is its being immaterial. Gilles, in the last analysis, does not matter." The novel concludes with the idea that we should remember Jeanne and forget Gilles. There is obviously a paradox here, since the novel calls up Gilles to remembrance. However, if Nye is speaking through Blanchet, he is suggesting that remembering Gilles leads nowhere emotionally whereas remembering Jeanne can be a valuable experience. Perhaps Nye wants to drive out the rehabilitators of Gilles or those who find some metaphysical significance in his crimes when there really is none.

In 1983, in *Gilles et Jeanne*, Michel Tournier did just that.[5] His is by far the most famous of the five novels under discussion, and he follows the tradition that has made Gilles and Jeanne a literary pair, already discussed in the context of Michel Ragon, whose novel is strongly marked by Tournier's. *Gilles et Jeanne* consists of twenty-seven easy-to-read short chapters, opening on 25 February 1429 with Jeanne on the day her destiny crossed with that of Gilles. Then the rest of the novel follows Gilles's life in chronological fashion, with only the next five chapters devoted to the period from 1429 to 1431. Tournier is more interested in Gilles as a practitioner of black arts and a murderer of children than as a sexual being. Thus, much of the middle section of the novel is given over to the arrival of Prelati, who eggs him on with blasphemies. For example, he reminds Gilles that Abraham was commanded to murder Isaac (1987: 89).

Tournier gives a very brief account of the trial, and he cuts off Poitou's graphic description. We read Poitou's interaction with Jean de Blouyn, the prosecutor:

> 'Did you witness what the Sire de Rais subjected those children to?
> 'Yes. The Sire de Rais, in order to take his carnal pleasure with these children, boys and girls, first took his member . . .'
> 'Silence! Not a word more !" (1987: 113)

At this point, de Blouyn puts his cloak over the crucifix as if Christ should not hear about such abominations (113). The description then begins again with Poitou saying, "[…]he took his member, rubbed it stiff, then stuck it between the child's thighs, avoiding, in the case of the girls, the natural passage" (113). As in the trial records, Poitou says that Gilles suspended the child, strangled him, and cut his throat. What is more important to Tournier is the killing and cutting of throats, as it connects back to the fairy-tale motif in which he is particularly interested. No complete episodes of Gilles at his sexual crimes is described. We do see him, however, on one night with a child:

> Gilles was there, surrounded by a group of ragged children, who observed him in deadly silence, the silence of birds hypnotized by a snake. Gilles was holding, close against his body, a boy of about seven or eight. The horseman's heavily gloved hand lingered over the boy's hair, then undid his clothes, closing at last around the delicate neck.
>
> It was at this point that Prelati's voice rang out: 'Seigneur Gilles!'
>
> Gilles looked like a sleepwalker who had just woken up. He stared around him wildly. He loosened his grip on the child, who immediately slipped sway to join his companions. They all then fled, with cries that might have been either triumph or of fear. (84-85)

The evil toward which Gilles descends is a metaphysical one, since he is determined to remain true to Jeanne, whose execution had convulsed him. Tournier writes, "Gilles now understood that if he wanted to follow Jeanne, he would have to continue the descent into hell that he had begun even before the Florentine's arrival" (88). Gilles is not evil as a youth, and he becomes so only when he is traumatized by the murder of a saint he deeply loved. Existentially, he tries to become as low as she has become elevated. At his trial, he provokes the court by reminding them that Christ said, "Let the little children come unto me" (119). Indeed they did, and perhaps the most striking episode of the story is one of the verbal pictures that the narrator offers up to illustrate what was being said about Gilles. It is a version of the story of Petit Poucet, and it has no happy ending. It concludes:

> The group plunges into the forest led by Poucet. Soon they arrive at the castle entrance. They knock on a postern. The gate opens as if by magic. They go in one by one. The gate shuts behind them. (48)

Later, Tournier does include quotations from the trial depositions of parents, who told how their children mysteriously disappeared. Whether or not Gilles was metamorphosed into an Ogre or Bluebeard or other fairy-tale villain has been debated, but Tournier suggests that he was. This idea is somewhat at odds with the existential import of the story, which leaves us with Gilles metaphysically luxuriating in the memory of his crimes and going to his death with the words, "Jeanne! Jeanne! Jeanne!" on his lips (124). Despite the fact that it follows the historical trajectory of Gilles's life and uses telling historical details, Tournier's story reads like a fable. Tournier avoids Ragon's concern with androgyny, Prouteau's with pederasty, Jacquemard-Sénécal's with sadistic same-sex attraction, and Nye's with sex crimes.

In conclusion, the case of Gilles de Rais has much interest for sexual politics. We can see that Tournier, an openly gay novelist and intellectual, does not call much attention to Gilles as homosexual torturer of boys but rather to Gilles as their murderer with the trappings of the fairy-tale ogre. It would seem that the only way that Gilles can be rehabilitated for queerdom is to insist along the lines of Prouteau that his trial was trumped up and that, unlikely as it seems, he did not commit the sex crimes and murders to which he confessed and which his two servants described in gory detail. Following the court record offers no way out to a new evaluation of Gilles' sexuality, as we can see through Blanchet as narrator of Nye's version. One novelist, Ragon, avoids the issue by not mentioning the sexuality, only the murders. Jacquemard-Sénécal, by leaving off Gilles' story before 1432, implies that Jehan de Malestroit had Gilles tried on trumped-up charges. However, in the end we are left with the problem that the least stereotyped and most queer view of Gilles, that of Ragon, is produced at the expense of any sexual details, the details that Prouteau interpreted as a dignified pederasty.

Most queer people will not be comfortable with a Gilles who has sex with eight to twelve-year-old boys. In contrast to some of these five novelists, some of us may wish to describe or even write off Gilles as criminally insane. Under the MacNaughton Rule introduced in Great Britain in 1843, an insane person can be held in court in some circumstances as responsible for his crimes, and as D. B. Lewis wrote in *The Soul of Marshall Gilles de Raiz*, in 1952, this evaluation seems to be applicable to the case of Gilles. In none of the five novels is Gilles criminally insane but rather a queer (Ragon), a pederast (Prouteau), a sadist in sex (Jacquemard-Sénécal), a sodomite (Nye), and a real-life Ogre (Tournier). There are as many views as there are novelists, and no consensus about the nature of his crimes emerges.

CARDINAL STRITCH UNIVERSITY

NOTES

[1] The MS. of the Procès de Gilles de Rais is found in the Archives Départementales de la Loire-Atlantique, Nantes, E. 189. The "Reclamation des héritiers de Rais contre la confiscation des biens du maréchal" is in the Bibliothèque Municipale de Nantes, mss. 2035 and 2036. See also René Blanchard, ed. *Cartulaire des sires de Rays (1160-1449)* (Poitiers, Société Française d'Imprimerie et de Librairie, 1888-1899).

[2] For early novels on Gilles, see Hippolyte Bonnelier, *Raiz*, 2 vols. (Paris: Allardin, 1834); Emilie Carpentier, *Les Memoires de Barbe-Bleu* (Paris: J. Vermot, 1865); Jean de Roche-Sevre, *Les Derniers Jours de Barbe-Bleu (Gilles de Rais)* (Nantes: E. Grimaud, 1888); S[amuel] R[utherford] Crockett, *The Black Douglas* (New York: Doubleday & McClure, 1899); Aime Giron and Albert Tozza, *La Bete de luxure, Gilles de Rais* (Paris: L'Edition Moderne, 1907); Roland Brevannes, *Les Messes noire: L'Ament de la demone; grand roman dramatique inedit,* 1908.

[3] Several French authors made briefer mention of Gilles : Voltaire in *Essai sur les moeurs*, Stendhal in *Mémoires d'un touriste*, Flaubert in *Voyage en Bretagne*, Rimbaud in *Les Illuminations*, and Artaud in "Le Théâtre de cruauté."

[4] See Joan Evans and Paul Studer, eds., *Saint Joan of Orleans; Scenes from the Fifteenth Century Mystère du siège d'Orleans*, trans. Joan Evans (Oxford: Clarendon P, 1926) ; V[icky] L[ou] Hamblin, ed. *Le Mystère du Siège d'Orléans : édition critique* (Geneva : Droz, 2003) [from a manuscript (Reg. lat. 1022) in the Biblioteca Apostolica Vaticana]. *Le Mystère* has been attributed to Jacques Milet.

[5] For discussions of Tournier's novel, see Giampiero Giampieri, "Gille de Rais e Francesco Prelati: A proposito di maghi e magie," *Città di Vita* 49.5 (Sept.-Oct. 1994): 401-10; Mireille Rosello, "Jésus, Gilles et Jeanne: 'Qui veut noyer son chien est bien content qu'il ait la rage'", *Stanford French Review* 13.1 (Spring 1989) : 81-95.

WORKS CITED

Bataille, Georges. "La Tragédie de Gilles de Rais."*Procès de Gilles de Rais : Documents précédés d'une introduction de George Bataille*. Paris: Club Français de Livre, 1959. 5-93. Rpt. Paris: Jean-Jacques Pauvert, 1965.

_____. "The Tragedy of Gilles de Rais." *The Trial of Gilles de Rais*. Trans. Richard Robinson. Los Angeles: Amok, 1991. 9-62.

Bayard, Jean-Pierre. *Plaidoyer pour Gilles de Rais: Maréchal de France, 1404-1440.* Etréchy: Editions du Soleil Natal, 1992.

Black, Candice. Introduction. *Dark Star : The Satanic Rites of Gilles de Rais*. New York: Creation Books, 2005. 5-8.

Bossard, Eugène. *Gilles de Rais, maréchal de France, dit Barbe-Bleue, 1404-1440: d'après des documents inédits*. Paris: H. Champion, 1885; Rpt with "Eugène et Gilles" by François Argelier. 327-334. Grenoble: J. Millon, 1992.

Fererro, Ernesto. *Barbablu: Gilles de Rais et il tramonto del Medioevo*. Casale Monferrato (Alessandria): Piemme, 1998. [Rev ed. of *Gilles de Rais : delitti e castigo di Barbablu* (Milan: Mondadori, 1975).]

Gabory, Emile. *La Vie et la Mort de Gilles de rais, dit —à tort—Barbe-Bleue*. Paris: Perrin, 1926.

Heers, Jacques. *Gilles de Rais*. Paris: Perrin, 1994.

Huysmans, Joris-Karl. *Là-bas*. Paris: Plon, 1891.

Hyatte, Reginald, trans. and ed. *Laughter for the Devil: The Trials of Gilles de Rais, Companion-in-Arms of Joan of Arc (1440)*. Translation of Marie Alphonse René de Maulde La Clavière's edition of the trials in Latin and Middle French published in Bossard's *Gilles de Rais*. Rutherford, NJ: Fairleigh Dickinson UP, 1984.

Jacquemard-Sénécal. *Le Printemps du loup: Une Jeunesse de Gilles de Rais; roman.* Le Château-d'Olonne: D' Orbestier, 1998.

Kaiser, Georg. *Gilles und Jeanne.* Potsdam: G. Kiepenheuer, 1923.

Lampo, Hubert. *De Duivel en de Maagd.* The Hague: A. A. M. Stols, 1955.

Le Coz, Martine, *Gilles de Rais: ignoble et chrétien.* Nantes: Editions Opéra, 1995.

Lewis, D. B. *The Soul of Marshal Gilles de Raiz, with Some Account of His Life and Times, His Abominable Crimes, and His Expiation.* London: Eyre & Spottiswoode, 1952.

Morgan, Val, *The Legend of Gilles de Rais (1404-1440) in the Writings of Huysmans, Bataille, Planchon, and Tournier.* Lewiston, NY: Edwin Mellen P, 2003.

Meurger, Michel. *Gilles de Rais et la littérature.* Rennes: Terre de Brume, 2003.

_____."L'Imaginaire de Gilles de Rais: La Bête, l'esthète, et Barbe-Bleue." *Le Visage Vert* No. 10 (April 2001): 20-55.

Nye, Robert. *The Life and Death of My Lord Gilles de Rais.* London: Hamish Hamilton, 1990.

Prouteau, Gilbert. *Gilles de Rais, ou le gueule de loup.* Monaco: Du Rocher, 1992.

Ragon, Michel. *Un Amour de Jeanne; roman.* Paris: Albin Michel, 2003.

Reinarch, Salomon. "Gilles de Rais." *Revue de l'Université de Bruxelles.* Dec. 1904: 161-82. Rpt. *Cultes, Mythes, et Religions.* 8 vols. Paris: 1912. 4: 267-99. Rpt. Ed. Hervé Duchêne. Introduction by Pierre Brunel. Paris: Laffont, 1996. 1026-42.

Thoma, Richard. "Tragedy in Blue." *Dark Star: The Satanic Rites of Gilles de Rais.* New York: Creation Books, 2005. 103-40.

Tournier, Michel. *Gilles & Jeanne; récit.* Paris: Gallimard, 1983.

_____. *Gilles and Jeanne.* Trans. Alan Sheridan. London: Grove Weidenfeld, 1987.

APPENDIX: Gilles de Rais in Literature Since 1975

A. Novels

Ragon, Michel. *Un Amour de Jeanne; roman.* Paris: Albin Michel, 2003.

Benson, Ann. *Thief of Souls.* New York: Delacorte, 2002.

Jacquemard-Sénécal. *Le Printemps du loup: Une Jeunesse de Gilles de Rais; roman.* Le Château-d' Olonne: D' Orbestier, 1998.

Obermeier, Siegfried. *Im Zeichen der Lilie: Der Roman über Leben und Zeit des dämonischen Ritters Gilles de Rais, Kampfgefährte der Johanna von Orléans.* Hamburg: Rowohlt, 1996.

Bérot, Violaine. *Jehanne.* Paris: Denoël, 1995.

Facon, Roger. *Moi, Gilles de Rais, noble capitaine de Jehanne.* Bruxelles: Éditions Savoir pour Être, 1994.

Prouteau, Gilbert. *Gilles de Rais, ou le gueule de loup.* Monaco: Du Rocher, 1992.

Nye, Robert. *The Life and Death of My Lord Gilles de Rais.* London: Hamish Hamilton, 1990.

Le Coz, Martine. *Gilles de Raiz, ou, La confession imaginaire: roman.* Paris: Seuil, 1989.

Natonek, Hans. *Blaubarts letzte Liebe.* Afterword by Juergen Serke. Vienna: Zsolnay. 1988.

Tournier, Michel. *Gilles & Jeanne; récit.* Paris: Gallimard, 1983. Trans. Alan Sheridan. London: Grove Weidenfeld, 1987.

Lucie-Smith, Edward. *The Dark Pageant: A Novel about Gilles de Rais.* London: Blond and Briggs, 1977.

B. Plays, Operas, Radio Plays

Claus, Hugo. *Gilles et la nuit.* Trans. Marnix Vincent. Adaptation by Jean-Claude Carrière. Paris: Calmann-Levy, 1995. [*Gilles en de nacht.* Amsterdam : Bezige Bij, 1989.]

Canat de Chizy, Edith, composer. *Tombeau de Gilles de Rias.* Libretto by Enzo Cormann, Paris Pierre Verany, 1995. Lionel Peintre, baryton; Feodor Atkine, Jean Boissery, recitants; Camillo Angarita, l'enfant; Brigitte Peyre, soprano; other soloists; Maîtrise de Paris; Patrick Marco, director; Ensemble musicatreize; Roland Hayrabedian; Philharmonie de Lorraine; Jacques Houtmann, conductor. PV795091

Cormann, Enzo. *La plaie et le couteau: tombeau de Gilles de Rais; suivi de, L'apothéose secrète Paris: Minuit* 1993.

Carrière, Jean-Claude, and Luis Bunuel. *Là-Bas.* Preface by Jean-Claude Carrière.Paris: Ecriture, 1993.

Clark, Sally. "Jehanne of the Witches." *Good Time Women from Way Back When* [with *A Woman's Comedy* by Beth Hurt]. Toronto: Playwrights Canada P, 1993. 7-142.

Boesmans, Philippe, composer. *La Passion de Gilles de Rais.* Libretto by Pierre Mertens. Paris: Ricercar, 1985 Peter Gottlieb; Carole Farley; Colette Alliot-Lugaz; Alexander Oliver; other singers; Chorus and Orchestra of the Opéra national (Belgium); Pierre Bartholomée, conductor. Recorded during the premiere performances on Oct. 25, 27, and 30, 1983, at the Théâtre Royal de la Monnaie, Brussels. RIC 024-025.

Mertens, Pierre. *La Passion de Gilles de Rais.* Le Paradou: Actes Sud, 1982.

Planchon, Roger *Gilles de Rais, l'infâme.* Paris: Gallimard, 1975.

The Virgin Martyr Updated:
"In the Garden of the North American Martyrs" as a Secular Saint's Life

Anita Hembold

The saints are like the stars. In his providence, Christ conceals them in a hidden place that they may not shine before others when they might wish to do so. Yet they are always ready to exchange the quiet of contemplation for the works of mercy as soon as they perceive in their hearts the invitation of Christ.

—Saint Anthony of Padua[1]

What has been said and done by the saints ought not be concealed in silence. God's love provided their deeds to serve as a norm of living for the people of their own times as well as of those years which have since passed; they are now to be imitated piously by those who are faithful to Christ.

—Saint Maximinus[2]

In his short story "In the Garden of the North American Martyrs," Tobias Wolff offers a modern twist on a medieval genre, the saint's life. He presents the reader with an unlikely heroine, Mary, a timid, mousy academic whose defining purpose in life has been "playing it safe," a pursuit she has embraced with dogmatic orthodoxy and nearly religious fervor. Wolff leads this unlikely saint on a three-part spiritual journey, through misguided complacency, to troubled insecurity, and finally, through a figurative act of martyrdom, to spiritual, moral, and intellectual authenticity.[3]

The medieval genre known as the "saint's life" enjoyed tremendous popularity in its own era;[4] indeed, it would be difficult to overstate its popularity or its influence throughout the Middle Ages. In the intervening years, however, the genre has fallen into disfavor, not only due to an increasing secularization in society, but because it defied disciplinary standards of worth: historians shunned it for its failure to provide documentary evidence, while literary scholars found such tales derivative and inartistic (Heffernan 17). Ironically, Wolff uses the saint's life, a form long held in disfavor by both literary scholars and historians, as a vehicle for presenting a literary story about the spiritual journey of his protagonist, a historian.

As is so often the case with generic labels, the term by which this literary form has come to be known offers a somewhat misleading perspective on the nature of the genre. "Saint's life" would seem to suggest a biographical account, perhaps even more specifically, a spiritual autobiography, and while hagiographies do concern themselves with issues deemed spiritually significant, they focus more intently on the spectacular and miraculous. Indeed, the label "saint's life" misleads, in that it calls attention to the life of the saint, whereas the capstone of the genre, its culminating purpose, is a description, complete with gory details, of the saint's martyrdom under exceptionally ferocious and cruel circumstances.[5]

Furthermore, a key aspect of saints' lives, and particularly of those of female saints, is the foregrounding of the "virginity at risk" topos. According to Jocelyn Wogan-Browne, the importance of the genre of the virgin saint's life cannot be overstressed: this literary form is "a, perhaps *the*, major Western form of representing women" (3; emphasis in original). In part, this significance derives from the high value placed on "the pervasiveness of virginity as a cultural ideal and a form of exemplary biography for women" (Wogan-Browne 3); virginity, in these saints' lives and in Wolff's story as well, "symbolizes a lost primal wholeness" (Wogan-Browne 20). Although Wogan-Browne's observations concern the genre in general, her statement that "virginity literature offers in many ways a liberatingly unofficial writing-space where professional knowledge is informally deployed" summarizes precisely what occurs in the climax of Wolff's short story.

The lives of female saints typically feature a virgin as martyr, with strong attention given to the issue of virginity, as well as a strongly defined virgin/pagan antithesis. Thus, martyrdom occurs not so much as a result of adhering to Christianity in the face of challenges from paganism as it does from keeping one's chastity in the face of sexual advances: the virgin-hero, resisting the attentions of some powerful pagan ruler, persists to the final extremity of martyrdom. In such stories, Christ defends his heroines, not by preventing the assault on their integrity, but by allowing, in a rhetorical mode, the triumph of the persecuted over the persecutor (Wogan-Browne 106).[6] What the martyrdom ultimately reveals is a pattern of events much larger than that over which the pagan powers presume to preside. At the heart of the saint's passion is a contest "not of strength, but of meanings" (Wogan-Browne 106), as revealed through language and rhetoric.

The female saint's life, because it served as a source of "inspiration, authority, and empowerment for women by suggesting a variety of relevant role models and experiences for them to admire, imitate, or to modify in order to fit their special needs or situations" (Tibbetts 56), provides an ideal vehicle for presenting the story of a woman seeking to preserve authenticity and yet ensure survival in a world attuned to the expression of only a limited range of values. So apt is this form for promoting the values which Wolff's story presents that Leslie Donovan's summary of the importance of the genre serves with equal accuracy as a summary of the significance of "In the Garden of the North American Martyrs": female saints' lives, like Wolff's story, represent women's genuine concerns

> about their own bodies, their physical vulnerability, their power in the world, and over their own selves. These lives represent the choices women had to make for themselves as well as portray their personal and public struggles to lead lives of value in the sociopolitical culture of Western Europe which restricted women's lives. Their stories offer a multilayered vision of women that is both historical and personal, radical and hegemonic, political and spiritual. (2)

While delivering up the miraculous in a sensational package may be the ultimate intent of hagiographic literature, the genre also offers social history. By placing these extraordinary stories within the context of the everyday, hagiographic writers reveal much about cultural contexts, often information about details of daily life, food and drink, the organization of rural and urban society, commercial and economic issues, gender and class relations, and, occasionally, specific dates related to military or political history (Hallsall). But from the perspective of purpose, these cultural matters are merely an aside: the function of hagiographic literature is to sustain and aid devotion by offering edifying and didactic tales to direct the reader to renewed faith and devotion.

Wolff builds an effective contemporary story onto these medieval foundations. In brief, this modernized saint's life runs as follows: Mary, a middle-aged history professor,[7] thrown out of work when the college at which she has taught for fifteen years closes, can find employment only at an unappealing college in Oregon. She takes the position but finds little contentment there; instead, she continues to apply to other universities. One day, she unexpectedly receives an invitation from a former colleague to apply for a position at the colleague's institution in New York. Mary travels there, only to learn that her invitation was merely a matter of form, a ploy to satisfy the school's affirmative-action policies. As part of what truly is a "mock" interview process, Mary must keep up appearances by delivering a classroom lecture, despite the fact that the interview committee had failed to inform her in advance of this expectation. What happens in this classroom provides the surprise martyrdom that concludes the story.

Unlike the heroines of many a medieval saint's life, Wolff's protagonist, throughout most of the story, is no paragon of virtue, but, rather, a flawed human being, so intent on saving her own life that she has in fact lost it. The first stage of Mary's spiritual journey, represented by her fifteen years of teaching at Brandon, marks the nadir of her spiritual development. At this point in the story—a point which accounts for the majority of Mary's professional life—Mary has made a career of making herself safe, ensuring her job security by a calculated retreat into inoffensiveness, since, as the very first line of the story reveals, "When she was young, Mary saw a brilliant and original man lose his job because he had expressed ideas that were offensive to the trustees of the college where they both taught. She shared his views, but did not sign the protest petition. She was, after all, on trial herself—as a teacher, as a woman, as an interpreter of history" (1611). In her estimate of the situation, Mary both errs and perceives accurately. Politically, she overestimates the importance of the paltry contribution made by adding her name to a petition: no doubt signers of the petition were neither fired nor censured *en masse*. Personally, however (although Mary herself does not necessarily perceive the application), Mary accurately recognizes this situation as a test, a trial: but she errs in perceiving that she passes, rather than fails, the test. Appropriately, it is on these very grounds—"as a teacher, as a woman, as an interpreter of history"—that Mary will be tried in her decisive New York interview.

Mary's retreat into spiritual, intellectual, and moral complacency comes at the cost of honesty, integrity, and self-expression. This retreat, however, associates her with the medieval virgin-saint, since "all good virgins' life-cycles begin in voluntary self-cloistering" (Wogan-Browne 26). Rather than speaking from her own store of knowledge and expertise, Mary fully scripts her lectures in advance. To be sure that she refrains from giving offense, she uses "the arguments and often the words of other, approved writers, so that she would not by chance say something scandalous" (1611).[8] Rather than adding to knowledge in her field, "Her own thoughts she kept to herself" (1611). Like the medieval virgin saint, Mary is "safely enclosed in her tower, bower, chamber, cave, or cell, and, most powerfully, within her own internalized sense of shame and decorum" (Wogan-Browne 24). A book that she publishes begins with the safety of certified fact, with words that Mary herself will come to perceive as inadequate: "It is generally believed that . . . " (1617). Her thoughts diminish, until it seems to Mary that "they shrank to remote, nervous points, like birds flying away" (1611). Coupled with this refusal to express herself comes a corollary disability: Mary develops a hearing loss, which she herself concludes comes from having strained too long to listen to all of the wrong voices (1612).

But ultimately, Mary's attempts at an inviolable self-protection fail. Although "no one at the college was safer than Mary," who, through a pattern of considered behavior and self-chosen eccentricities, was "making herself into something institutional, like a custom, or a mascot—part of the college's idea of itself" (1612), the institution itself folds as a result of financial mismanagement. Astray and adrift, and reaping the consequences of years of intellectual mediocrity, Mary can find work only at a new "experimental" college in Oregon, an institution more like an elementary school than a university: "The college was in one building. Bells rang all the time, lockers lined the hallways, and at every corner stood a buzzing drinking fountain. The student newspaper came out twice a month on mimeograph paper which felt wet. The library, which was next to the band room, had no librarian and no books" (1612).

Mary's understandable disappointment at acquiring so unsatisfactory a position leads her to continue to search for more appealing employment, but her problems in Oregon go far beyond mere job dissatisfaction. Indeed, Mary's dissatisfaction (or lack thereof) with the status quo serves a crucial function in defining her character. At Brandon, she had tolerated the sacrifices she made for security, notwithstanding the twinges of regret that she allowed herself to feel on occasion. For example, while at Brandon, she had wondered, from time to time, "whether she had been too careful" (1612). She recognized the deficiency of her contributions: "The things she said and wrote seemed flat to her, pulpy, as though someone else had squeezed the juice out of them" (1612).[9] And an image reflected in a glass, of herself straining to catch a colleague's voice, positively "disgusted" Mary.[10] But these trivial considerations seem too slight to shake Mary out of the cage of her complacency.

Not so in Oregon, where the whole of Mary's experience is described as a series of disappointments and malfunctions and where Mary's dissatisfaction begins to have a salutary effect on her willingness to compromise to achieve safety and security. Her professional life unrewarding, Mary finds things beginning to unravel in her personal life as well. Try as she might, she can no longer achieve the comfort which had cocooned and imprisoned her:

> The [Oregon] countryside was beautiful . . . and Mary might have enjoyed it if the rain had not caused her so much trouble. There was something wrong with her lungs that the doctors couldn't agree on, and couldn't cure; whatever it was, the dampness made it worse. On rainy days condensation formed in Mary's hearing aid and shorted it out. She began to dread talking with people, never knowing when she would have to take out her control box and slap it against her leg. (1612)

In Oregon, Mary can neither breathe nor hear properly, and her "control box" no longer allows her to be in control; her coping strategy has become not an asset but a liability. Her physical symptoms reflect her moral and spiritual decay. Mary recognizes the danger of continuing on in the present way: comparing herself to the junk cars that she sees propped on blocks in people's yards, she thinks of herself in a mechanized, dehumanized way, as "rusting out" (1612). Furthermore, although "Mary knew that everyone was dying, . . . it did seem to her that she was dying faster than most" (1612). In reality, little has changed in Mary's situation between Brandon and Oregon, save that in Oregon, Mary becomes newly sensitized to the inadequacy of her situation.

Fortunately, salvation is about to arrive, in the form of an invitation to interview at a prestigious college in New York. In preparation for the climactic scene in which Mary finds herself "on trial," Wolff imbues each paragraph of this portion of the story with rising significance, and he enmeshes his heroine and her antagonists in a complex web of Biblical and historical allusion. From Mary's arrival in New York State to the scene of her academic martyrdom, Wolff heightens the spiritual stakes attendant upon the characters' actions and reveals the callous heartlessness and cruelty of Mary's antagonists.

The New York opportunity seems to awaken something in Mary; she looks upon the event as a kind of homecoming. Thus, "[s]he read about the area with a strange sense of familiarity, as if the land and its history were already known to her" (1613). When she relates these feelings to Louise, the former colleague who has arranged the interview, Louise dismisses Mary's strange sense of *déjà vu* as "a hoax . . . just a chemical imbalance of some kind" (1613). But Mary is right and Louise is wrong. For Mary, the trip indeed constitutes a spiritual homecoming, during which Mary will find the authentic—and rather prophetic—voice of her spirit, and Mary's premonition of familiarity attests to her increasing spiritual sensitivity. Louise, on the other hand, displays her disdain for the spiritual realm; she attempts to explain Mary's spiritual intuitiveness on the basis of biology, and she cannot accept Mary's sense of call, destiny, and belonging.[11]

The story, however, does associate Louise with a different kind of spirituality. Louise, after picking Mary up at the airport, asks her fellow historian point-blank, "Tell me now—honestly—how do I look?" (1613). Mary recognizes that a lie is expected and responds according to form. But her real perception is that Louise "seemed gaunt and pale and intense. She reminded Mary of a description . . . of how Iroquois warriors gave themselves visions by fasting" (1613). Thus, Louise is a representative of pagan spirituality—and an opponent of the Christian spirituality which Mary represents. But this allusion to the Iroquois not only makes this association: within the context of the story, it serves a more much specific function as well. By associating Louise specifically with the Iroquois, the confederation of tribes responsible for the martyrdoms of the Jesuits who came to be known as the North American martyrs, Wolff designates Louise and her colleagues as their modern-day moral and spiritual descendants. Mary does, indeed, know the land and its history: she has heard this story before, and she and her colleagues are about to reenact, symbolically, another North American martyrdom.

Although Mary responds easily to Louise's question with the expected lie about her appearance, Louise's next utterance provokes the first moral quandary of Mary's visit. Louise attributes her imputed healthy appearance to the fact that "I've taken a lover," a decision that she reports as if it were a standard health-care measure prescribed by physicians: "My concentration has improved, my energy level is up, and I've lost ten pounds. . . . I recommend the experience highly. But you probably disapprove" (1613). This time, however, Mary "didn't know what to say," although she manages to make a non-judgmental comment. Throughout the story, Mary's challenge has been knowing what to say—whether to speak out truthfully or to retreat into the protection of silence.

This interchange between Louise and Mary also serves an additional function: it helps to highlight Mary as virgin heroine. Louise speaks openly and freely of her husband, lover, and children, and, by contrast, the reader realizes that Mary has been associated with no such relationships. Although the story does nothing to rule out Mary's acting on the sexual side of her nature, it also fails to ever associate her with an exercise of her sexuality. The stark contrast with Louise's outspoken sexuality renders Mary virginal by comparison, and Mary's name, allusively calling to mind the Virgin Mary, heightens her association with virginity.

But it is not Mary's sexual chastity to which the story attaches the greatest significance; rather, it is her academic and intellectual integrity which the story tempts her to violate. When Louise, *en route* to Mary's lodging, alludes for the first time to the classroom lecture that Mary must deliver on the following afternoon, Mary responds with horror at the thought of having to extemporize. Temptation arises when Louise "solves" the problem by telling Mary that she can read a lecture of Louise's instead, passing it off as her own. Over the course of the next twenty-four hours, this dilemma changes Mary's life; in fact, it results in her "martyrdom." Thus, the story's structure follows the ideological trajectory of the medieval saint's life: it "provide[s] an occasion for the display of intellectual debate and raise[s] questions of public social importance," as well as "examines the strength of individual conviction under duress" (Heffernan 273).

Mary's surrender to authenticity occurs gradually between the time Louise suggests the plagiarism and the time of the classroom lecture itself. Mary's first thought is that presenting Louise's work as her own was "wrong," but then "it occurred to her that she had been doing the same kind of things for many years, and that this was not the time to get scruples" (1614-15). For the first time, Mary confronts and admits the extent of her own intellectual compromise, and she recognizes it as wrong. But she cannot let the matter rest so easily and merely justify the present indiscretion on the basis of past errors; Mary cannot ignore the seriousness of what she proposes to do.

Wolff helps to build to the climax of the story by couching Mary's approach to the site of her upcoming martyrdom in imagery of intensifying contrasts between light and dark and by portraying Mary's movement as an ascent. As they approach the cabin at which Mary will spend the night before her fateful interview, they rise through the hills, into the wilderness and into the darkness. The few lights serve only to make "the darkness seem even greater" (1614). Louise drops Mary off at the cabin, where the wood for the fire is already laid, but she does nothing herself to dispel the cold and darkness in which she leaves Mary. But Mary is finding her way: here, she can both breathe and see: "She filled her lungs, to taste the air: it was tart and clear" (1615), as her lecture on the morrow will be. And she receives a kind of illumination, as well: "She could see the stars in their figurations, and the vague streams of light that ran among the stars" (1615). By the following afternoon, Mary's transformation will be completed, and her augmented seeing and breathing will be accompanied by a renewed kind of hearing, as well.

But as yet, in the proverbial darkness before the dawn, Mary continues to struggle. She cannot easily reconcile herself to reading Louise's lecture as part of her candidacy, because "It would change her. It would make her less—how much less, she did not know. But . . . [s]he certainly wouldn't 'wing it.' Words might fail her, and then what? Mary had a dread of silence. When she thought of silence she thought of drowning, as if it were a kind of water she could not swim in" (1615). Ironically, however, silence is precisely what Mary has been drowning in throughout most of her academic career. Wolff's careful phrasing, rendering Mary's thoughts about extemporizing as something she "wouldn't," as opposed to "couldn't" do, emphasizes the decision of the will involved in Mary's refusal to speak her own thoughts and signal the potential, lurking just below their surface, that she could choose to do otherwise.

Further encounters with the institutional ethos strengthen Mary's resolve to conduct herself with integrity. Louise returns to the cabin late that night, interrupting Mary's sleep with ongoing self-pitying complaints about the status of her extra-marital affair. On the following morning, a tour of the campus reveals the college's self-serving motto: "God helps those who help themselves." Glancing over the names of graduates, Mary sees how thoroughly the institution's graduates had done just that: "They had helped themselves to railroads, mines, armies, states; to empires of finance with outposts all over the world" (1616). As she reviews a plaque dedicated to alumni killed in wars, the paucity of names prompts her observation that "Here, too, apparently, the graduates had helped themselves" (1616). Her student tour guide, Roger, embodies the twisted institutional values: he becomes "reverent" gazing upon the power plant; for him, "this machine was the soul of the college" (1617). Unwittingly, he reveals both his (and the school's) sexist attitudes, as well as the real reason for Mary's having been granted an interview. Seeking to assure Mary of the college's progressivism, he explains, "People think the college is really old-fashioned, but it isn't. They let girls come here now, and some of the teachers are women. In fact, there's a statute that says they have to interview at least one woman for each opening" (1617). Though the full significance of these remarks does not become apparent until Mary's interview, the stage is being set for a conflict structured around the issue of gender, the essential battleground of the female saint's life.

After a travesty of an interview, in which Mary's qualifications for the position never enter into the desultory small talk which constitutes the dialogue, Louise reveals, under Mary's prodding, that she chose Mary to undergo the sham interview because Louise hoped to benefit personally: "I've been unhappy and I thought you might cheer me up. You used to be so funny" (1618). When Mary, understandably wishing to forego further humiliation, digs in her heels and refuses to deliver Louise's lecture, Louise insists that "All you have to do is read this. It isn't much, considering all the money we've laid out to get you here" (1618). Treating the proposed dishonesty as immaterial, Louise attempts to shame Mary into prostituting herself to uphold appearances. This scene is essential for establishing the context of virgin martyrdom that structures the narrative. Since the female saint's possession of virginity (here, figured as academic honesty) is not in itself sufficient to assure the saint's blessedness, but only a virginity heroically maintained against external assault (Heffernan 278), Louise's challenge to Mary's integrity provides the plot element necessary to ensure the efficacy and merit of Mary's sufferings. Louise, with her foreknowledge of her colleague's reticence about expressing her own opinions, no doubt believes she has successfully bullied Mary into submission and collusion. But Mary is about to emerge as virgin heroine, a powerful antagonist who will, like her medieval forebears, "[upset] everyone's expectations of her" and who will deceive, rebuke, outwit, display more courage than, and ultimately, triumph over men (Heffernan 292).

Wolff portrays the packed lecture hall into which Louise ushers Mary as a scene of martyrdom. The professors sit in the front row, with their legs "crossed." The sun that streams through the stained-glass windows of the room "paints the faces" of the audience and thus renders them Iroquois warriors set to do battle; it also evokes the hallowed atmosphere of a church. Audience and setting combine to picture Mary burning at the stake: "Thick streams of smoke from [a] young professor's pipe drifted through a circle of red light at Mary's feet, turning crimson and twisting like flames" (1618). The night before, at the cabin, Louise had observed to Mary, "they've laid a fire for you. All you have to do is light it" (1615). And so Mary does, both at the cabin and in the classroom.

Mary has come to the podium "unsure of what she would say; sure only that she would rather die than read Louise's article" (1618). Announcing that the room in which they find themselves is "the Long House, the ancient domain of the Five Nations of the Iroquois" (1618), she goes on to describe the Iroquois as cruel and pitiless: "[b]ecause they had no pity they became powerful, so powerful that no other tribe dared to oppose them" (1619). To her "tormentors'" increasing discomfort, she describes the deaths of the North American martyrs, but as she is about to deliver Jean de Brébeuf's last words, she arrives at "the end of her facts. She did not know what Brébeuf had said. Silence rose up around her; just when she thought she would go under and be lost in it she heard someone whistling in the hallway outside, trilling the notes like a bird" (1619). She finds the truth of Christ's words to his disciples: "On my account you will be brought before governors and kings as witnesses to them and to the Gentiles. But when they arrest you, do not worry about what to say or how to say it. At that time you will be given what to say, for it will not be you speaking, but the Spirit of your Father speaking through you" (Matthew 10:18-20).

Mary denounces their corruption, using the words of the Old Testament prophets: "Mend your lives. You have deceived yourselves in the pride of your hearts, and the strength of your arms. Though you soar aloft like the eagle, though your nest is set among the stars, thence I will bring you down, says the Lord. Turn from power to love. Be kind. Do justice. Walk humbly" (Obadiah 1:4; Micah 6:8; Wolff 1619).[12] Ignoring Louise's frantic waving and shouts of protest, the story ends—or perhaps merely begins—as Mary turns down her hearing aid, finding that she has "more to say, much more" and determined that "she would not be distracted again."[13]

In this final act of rebellion, which becomes an act of self-realization, Mary completes her transgression of boundaries. She joins the family of virgin martyrs who "breach marriage customs, sexual responsibilities, familial authority, and political status. Most of all, they insist on the supremacy of their own will as a vehicle of their faith and, in so doing, make themselves objects of public regard and controversy" (Tibbetts 15). No longer do Mary's true thoughts remain unvoiced. By sacrificing her regard for personal safety in her professional life, Mary ensures the future malice and ill will of the members of the interview committee. More promisingly, however, her decision to speak out may gain for her other admirers and might open the door for greater opportunities for her future at other institutions. Again, Wolff's story mirrors the dual effects of its medieval models, since "all saints, by their lives, stretch the boundaries of what we have conceived of as human possibility, and their zeal in breaking through conventional limitations can be both attractive and repellent, pointlessly mad and unshakeably [sic] sane at the same time" (Petroff 161). As the Apostle Paul observes, "the foolishness of God is wiser than man's wisdom, and the weakness of God is stronger than man's strength" (I Cor. 1:25).

In the brief but powerful climax of Wolff's story,[14] his virgin-hero Mary blazes brightly, emboldened and empowered as she experiences the power of a life paradoxically transformed. At the lowest and most desperate point of her academic career and moral life, Mary ascends to dazzling heights. Utterly victimized and utterly powerless, she finds the courage and power to speak the truth. Having resolved to lose her life, she finds it; having come to the moment of greatest weakness, she finds that God's strength is made perfect in her weakness. In her ultimate trial "as a teacher, as a woman, as an interpreter of history," Mary's sacrifice becomes a triumph. In this saint's-life-for-our-time, Christ prevails, wresting power from the powerful; bringing his representative through the flames and into the light; showing himself to be the friend and defender of the weak, the helpless, and the despised; and transforming suffering into glory. Wolff demonstrates what Hrotsvitha, a tenth-century nun and author of plays about virgin martyrs, affirms: "more glorious [is] the victory of those shown triumphing, especially when womanly frailty emerges victorious, and virile force, confounded, is laid low" (qtd. in Dronke 69).

But Wolff's story, like all good saints' lives, does not properly end with the words inscribed on the page, but in the response in the life of the reader. Saints' lives were never written merely as entertainment, but as models to be followed. Thus, Wolff's story serves as more than a merely Pyrrhic victory for Mary or as a neatly virtuoso display of poetic justice. Rather, just as Mary's newly awakened capacity for speaking out poses challenges to her fictive audience, it challenges the readerly audience as well. "In the Garden of the North American Martyrs" raises a number of troubling questions about workplace and gender politics: about the extent to which political correctness and power relations muzzle the free interchange of ideas which should characterize the functioning of a university; about the marginalization of Christian discourse within the academy; about the extent to which patriarchy continues to oppress and confine women and to dictate their roles for them. Finally, the story asks each reader to examine his or her own conscience and to consider the degree to which one's own practices serve either to further or to challenge the aims and practices of the systems and institutions which conspire to degrade the human spirit, to anesthetize one's moral sensibilities, and to silence the prophetic voice of truth.

TAYLOR UNIVERSITY COLLEGE

NOTES

[1] Although this statement from St. Anthony is widely quoted, I have not been able to locate its specific point of origin in his writings.
[2] This quotation comes from a life of St. Maximinus written by Bertholdus of Micy, 1:592.

[3] Alternatively, the three stages in Mary's journey could be classified according to the three-phase archetypal scheme which Thomas Heffernan finds operative in the medieval saint's life: renunciation, testing, and consummation. (For a description of these terms, see his chapter on "Virgin Mothers," especially pages 265-75). While for Heffernan (and for the medieval saint's life) "renunciation" means a rejection of the world, for Mary, renunciation consists not of withdrawal into hermetic sanctity but of a withdrawal from authenticity, a movement away from the desired goal. Nevertheless, Mary's renunciation serves precisely the function that Heffernan describes: it consists in "the rejection of one belief system [or, more accurately, in Mary's case, the repression of her primary belief system] in order to accept a new one which selectively controls the choices made as the narrative unfolds" (266).

[4] Linda Coon, in her chapter on "Hagiography and Sacred Models," offers a useful and wide-ranging introduction to the genre.

[5] The term "saint's life" does not necessarily refer to a unitary phenomenon. William Calin distinguishes two basic variations: stories of martyrdom and stories of exemplary asceticism. Alternatively, Rachel Anderson distinguishes between the *passio*, which portrays the suffering saint resisting opposition and undergoing martyrdom, and the *vita*, which serves a more classically biographical function. David Townsend defines the saint's life proper as the *vita*, of which he argues the *passio* to be an abbreviated form. These various distinctions notwithstanding, however, the term *vitae* is most often applied to the genre as a whole rather than to a particular form of narrative.

While the martyrdom narrative is the most familiar variety of saint's life, it reflects a development relevant to the earliest years of the Christian faith. Once the period of persecution had largely passed and the church emerged, in the fourth century, as a legitimate institution, the focus of saints' lives shifted from emphasizing heroic death to focusing on stories of "holy endurance" and, often, asceticism (Coon 4). While martyrdom constituted the greatest heroic virtue practicable by a believer when Christianity was an outlaw religion, in the Christian era, virginity came to replace martyrdom as the highest form of spiritual sanctity to which one could aspire (Heffernan 249, 252-53).

[6] Wolff has constructed an original tale, but one highly indebted, in a generic sense, to the genre of the saint's life. For example, his story offers many instructive parallels with the martyrdom of St. Katherine, as recounted in the Katherine group, an early thirteenth-century collection telling the stories of three virgin martyrs, Saints Katherine, Margaret, and Juliana. These texts, according to Julie Hassel, all "articulate powerful images of autonomy for unmarried women" (1). All three of these tales reach their climax in the public conflict between saint and pagan, in contests that "allow these women to demonstrate, and in narrative terms create, their own saintly lives" (Hassel 51). In the Katherine legend, the climactic encounter takes the form of a public debate. Katherine accuses the philosophers who oppose her of participating solely for financial reward, just as Mary will indict the materialism of her opponents. Like Katherine, Mary is given the opening role in the debate, traditionally, the inferior position, since it leaves her open to rebuttal from her opponents. But like the medieval saint, whom Hassel describes, Wolff's Mary "cleverly shifts the terms of the debate firmly to her own ground" (Hassel 59). Again, Hassel's description of the Katherine legend applies equally to Mary's martyrdom: she "refuses to debate them using pagan sources, their only body

of knowledge" (59); instead of reading Louise's paper, Mary takes a Biblical text as the starting point for her oration. In both cases, "[t]he philosophers do not challenge the new terms of the debate and instead are on the defensive, respondents to her argument" (Hassel 59). Again analogously, in both stories, the saint's opposition seeks not the woman's physical death, but the overcoming of her will (Hassel 60). Finally, and perhaps most tellingly, the two virgin heroes share similar traits. Hassel describes Katherine in terms fully appropriate to Mary: "Katherine emerges . . . as a powerful example of female autonomy and faith. She is an intellectual, capable of persuasive speech, and visionary" (62), eloquent in her use of theology as she presents her case before those who oppose her.

[7] In keeping with the medievalism of the chosen vehicle for this story, Wolff fails to provide last names for his characters. Mary is simply "Mary"; the colleague who invites her to interview in New York is merely "Louise"; we learn that she has a husband named Ted and a lover named Jonathan. The student who escorts Mary around the New York campus is simply "Roger." One exception to this rule occurs, and Wolff specifically identifies it as such: Louise "introduced Mary to the men [on the interview committee], but with one exception the names and faces did not stay together. The exception was Dr. Howells, the department chairman" (1617). Even here, Wolff follows the medieval form: while most characters in a medieval saint's life would be identified by first name only (and perhaps a toponymic), the chief pagan opponent, such as a duke or king, the ranking pagan authority, would, by contrast, be identified by title ("the King of . . . ") rather than by name. Wolff remains strikingly true in his adherence to the conventions of the saint's life. It is perhaps no coincidence as well that in choosing the name "Mary" for his protagonist, Wolff has chosen a name evocatively close in spelling to the word "martyr."

[8] Mary's refusal to speak her own ideas is a form of silencing, a response to authoritative strictures which prescribe the limits of speech. Such silence has often been associated with, and expected from, the virgin female, but Mary, as virgin martyr, will ultimately speak out, as her literary and historical predecessors have done, speaking, as it were, "in [a court] of law in order to restore justice" (Carlson and Weisl 7).

[9] Despite Mary's recognition of the poverty of her work, it is interesting to note that her awareness does not extend to agency: she feels, tellingly, as though "someone else" has impoverished her work. At this stage in her spiritual journey, Mary is ready neither to recognize nor to take responsibility for her failures as a scholar and as a person.

[10] Interestingly, the iconography of this scene, as described in the text, suggests medieval miniatures which portray acceptance of divine guidance as an act of hearing: thus, the text clearly represents Mary as straining to hear the wrong voices, a point which Mary's own disgust underscores.

[11] Not only does the story distance Louise from Mary spiritually, it also distances the two women in terms of gender. Virgin saints' lives pit women against men; so strong is this motif of female solidarity that "the polarization of the sexes . . . is found in almost all virgin martyr legends" (Winstead 8). In the typical virgin martyr's story, "Women are rarely persecutors but are frequently sympathetic bystanders who protest the virgin's persecution and offer emotional or material comfort during their trials" (Winstead 6). Wolff inverts this gender solidarity and places Louise in the men's camp: he makes

her a source of emotional torment, rather than comfort, to Mary, as well as her chief persecutor.

Furthermore, in subtle ways, Wolff portrays Louise as masculinized. When a distraught Louise disturbs Mary's sleep the night before the interview, her outburst has apparently been occasioned by her lover's criticism of her as lacking in femininity. What Louise reminds Mary of is not an Iroquois woman, but a warrior: clearly a man's role, and an aggressive one at that. Louise's success and her strategies for pursuing it, as well as her habits of speech and personal bearing, all portray Louise as having had to sacrifice herself as a woman and, essentially, to function as a man, in order to succeed.

[12] In the text, Mary's utterance is offered as her own words; the Biblical provenance is not alluded to in the story itself. This presentation is in keeping with the conventions of the saint's life, in which "Bible passages may be quoted verbatim, Bible stories are alluded to, and Biblical expressions are used without any indication of the source" (Ferguson 118). Thus, the saint's life uses Biblical terminology naturalistically, calling upon the language of Scripture as a verbal resource suitable for appropriation. Indeed, as Ferguson goes on to remark, the use of interpolated Scripture as a developmental technique for the saint's life "seems to have been highly valued and recognized as a mark of good writing for the genre" (118-19).

[13] Appropriately enough, Mary's ultimate challenge to her oppressors is delivered in the form of an oral address rather than a written statement, as befits the medieval context which governs the organizing logic of the story. Mary's ascendancy at the close of the story is not merely verbal, however: the power that she has achieved through her response to her ordeal enacts the fundamental victory at the heart of the saint's life. (See Kitchen, 156, for a description of the various ways in which saints' lives demonstrate the power of the martyred victim.)

[14] The lecture-hall scene occupies less than a full page of text and feels, to the reader, surprisingly short, given its structural importance to the story and the heavy ideological weight it must bear. Nevertheless, even here Wolff's structuring reflects that of the medieval saint's life. Thomas Heffernan's summary of the climactic moments of such stories is instructive and entirely applicable: "The consummation is the shortest sequence of actions in these lives. Its brevity serves both a thematic and a structural purpose. A rapid denouement serves as a catalyst to focus all the elements of the narrative together in one moment of grand drama, the blood sacrifice of the young woman and her consequent achievement of salvation" (273). Appropriately, Mary's suffering and torment occurs *prior* to the martyrdom scene, which Wolff presents with powerful, exemplary brevity.

WORKS CITED

Anderson, Rachel. "Saints' Legends." *A History of Old English Literature*. R. D. Fulk and Christopher M. Cain. Blackwell Histories of Literature. Malden, MA: Blackwell, 2003. 87-105.

Bertholdus of Micy. "Vita s. Maximini." *Acta sanctorum ordinis sancti Benedicti*. Ed. Luc d'Achéry and Jean Mabillon. 1st ed. 9 vols. Paris, 1668-1701.

Calin, William. "Saints' Stories: The Literary Quality of Anglo-Norman Martyr Hagiography." *The Shaping of Text: Style, Imagery, and Structure in French Literature: Essays in Honor of John Porter Houston*. Ed. Emanuel J. Mickel, Jr. Toronto: Associated UP, 1993. 24-44.

Carlson, Cindy L., and Angela Jane Weisl. Introduction: Constructions of Widowhood and Virginity. *Constructions of Widowhood and Virginity in the Middle Ages*. Ed. Carlson and Weisl. The New Middle Ages. New York: St. Martin's, 1999. 1-21.

Coon, Linda L. *Sacred Fictions: Holy Women and Hagiography in Late Antiquity*. The Middle Ages Series. Philadelphia: U of Pennsylvania P, 1997.

Donovan, Leslie A. *Women Saints' Lives in Old English Prose*. Library of Medieval Women. Cambridge: Brewer, 1999.

Dronke, Peter. *Women Writers in the Middle Ages: A Critical Study of Texts from Perpetua († 203) to Marguerite Porete († 1310)*. Cambridge: Cambridge UP, 1984.

Ferguson, Charles A. "Devotional Reading and Science Fiction: The Medieval Saint's Life as a Form of Discourse." *Language in Global Perspective: Papers in Honor of the Fiftieth Anniversary of the Summer Institute of Linguistics, 1935-1985*. Ed. Benjamin F. Elson. Dallas, TX: The Summer Institute of Linguistics, 1986. 113-22.

Halsall, Paul. "Saints' Lives: Introduction." Internet Medieval Sourcebook. Ed. Paul Halsall. 4 Mar. 2001. The Online Reference Book for Medieval Studies. 15 July 2004 <http://www.fordham. edu/halsall/sbook3.html#int>.

Hassel, Julie. *Choosing Not to Marry: Women and Autonomy in the Katherine Group*. Studies in Medieval History and Culture 9. New York: Routledge, 2002.

Heffernan, Thomas J. *Sacred Biography: Saints and Their Biographers in the Middle Ages*. New York: Oxford UP, 1988.

Kitchen, John. *Saints' Lives and the Rhetoric of Gender: Male and Female in Merovingian Hagiography*. New York: Oxford UP, 1998.

Petroff, Elizabeth Alvilda. *Body and Soul: Essays on Medieval Women and Mysticism*. Oxford: Oxford UP, 1994.

Tibbetts, Jane Schulenburg. *Forgetful of their Sex: Female Sanctity and Society, ca. 500-1100*. Chicago: U of Chicago P, 1998.

Townsend, David. "Hagiography." *Medieval Latin: An Introduction and Bibliographical Guide*. Ed. F. A. C. Mantello and A. G. Rigg. Washington, D.C.: The Catholic U of America P, 1996. 618-28.

Winstead, Karen A. *Virgin Martyrs: Legends of Sainthood in Late Medieval England*. Ithaca, NY: Cornell UP, 1997.

Wogan-Browne, Jocelyn. *Saints' Lives and Women's Literary Culture c. 1150-1300: Virginity and Its Authorizations*. Oxford: Oxford UP, 2001.

Wolff, Tobias. "In the Garden of the North American Martyrs." *The Norton Anthology of Short Fiction*. Ed. R. V. Cassill and Richard Bausch. 6th ed. New York: Norton, 2000. 1611-19.

Where the Falling Angel Meets the Rising Ape

Cory James Rushton

In May 2006, a potentially shocking story of inter-species sex hit the media: early humans, announced David Reich of Harvard University, may have had sexual relations with chimpanzees; more shocking still, at least one of these unions seems to have led to a "fertile female hybrid, who then could have mated with either a male chimp or human, and produced offspring that went on to have children of their own."[1] The DNA evidence is said to be compelling. What is surprising is that, as of this writing, there was no great outcry among the proponents of intelligent design, let alone any vast soul-searching or disbelief in the media at large: the story that early humans mated with chimpanzees after the species split from each other was apparently taken in stride. The initial response to Darwin's theories, exemplified by cartoons produced over a century ago which depicted humans as the descendents of apes dressed like stereotypical grandparents, was entirely missing here.[2] This essay deals with a literary tradition, rather than a scientific one: the evolution of a motif, the motif of the half-breed, of what is scientifically called miscegenation, sexual union between people of different races, in these texts between different sentient species. Just as society at large seems to accept evolutionary principles on some level (even intelligent design heralds an abandonment of what were once key facets of Creation science), society is also much more open to marriage and child-bearing between different ethnic groups. The literature of the fantastic—medieval romance (*Sir Gowther*) and fantasy novel (those of J.R.R. Tolkien and Terry Pratchett)—allegorizes this acceptance, even though central elements have changed, among them the meaning of miscegenation and the role it plays in the gradual unfolding of the universe (divinely ordained or random, as the case may be).

"Miscegenation," of course, is not a medieval word: medieval theologians used "sodomy" to describe not just homosexuality but also "sexual relations between Christians and heretics, for example, Christians and Saracens; it could encompass intercourse with animals or other "unnatural" liaisons.[3] John Boswell attempted to eliminate the word "sodomy" altogether from his landmark study on homosexuality in the Middle Ages, arguing that the word "is so vague and ambiguous as to be virtually useless" because "it has connoted in various times and places everything from ordinary heterosexual intercourse in an atypical position to oral sexual contact with animals."[4] The word itself comes from the ancient story of Sodom in Genesis 19, where *cognoscare* has been translated as "to know" in a sexual sense, implying that the men of Sodom are punished for wishing to have homosexual sex with Lot's angelic visitors, possibly by raping them (two different crimes in Jewish law). Complicating the matter is Boswell's argument that "to know" simply meant to identify them, as Lot had apparently not received permission from the city elders to allow strangers within the city walls at night; Christ may well have implied in Matthew 10:14-15 that a lack of hospitality was the real sin of the Sodomites.[5] Alain of Lille (1199-1202) defined sodomy as "the sin against nature as expending one's seed outside the proper vessel" which "frustrated the conception of children."[6] That frustration could, I argue, imply not only barrenness but of mixed-species children, monsters in need of salvation (as in Wolfram von Eschenbach's piebald Fierefiz, son of an Angevin prince and a Saracen princess) or extermination (as in Grendel, descendent of Cain, 1258-65).[7] For my purposes, I will assume that the sin represented in Genesis 19 was sexual in nature (and that medieval writers understood the story in that way), possibly homosexual but possibly also a matter of miscegenation: the angels appear as men, but are also of a different species.

Genesis also records that the heroes and giants of ancient days were the result of breeding between the daughters of men and angelic beings, and were called the Nephilim; this story seems to be recalled directly in the romance *Sir Gowther*.[8] Alternatively, the identity of Cain's wife, unnamed in the Bible and of uncertain origins, was said to be a short-hand term for a succession of animals.[9] This might explain the monstrous nature of Cain's descendents but also opens up the possibility that most humans had some non-humans in their family trees. Some exegetes insisted that the "sons of God" were the sons of Seth, virtuous humans who nonetheless eventually bred with the daughters of Cain's lineage, but the idea that something supernatural, something angelic, existed in human bloodlines was present throughout the medieval period.[10] Complicating an already complicated picture was the Bible's insistence that Cain and his descendents invented what more or less constitutes civilization: Cain built the first city, separating humanity from a pastoral and peaceful past, creating boundaries between peoples and individuals; his descendent Tubal-Cain invented metalwork, specifically imagined in the medieval period as weaponry, which allowed an extension and perfection of Cain's initial invention, homicide.[11] Where most mythologies created culture heroes to explain the origins of civilization, some medieval exegesis implies that civilization is itself an evil.

Modern fantasy is the most direct heir to various medieval traditions, and the half-human is no exception. Tolkien may seem to stand at the source of the modern fantasy genre, although he himself would have used the phrase 'fairy-story' to describe his particular type of world-building. Yet it is exactly this emphasis on linguistic invention and the near-obsessiveness of the details which separates Middle-earth as unique in the fantasy genre, as well as the well-head from which most later practitioners take their mark. There is a world of difference between creating a fantasy world and trying to create a mythology for England, and the plethora of detail leads to (perhaps "allows" is a better word) a more complicated series of theoretical explorations. Pratchett's genre is fluid, as he himself has implied: "It's quite hard to explain the difference between a genre author and, well, a normal one, especially if you take the view that there are rather more genres around than serious literary editors would care to admit … I think I write fantasy."[12] Discworld began as a parody of fantasy novels, then became a series of fantasy novels, and now, with the attention of literary heavyweights like A. S. Byatt, seems to have become something else altogether, "grimmer and not so calmly comic."[13] The contradictions and philosophies of half-human hybrids within the historical structure of Middle-earth demand attention. If we agree with Elizabeth Grosz that "[c]arnal experience is uncertain, teleological, undirected" in actual practice,[14] it is anything but in literature and mythology. Sex drives history, from the Trojan War to Clinton's White House, and the children of literary sexual unions between unlikely partners (based, always, in someone's desire for someone or something else) are almost always the agents of destiny (sometimes planned teleologically, sometimes not). The stranger the union, the more pronounced is the child's centrality to the unfolding of history. Both Tolkien and Pratchett inherit something ambiguous and dangerous from the Middle Ages, something which they partially redeem for their own purposes: this essay can only provide snapshots of a motif in transition.

Devilkin: Sir Gowther

A poem like *Sir Gowther* moves between genres as the scholars who study it find necessary: for a romance conference, it is a romance; for a volume of Breton *lais*, it is a Breton lay.[15] Some scholars consider it a kind of hagiography. *Sir Gowther* is still unfamiliar enough to require a synopsis, borrowed here from Alcuin Blamires:

> Gowther is the name of the son born to a hitherto childless duchess after she is first threatened with repudiation by her husband and then apparently impregnated by a devil out in an orchard. This son grows up to pursue a life of reckless helter-skelter sadism. However, when an elderly earl of the region alleges that such tyranny proves he cannot be of human stock, Gowther coerces his mother to admit the devilish identity of his father. He recoils from this revelation into a course of abject penitence. Under the pope's instruction he embraces complete voluntary silence and undertakes a startling regime of self-humiliation, accepting food only from the mouths of dogs. Gowther's spiritual rehabilitation is subsequently consolidated through the agency of an emperor's mute daughter, whom he delivers from

the prospect of a forced marriage to a Sultan by thrice fighting the Sultan's forces, in successive suits of armor miraculously supplied in response to prayers. Although the daughter falls from her tower when she sees Gowther wounded on her behalf, she arises after three days of 'death' and escapes also from her mute condition to proclaim news of his divine forgiveness. Gowther marries her and they inherit the empire.[16]

The poem exists in two versions: British Library Royal MS 17.B.43 (Royal, or B) and National Library of Scotland MS Advocates 19.3.1 (Advocates, or A). Both versions proclaim that Gowther becomes a saint after his death, healing the mute, the blind, and the crippled; Royal associates him with an English saint called Guthlac, who was quite a distinct and certainly historical figure.

Gowther's list of crimes is extensive, and range from the unwitting to the appropriately diabolical. The first sign of Gowther's devilish nature comes when the Duke provides a wet-nurse for him, and Gowther literally sucks her dry: "He sowkyd hom so thei lost ther lyvys" (113). He does the same thing with eight other wet-nurses before the local supply of "gud knyghttys wyffys" apparently runs out (109-20); when his mother attempts to nurse him, he bites off her nipple (127-31). Gowther grows at a prodigious rate and wields a falchion which no other man can carry by the time he's fifteen; the falchion, a weapon associated with the heathen east, is another sign of Gowther's difference. Jeffrey Cohen is right to note that Gowther is, in fact, a giant as well as a devil's son; for Cohen, giants are primal and masculine, suffering from enjoying vast appetites for food, rape, and destruction.[17] This teenaged half-demon terrorizes the local neighborhood: "Erly and late, lowed and styll, / He wold wyrke is fadur wyll" (176-77); as Cohen notes, the narrator's comment obscures the fact that Gowther "has no idea who his father is."[18] The Duke knights him despite his wickedness; this has been seen as a comment on the ineffectiveness of the ritual of knighthood, "a last-ditch means" of curbing Gowther's violent excess and encouraging "an adult sense of responsibility" (his earlier baptism had no effect, either).[19] The Royal version specifically notes that the Duke gives Gowther "his best swerde" and therefore "implicates himself" as Gowther's father, partially responsible for the "mayhem consequently caused by the son with this sword."[20]

The problem, of course, is that Gowther takes after his real father: his demonic heritage wins out over his human heritage (although Blamires makes a good case for acknowledging his earthly father's contribution). It is worth noting, with Henry Vandelinde, that *Sir Gowther* is the only poem in this family of texts (based on the legend of Robert the Devil) in which the protagonist's origins are literally demonic.[21] As such, this story is overtly concerned with the mingling of different sentient beings, earthly and supernatural, and thus it is a tale of miscegenation as well as redemption. The Christian faith of the medieval

West believed, strongly, in choice: Gowther either has no choice because he is inherently evil, or he makes the wrong choices, until he confronts his mother and she tells him the terrible truth:

"Son, sython Y schall tho soothe say:
In owre orcharde apon a day,
  A fende gat the thare;
As lyke my lorde as he might be,
Underneyth a cheston tre." (226-30)

The duchess is not lying; when the fiend appeared to her, the narrator uses this precise line, "As lyke hur lorde as he might be" (67). He reveals his demonic nature only after he has his way with her (68-72), when he appears as a "felturd fende" or shaggy fiend; she does not, it appears, commit the sin of demoniality, knowingly having sexual relations with the demonic.[22] She does lie to her husband the Duke, saying that an angel appeared to her in the orchard and revealed that her barren-ness would end if they made love that very night (80-85). This is fast thinking, although it is difficult not to see a parody of the Annunciation to Mary here; the real story of miscegenation between human and devil, a possibility not universally accepted by medieval theologians, is masked by a reference to the one theologically undeniable case of historical miscegenation, that between human and holy spirit.

The *Gowther* poet seems defensive about his subject matter. He begins the poem by relating the skepticism about demonic sexual assault: it is a "selcowgh thing...to here" that demons can impregnate women (13-15). He says that clerks make this claim, and that he would be shamed to repeat the arguments made by, among others, Aquinas.[23] In short, the theory is that demons cannot impregnate mortal women: they are things of the spirit, and corrupt besides. What they can do is disguise themselves as women, sexually assault men in their sleep, and steal their semen (draining them, in a sense, as Gowther is said to drain his wet-nurses: demons are a hungry breed). In this form, they are called *succubi*. They then change their form to that of a man, sexually assault women in their sleep, and leave the stolen semen behind. Now, they are called *incubi*. The semen is somehow changed in the course of its theft and delivery, and the resulting child can be called the devil's.

The wizard and prophet Merlin is also said to be the devil's son. Geoffrey of Monmouth's account of Merlin's early life includes a philosopher, who theorizes that an incubus appeared to Merlin's mother and begot Merlin; he further tells us that incubi "have partly the nature of men and partly that of angels" and "live between the moon and the earth.[24] The *Gowther* poet makes the connection between the two characters explicit: he begins his poem by stating that the devil once had the power to appear in the guise of husbands and sire children like "Merlin and mo" (7-12). He later claims that Merlin is

Gowther's half-brother, because the "won fynd gatte hom bothe" (94-6). Yet Merlin's story is very different from Gowther's. Gowther's conception seems inadequately motivated: the fiend simply says that Gowther "in is yowthe full wylde schall be" and that he will be good with weapons (73-5). Merlin, on the other hand, is the centerpiece in a diabolical plan hatched during a council meeting in Hell. Smarting from Christ's post-crucifixion Harrowing of Hell (in which he frees the souls of the righteous pre-Incarnation dead), the devils decide to create an anti-Christ by impregnating a nun. They seduce her through the time-honored method of killing her family; when that does not work, the chosen demon waits until she forgets to say her nightly prayers and rapes her in her sleep. The plan is foiled when baby Merlin is born, covered in hair (shaggy, like Gowther's father); the attending hermit quickly baptizes Merlin, the hair falls off, and Merlin inherits full knowledge of the past from his demonic father and is given full knowledge of the future by Divine forces seeking to use him for their own ends.[25]

We might expect, then, that Gowther's problem is that he is not baptized. Yet, he is indeed christened in a church soon after his birth (103-5) and, further, undergoes the ritual of knighthood. Nothing works, and where Merlin becomes the servant of the Good, Gowther remains the devil's spawn until confronted with the awful truth of his demonic origins. The problem, perhaps, lies in his conception. Where Merlin's mother is usually depicted as an innocent, Gowther's mother may not be. The demonic visitation in the orchard is not, narratively speaking, entirely unexpected: fleeing her husband's threat to repudiate her, she prays in the garden:

Scho preyd to God and Mare mylde
Schuld gyffe hur grace to have a child,
On what maner scho ne rogth. (61-3)

She prays for a child and does not care how she gets it. The demon intercepts this foolish and imprecise speech act (a variant of the Rash Promise topos) and fulfills it. His words to her are quite accurate: Gowther is "full wild" as a youth. It is Gowther's adult years that will be in question. Complicating the issue further is the predominant medieval theory of conception, which required consensual sex; and consensual sex always resulted in orgasm for the woman. As Cohen notes, Gowther's conception occupies an ambiguous space: "Was it rape? Was it desired? A rape-in-desire? How does one judge such an event?"[26] Is it enough that the woman thought the fiend was her husband, as Ygraine thought Uther was Gorlois? What about Merlin's mother: can desire be expressed by the unconscious mind? If so, it was clearly not a source of shame for her, at least in most versions of Merlin's conception. For Gowther's mother, the fault lies in her imprecise prayer, which should not surprise us in a poem which also features a virtuous but mute princess and a hero who takes a vow of silence.

Therefore, it is also not surprising that Gowther's rehabilitation should begin when his mother finally tells the truth about his conception. She once told her husband that divine visitation assured her that the child would be his; when Gowther confronts her, her first reaction is to repeat that he is, indeed, the Duke's son. Only when she tells the truth does the story change direction. Gowther finds the old earl who questioned his parentage:

'Tho soothe tale tolde thou mee.
Y wyll to Rome to tho apostyll,
That hemey schryfe me and asoyll:
Kepe thou my castyll free' (246-9)

He being no longer a youth, Gowther's journey into maturity begins with a traumatic revelation and the start of a pilgrimage through what Cohen calls "the wilds of identity, a monstrous route to becoming male in the Middle Ages."[27] Gowther vows to "lerne anodur lare" (234), but I would suggest that Gowther's route is not exclusively towards masculinity, but to Christianity and humanity—categories which are sometimes inseparable for the medieval West.

Gowther's progress from half-breed to full human is marked in two ways. The first is his sojourn among the dogs. Sometimes dogs are sent by divine providence to feed him, sometimes he steals food from their mouths as though he were as bestial as they are. Gowther's spiritual journey mirrors Cain's physical path, but in reverse. On one memorable occasion, the mute princess sends him food by canine courier, making sure to wash the dog's mouth with wine first. Gowther makes himself less than he was in order to achieve a higher status. According to Cohen, who draws on Deleuze and Guattari, "Gowther and the hound...enter into a masochistic relationship. He seems to be imitating the dog but in fact is engaged in a more complex process of inter-subjective embodiment."[28] Gowther's "wild, molecular identity is constrained through a mapping across an animal body," becoming human "only after this interstitial (transitional, transferential) form has been successfully passed through"; Gowther is briefly "a dog-man," but eventually his "body passes out of its freakish hybridity to be inscribed more fully than ever into the secure space of the human."[29] This is not to ignore more traditional readings of the poem: Hopkins also notes that "Gowther becomes more human as his penance progresses; he grows a soul." She locates that growth in the movement towards God, a movement through which "he becomes more affectionate, loyal, grateful, generous, and noble" as he leaves behind the "animal-like" qualities he had while under the devil's rule.[30] Later, during the battles with the Sultan's forces which Dieter Mehl feels are more central to his penance than his time among the dogs, Gowther receives further divine aid in the form of armor, each suit of a different color: first black, then red, then white.[31] The white armor represents, quite opaquely, the purification of Gowther's soul in the fires of physical mortification, the humiliation of his ascetic vows, and the rigor of battle. Gowther is becoming human, and further (at least in the Royal text) he becomes associated with a particular saint, implying that (like all saintly figures) Gowther's role is divinely ordained.[32] His story is an *exemplum* illustrating the ultimate triumph of good over evil, utter proof that anyone can be saved.

Gowther's path might be difficult, but the choice to convert was a simple one and, as any good conversion should be, accompanied by bitter tears shed by both himself and his mother. For a medieval Christian poet, it could not really be otherwise: the war between Heaven and Hell has only two sides. For later authors adopting medieval material, the matter of miscegenation and the resulting choice between cultures is not so simple, even when the author feels himself to be closely in tune with medieval thought and culture, as J.R.R. Tolkien clearly did.

Bloodlines: Elves and Orcs

In Tolkien's works, the most prominent examples of miscegenation are not between demons and humans, but between mortal men and Elves. Racial interbreeding also takes place between human ethnic groups. The Numenoreans become the Dunedain precisely because of their blood, a mingling of half Elf and Human is subsequently diluted by the blood of lesser men, the Haradrim who comprise much of the population of the Numenorean Empire. It is this racial impurity which lead to a civil war in Gondor in the mid-Third Age, a war between the followers of the half-Northman Eldacar and his cousin, Castamir, seen as pure Numenorean but ironically the ancestor of the Corsairs, mixed-race pirates who are later counted among Sauron's allies in the War of the Ring. Much has been made of Tolkien's perceived racism, and the most recent defense of Tolkien claims that, because "fear or death and envy of immortality" are the primary divisions between the human groups in Middle-earth, Tolkien's work "reveals the artificiality of racial difference, since Numenoreans and Haradrim alike are subject to death and can be manipulated by fear of it."[33] Yet there is a real racial difference present precisely because of the Elves, God's first children and therefore a sibling race, one which has changed the fate of some, but not all, human groups. In the Appendices to *The Lord of the Rings*, Tolkien tells us that there were three unions between Elves and Men, "the Eldar and the Edain": Beren and Luthien, Tuor and Idril, and Aragorn and Arwen (*LOTR* 1071).[34] The last couple, whose story is told in one of these appendices but was brought into sharp relief by the recent films, are descended from the first two couples. These three major unions—there may be others less heralded—change the course of history, and each union in turn plays a beneficial role in the unfolding of events: Elven marriage with humans is a matter of Divine Providence.

Arwen's choice, to be mortal or immortal, became one of the film trilogy's central threads. As in the books, Arwen's father, Elrond (who appeared in both *The Hobbit* and the trilogy), has a twin brother, Elros. They were the sons of Elwing and Earendil, who survived until the end of the First Age, a time of war between Elves and the first Dark Lord, Morgoth. Because the blood of both Elves and Men ran through their veins at a moment when the world was being sorted out, they are given a choice between their two peoples. Elros chooses mortality and goes to rule over the island of Numenor, poised halfway between the immortal land of the gods and the mortal world, but still subject to mortal law (*LOTR* 1071-2). Elrond chooses his Elvin nature and settles in Middle-earth. Earlier individuals in similar circumstances (Beren and Luthien, Earendil and Elwing) were given a more limited choice: like Elros and Elrond, "they must be either Elven or human…separated from humanity, having transgressed the human and nonhuman boundary."[35] This difference is primarily because the characters in question have seen Valinor, an experience which cannot and should not be communicated to mortals.[36]

The nature of this choice and how it is offered to the sons of Earendil is only hinted at, but the end of the First Age is a time when gods walk among mortals, and it can be assumed that they are offered a choice directly. Arwen's choice is different. Elrond tells Aragorn that her choice is tied to himself (*LOTR* 1097). As long as she stays with Elrond, either in Middle-earth or in the West, she will be Elven—immortal. If she stays with Aragorn, she will be mortal. When Aragorn is dying, he tells Arwen to take ship for the West; she tells him, "that choice is long over," implying that the method of choosing had been different in nature to that of her father (*LOTR* 1100). The films, to their credit, actually do pick up on this battle between father and fiancé for the love of Arwen but also manage to muddy the waters by providing a thinly sketched alternative explanation for Arwen's sudden mortality. In a scene largely new to the film, Arwen protects a dying Frodo from the Black Riders, the Nazgul, when he has been stabbed by a Morgul knife, the blade of which has snapped off in the wound and is making its way to his heart. She whispers over him, praying that whatever grace is within her should pass to him.[37] Her father then heals Frodo, as he does in the book, but Arwen's later illness seems linked with this moment; Elrond tells Aragorn that she is now tied to the Ring, but the films (particularly the first) is never very clear on the circumstances of Arwen's choice or the nature of her illness. As Cathy Akers-Jordan notes, in an early scene Arwen speaks to Aragorn of her choice in a way that makes it look as though the matter is decided; in a later scene, Galadriel will say that Arwen's choice is not yet made.[38] For Akers-Jordan, the moment of Arwen's choice is her return to Rivendell at the end of *The Two Towers*, noting that this is linked with her insistence that Aragorn's ancestral sword be at last reforged: "She starts a chain of events which…at last sets Aragorn on the path he has been resisting out of self doubt."[39] The success of the forces of good in the films rests on the decision Arwen makes, which ties in neatly with a major theme in Tolkien's work: the importance of Arwen and Aragorn's union as the third of the divinely ordained unions between species.

The children of these unions between Elf and Man are said to be the best of both peoples, superlative individuals; the son of Aragorn and Arwen, glimpsed briefly in the films, is named Eldarion, meaning "of the Eldar," of the Elves. Through him, the physical and moral superiority of Aragorn's people, the ancient Numenoreans of Dunedain, is restored. This is an uncomfortable aspect of Tolkien's work, this racial superiority inherent in the Numenorean line. To some extent, Tolkien attempts to evade this by painting many of the Numenoreans as aggressive imperialists, but the fact remains that throughout his work, lesser peoples are either threats to be overcome or raw material to be developed: Tolkien was himself a child of Empire, growing up in South Africa. Nevertheless, miscegenation between Elves and Men is beneficial to the world, but Tolkien is capable of a darker view of miscegenation: the Orc. While Jane Chance is correct to note that Tolkien consistently "promotes the intermarriage of races—Maiar, Elf, and Man…in order to blend their strengths in governance and parliamentary representation,"[40] the Orc remains a mirror image: the Orc's strength is physical, his sole contribution to governance a craven obedience to those who are stronger and a dedicated sadism towards those who are weaker. Ruth Noel notes that Orcs are named for "a god of the underworld, the Latin Orcus, and are reflections of all the demons that plague mankind in mythology."[41] Shippey believes, with some justification, that the word derives from the Anglo-Saxon *orc-neas*, a term used in *Beowulf* to describe Grendel's kin;[42] as Tolkien's later meditations on the subject make clear, the Orc might also be partially human, just as Grendel has human blood within his savage body.

The origin of Orcs is unknown, although in his copious letters and notes (now mostly published by his son Christopher), Tolkien hints that Orcs are Elves corrupted by the tortures of Morgoth, an explanation also found in *The Silmarillion*:

> Yet this is held true by the wise of Eressea, that all those of the Quendi who came into the hands of Melkor, ere Utumno was broken, were put there in prison, and by slow arts of cruelty were corrupted and enslaved; and thus did Melkor breed the hideous race of Orcs in envy and mockery of the Elves, of whom they were afterwards the bitterest foes (*Sil* 58).[43]

This is possible because Elves, like the gods in the West, have some control over their physical forms: they are, like Geoffrey of Monmouth's incubi who live between earth and moon, "partly of the nature of angels and partly of humans." Their appearance can reflect their inner being, but once the transformation from Elf to Orc has been made, it is apparently irreversible: Orcs are born inherently evil, like Gowther but without the possibility of redemption. Their ability to speak makes them, in medieval terms, more like humans than they are unlike them, but even W.H. Auden (generally a supporter of Tolkien's work) suspected that an irredeemable race might be heretical.[44] As Shippey has noted, the few Orcish conversations in the trilogy heavily imply that "orcs are moral beings, with an underlying morality much the same as ours" but which has "no effect at all on actual behavior": they are capable of condemning cowardice in Elves, despite the hypocrisy prevalent in that position.[45] In one note, Tolkien reflects that Elves considered it a mercy to kill an Orc. Tolkien opines on another occasion that Orcs were, in fact, demons in origin and not Elves, and were then cross-bred with Men, whose natural predilection for cruelty and immorality made them natural candidates for corruption, both enforced and chosen.[46] Randel Helms compares Tolkien's Orcs with the fecund Orc of Blake's *America: A Prophecy*, a positive figure who escapes sexual repression, an escape which metaphorically stands for political revolution; as Helms notes, while the difference far outweigh the similarities, Blake and Tolkien both see the Orc as "libidinous" and procreative: Tolkien's "Orcs are rabbit-like in their breeding and swarming."[47] While Helms sees the Hobbits as opposite to Orcs because they marry late and presumably have less offspring as a result, the true opposites are found higher in Tolkien's imaginary chain of being: the Dunedain and the Elves often have two children or fewer in the course of very long lives. Tolkien's notes, published fifteen years after Helms wrote, would confirm some of this: "The Orcs of the later wars...bred and multiplied rapidly whenever left undisturbed," and they "continued to live and breed and to carry on their business of ravaging and plundering after Morgoth was overthrown" (*MR* 416-8). Helms is probably correct, at least partially, that the Orc represents a kind of "unfettered Eros [which] is the ally, even the servant, of Thanatos."[48] As Shippey argues, despite "several explanations for them [Orcs], their analogousness to humanity always remained clear."[49] Certainly, the Uruk-hai (stronger Orcs able to withstand sunlight and think a little faster than their brethren) are openly said in the trilogy to be the result of genetic experimentation: Sauron and Saruman both breed Orcs with humans in the race for an all-conquering hybrid. The libidinous and sometimes deliberately created Orcish soldier is the Gowther poet's vision of demons impregnating women turned into an assembly line, reminding us that one of Tolkien's most prominent themes is the nightmare of industrialization. Sauron's armies are led by a thousand Sir Gowthers.

The choices in Tolkien, when the character has a choice, are no longer as diametrically opposed: good and evil still exist, but the presence of different, sentient species (Elves, Men, Dwarves, Orcs) means that there are different approaches to the problem of morality. The fates of these species are different: Elves go to the Undying Lands in the West, to await a rumored oblivion; Men go to join the One True God, unless they have been allied with the Darkness; Dwarves believe they go to an afterlife of their own. The unions between Elves and Men happened to strengthen Men, not to initiate a free-for-all of Elf Love. More than once, Tolkien repeats the assertion that there were only three such unions (as opposed to an unknowable and unthinkable number of forced unions between Men and Orcs). His own extensive corpus undermines this: to take one example, the princes of a Gondorian province called Belfalas are said to be descendents of a nameless Elven handmaiden, lost in the mountains, who marries a local noble. Legolas, seeing a prince of this line, thinks that "here indeed was one who had elven-blood in his veins" (*LOTR* 906). This exception aside, the fact remains that, for Tolkien, some cases of miscegenation are part of the unfolding of divine providence, while most other instances are active, if unsuccessful, rebellion against that providence.

Genetics Passed Through the Soul

My last stop is Terry Pratchett, who began writing the Discworld series in 1983, six years after Tolkien's death, with *The Color of Magic*. Some of the early books remain extremely popular as both novels and plays: *Equal Rites*, *Wyrd Sisters*, *Guards Guards*, and, important for my purposes here, *Mort* and its direct sequels, the Susan Sto Helit trilogy. There are four main strands in the series: the cowardly wizard Rincewind, the witches, the city guards, and Death. Death, as a character, appears in almost every book in the series; Colin Manlove, who believes that "creativity is a continual theme" throughout the series, sees no surprise "that [Pratchett] has also written about its uncreating opposite, Death."[50] Yet if Death opposes creativity in the Discworld, he does so in a particularly creative way, constantly mimicking humanity and its drive to create (whether art or comfortable homes). In *Mort*, first of the books fully focused on Death, Death wishes to take an apprentice, and he chooses the appropriately names Mort; Death has previously adopted a daughter, Ysabel. Mort proves to be an inadequate apprentice, in large part because he is human: he cannot see matters of mortality as Death, the personification of mortality, sees them. Mort saves a princess from assassins when he should have let things take their course. In the end, Death allows Ysabel and Mort to go back to the world, leaving the changes Mort has made to weave their way into the fabric of reality. Mort and Ysabel are married, and the princess rewards them with the duchy of Sto Helit. However, it is revealed that Mort and Ysabel did not long survive their return to the world; Death watches as their carriage plunges from a cliff. They did, however, have a daughter—Susan Sto Helit, when we first meet her in *Soul Music* (*SM*), is an orphan living at a girls' boarding school. Susan, it is revealed, is not entirely human; her journey, so far, continues in *Hogfather* (*NF*, a Christmas spoof) and the recent *Thief of Time* (*ToT*).[51]

In *Soul Music*, Death once again interferes in the fabric of reality, this time experimenting with the human ability to forget painful memories (a trait he, as an anthropomorphic entity, does not share). His interference is the result of his own creation by humans and his long subsequent contact with them. His fellow Horsemen suffer the same fate:

> To be human was to change, Death realized. The Horsemen…were horse*men*. Men had wished upon them a certain shape, a certain form…. They would never *be* human, but they had caught aspects of humanity as though they were some kind of disease.

Once humanity dreams up a personification, "once they gave him his arms and legs and eyes, that meant he had to have a brain. That meant he'd think: (*ToT* 277). Non-human characters who are either created or incarnated in human form often find themselves at the mercy of their suddenly-human brain, a thing of primitive instincts under the veneer of intellect, a thing prone to the body's physical senses: Lady LeJean, one of the colorless opponents of life known as the Auditors, experiences the chaos of humanity's physicality following her incarnation:

> She had been human for two weeks, two astonishing, shocking weeks. Whoever would have guessed that a brain operated like this? Or that colors had a meaning that went way, way beyond the spectral analysis? How could she even begin to describe the blueness of blue? Or how much thinking the brain did by itself? It was terrifying. Half the time her thoughts seemed not to be her own. (*ToT* 200).

Even the anthropomorphic representations must think about something other than their work occasionally. "THANK GOODNESS," Death thinks, contemplating this, "THAT I AM UNCHANGED AND EXACTLY THE SAME AS I EVER WAS" (*ToT* 277). Pratchett's point, of course, is that Death is not immune to the effect of personification (a word I am using here as a process and not a noun). While Death has a function, his role seems to be entirely contingent upon what humanity makes of him and what he chooses to make of himself: his role is not divinely ordained but the stuff of random circumstance and personal, predictable evolution.

The plot of *Soul Music* is relatively lightweight, concerning itself with the invention of rock music by a supernatural entity. Susan can make herself invisible—not literally, but invisible enough that people do not notice her. She can walk through walls. When she begins work as a governess, she can spot the monsters under the bed, pull them out by the hair, and beat them with her umbrella until they promise never to do it again. She can instantly move a classroom full of children (including desks) from city to city to teach them about other cultures (*ToT* 34-9). And she is haunted by the supernatural harbingers of her grandfather Death, who constantly call upon her to help her grandfather save the universe.

The problem, *Thief* explains, is that "some genetics are passed on via the soul" (*ToT* 94). Susan should be completely mortal, but Ysabel and Mort's time in Death's domain have affected their daughter; as Death's servant Albert explains, after some early childhood visits, Ysabel and Mort sever all ties with Death in an attempt to give Susan a normal life:

> "Your Mum and Dad thought it best if you forgot," said Albert. "Hah! It's in the bone! They were afraid it was going to happen and it has! You've inherited." (*SM* 84).

Death notes that naming her "Susan" was a particularly clumsy attempt at prosaicness:

> I DID SAY UNIQUE. YOUR NAME IS –
> "Susan, but…"
> SUSAN? said Death bitterly. THEY *REALLY* WANTED TO MAKE SURE, DIDN'T THEY? (*SM* 150)

Susan herself notes that Death's granddaughter "*should have better cheekbones, straight hair and a name with Vs and Xs in it*" (*SM* 293, italics in original). As with Gowther and the Duke, and Elrond and Arwen, we see a parent-figure attempt to impose normality upon a child who lives between worlds…and as with these earlier figures, the attempt fails. Susan, like others in the Discworld, understands something of genetics: "It's all about mice and beans and things" (*SM* 84); heredity is not supposed to allow Susan to inherit a scar from a blow her father suffered at Death's skeletal hands (*SM* 148), although a birthmark indicating a person's extraordinary origins is a standard fairytale motif. Gowther is always something more than human, whether devil or saint; Arwen chooses differently than her father would like. What is perhaps most interesting with Susan Sto Helit is that she is never really allowed to choose at all, although Death seems to think she does; he watches her sobbing at the end of her first harrowing adventure as Death's heir:

> Far above the world, Death nodded. You could choose immortality, or you could choose humanity. You had to do it for yourself. (*SM* 375)

Unfortunately, Susan's unwillingness to participate in her grandfather's life is never heeded, even when he has promised to leave her alone. Susan suspects, at the start of the third volume, that this is because "each of them had no-one else but each other" (*ToT* 103). While she does not always get along with her grandfather, she likes him enough to ask him to come and speak to her class on one occasion—and Death duly keeps the children's drawings of him on his unnecessary fridge. (*ToT* 89-90, 104).

At the same time, despite her profound distaste for her immortal heritage, she also embraces aspects of it:

> Not a day went by but she regretted her curious ancestry. And then she'd wonder what it could possibly be like to walk the world unaware at every step of the rocks beneath your feet and the stars overhead, to have a mere five senses, to be almost blind and nearly deaf… (*ToT* 104).

In one moment of self-candor, Susan reflects that she often "wished she'd been born completely human and wholly normal, but the reality of it was that she'd give it all up tomorrow" as long as this did not mean giving up Binky, Death's pale horse (*ToT* 220). She makes attempts at living a normal life, at "being her Own Person and holding down a Real Job" (*HF* 14), but while she hides her special abilities, she makes no attempt to disavow them: on one occasion she uses Death's peculiar commanding voice, which she has inherited, to negotiate a pay raise from the school where she works (*ToT* 121). She can "put time on and off like an overcoat" and she prides herself on her ability to "see things that were really there" (*ToT* 103-4). "The Look" is effective in cowing everyone Susan meets in her later career as a teacher: students, parents, and employers alike (*Tot* 33); the Look is described as her "terrible ability to give you *her full attention*" (*ToT* 86, italics in original). Her attempts at normality are sometimes bizarre: her work as a governess is complicated by her employer's awareness that Susan is, in fact, a duchess.

> You couldn't be a duchess and a servant. But it was all right to be a governess. It was understood that it wasn't exactly what you *were*, it was merely a way of passing the time until you did what every girl, or gel, was supposed to do in life, i.e. marry some man. (*HF* 87)

Her employer, Mrs. Gaiter, never knows whether or not she should curtsey to Susan (*HF* 15); "she treated Susan with the kind of deference she thought was due to anyone who'd know the difference between a serviette and a napkin from *birth*" (*HF* 87). For Susan, the choice should be Death's granddaughter or Duchess of Sto Helit, implying that she is twice a border figure: mortal/immortal, woman/aristocrat.

Of some interest here is the character of Death's servant, Albert. Albert lives in Death's domain as a way of avoiding his otherwise imminent demise: in *Soul Music*, we learn that he has a mere" [n]ineteen days left in the world" (*SM* 288), some of which he has since used up. Albert's devotion to "the Duty" of collecting souls is second only to Death's (and even that small hierarchy is debatable); he complains that both Mort and Susan fail to understand that

Duty. When Susan repeats her father's mistake in attempting to save the life of a love interest, Albert tells Death:

> "She's trying to save the boy, Master!" he said. "She doesn't know the meaning of the word Duty --"

BUT WE DO, DON'T WE? said Death bitterly. YOU AND ME. (*SM* 342)

Death's bitter reaction may imply that Albert is as much a border figure as Susan and her parents; although he does not share their gifts or their immortality, he has taken on a respect for and dedication to the Duty even as Death's adherence sometimes wanes. Albert's status as a domestic servant masks a secret past: he was once Alberto Malich, the most powerful wizard in the Discworld, the founder of the Unseen University where wizards are trained, a man who sought immortality and "the mantel of Goddes"(*Mort* 154, 179). Wizards are already border figures—the current Archchancellor of the Unseen University is the only character who can consistently see Susan, even when she is acting as Death—and Albert is no exception. His name might be intended to remind us of Albertus Magnus, a medieval philosopher whose work and reputation are heavily linked with the tradition of alchemy; if so, perhaps we are meant to see Albert Malich as someone who becomes a border figure through transmutation (alchemy) rather than adoption (genetics). His transformation, however, is incomplete: the Albert who fries everything he cooks and who plays the domestic for Death is neither Albert Malich the Sorcerer nor Albert Malich the God. In Pratchett's world, power of Death's kind is inherited and not stolen.

In the end, Susan remains what she is, although sometimes reluctantly. Susan's role is not the fulfillment of history and she is not an example (like Gowther) to be heeded; Death seeks her out because, while he sees the future, her special status as a border figure allows her to change history (*ToT* 109); her immortal powers are at the service of the human intellect. At the end of *Thief of Time*, there is a further reconciliation between Susan and the world: Lobsang Ludd, the son of the incarnation of Time and a mortal priest, seems to fall in love with her and share with her "a perfect moment" (*ToT* 430. "TIME HAD A SON," Death says. "SOMEONE MOSTLY MORTAL. SOMEONE LIKE YOU" (*ToT* 111). That the similarities end there—Susan reflects that she had known her parents, but Time had been forever unable to touch her own child (*ToT* 125)—allows Susan a partially maternal role, uniting her career as a teacher and a quasi-immortal: she will teach Time's son to be both human and unique, finding a balance that is unknown to Gowther (evil then good, half-demon then half-saint) and Arwen (Elven and then human). Susan and Lobsang Ludd are two of a kind, both human and immortal, and in a relativistic world they need only choose each other—but this is, whether Pratchett's intention or not—partly because their choices are so limited. There is no sense of destiny at work in Susan's life: while the lives of individuals are recorded within Death's domain, they are recorded as they occur and not before. Time itself is said to be often broken and often pieced back together, obliterating any sense of divine providence; there are rules (the Horsemen should ride out, the book's villainous figures are the Auditors, who clearly audit the universe on someone's behalf), but no plan. For Tolkien, the unions between Men and other sentient races were a significant part of providential history, however mediated by individual choice and emotion; for Pratchett, Death's interference in the unfolding of history is the accidental result of individual experimentation.

Conclusions

Each of the three texts highlighted here represents its own era in ways that go beyond the narrow theme of this essay: *Sir Gowther* is deeply concerned with crusading ideology; Tolkien helps to foster a vast if sometimes derivative fantasy literature which does not share his concerns with medieval antecedents or his experience of the First World War; Pratchett's Discworld is part of a wider movement within fantasy to reinvent the genre but, like Tolkien, there are as many links to non-generic fantasy literature as there are to the genre itself as the series moves from pure parody to something more serious. What I hope to have demonstrated is the continuation of the idea of inter-breeding between humans and immortals as a motif uniquely concerned with the unfolding of history, planned or otherwise. The characters presented here are border figures whose ability to move between worlds (uni-directionally in *Gowther* and Tolkien, ambiguously in Pratchett) is essential to the maintenance of social and political norms within those worlds, and is often essential in preserving the integrity of those different spheres.

In a longer essay, I would attempt to forge a stronger link between social attitudes to miscegenation and the depiction of extra-human liaisons in the genre fiction of the fifteenth, twentieth, and twenty-first centuries. Certainly, public perception of mixed race marriages has come so far in the West that the word "miscegenation" is rarely used, and "half-breed" seems to have a usage limited solely to the genre of the western. Even J.K. Rowling does not use "half-breed" to describe a wizard with mortal, or "Muggle," blood: her villainous characters use the term "mudblood" instead, making the very concept of prejudice against mixed-race characters seem somehow alien (it is perhaps also important that only her villains seem to plan anything at all, while the forces of good merely react—no divine providence here, merely Satanic scheming). To bring us, perhaps, full circle, it is worth noting that in the *Omen* film series, one of the many warnings received by the parents of the young Anti-Christ, either half-devil or half-dog, is the agitation of humanity's near relatives. In the original 1976 *Omen*, Damien's presence agitates baboons in a nature preserve; in the

2006 version, the most agitated creature is the gorilla, who repeatedly throws himself at the glass in a clear attempt to reach and destroy Damien. We have come so far that our nearest genetic relatives, far from being alien, are more like us than not—they may be more sensitive to the presence of evil, but they are not in themselves evil. In fact, they might be our allies against the supernatural, rather than representative of it.

ST. FRANCIS XAVIER UNIVERSITY

NOTES

[1] "So that's what monkey business means." *Globe and Mail*, Thursday, May 18, 2006, A10.

[2] Darwin studies is a large field, but a reliable introduction to the controversy which followed the publication of his theories is E. Janet Browne, *Charles Darwin, Vol 2: The Power of Place* (London: Jonathan Cape, 2002).

[3] Robert Mills, *Suspended Animation: Pain, Pleasure, and Punishment in Medieval Culture* (London" Reaktion Books, 2005), 91; see also Jeffrey Richards, *Sex, Dissidence and Damnation: Minority Groups in the Middle Ages* (London: Routledge P, 1991), 132-49.

[4] John Boswell, *Christianity, Social Tolerance, and Homosexuality* (Chicago: U of Chicago P, 1980), 93 n.2.

[5] Boswell, 93-4.

[6] Richards, 141.

[7] The links between Grendel and his mother and the motif of Satan and his mother are explored briefly in Jeffrey Burton Russell, *Lucifer: The Devil in the Middle Ages* (Ithaca and London: Cornell University Press, 1984), 147-51. See also Ruth Mellinkoff, *The Mark of Cain* (Berkeley: University of California Press, 1981) and David Williams, *Cain and Beowulf* (Toronto: U of Toronto P, 1982).

[8] Jeffrey Jerome Cohen, *Of Giants: Sex, Monsters, and the Middle Ages* (Minneapolis: U of Minnesota P, 1999), 124. Cohen explores a modern book entitled a modern book titled *Giants: A Reference Guide from History, the Bible, and Recorded Legend* by Charles Deloach (Metchuen, NJ: Scarecrow, 1995). Deloach argues that "Lucifer and the many angels loyal to him … started playing around with the animals," and they "probably derived their greatest fun and pleasure from matings"; Cohen notes that Deloach thus achieves "a complete resolution of the incommensurable accounts of human origin offered by Genesis and evolutionary biology" (Cohen, 31-33). "Goats and monkeys," as Othello (that other great symbol of miscegenation) might exclaim.

[9] Williams, *Cain and Beowulf* 28.

[10] Williams, *Cain and Beowulf* 31.

[11] Williams, *Cain and Beowulf* 28-29.

[12] Terry Pratchett, "Imaginary World, Real Stories," *Folklore* 111 (2000), 159-68 (159-60).

[13] A. S. Byatt, "A comforting way of death," <u>Guardian</u>, November 9 2002. http://books. guardian.co.uk/reviews/sciencefiction/0,,836250,00.html. Accessed February 1 2007.

[14] Elizabeth Grosz, "Animal Sex," in Elizabeth Grosz and Elspeth Probyn, eds., *Sexy Bodies: The Strange Carnalities of Feminism* (London: Routledge, 1995), 278-99 (286).

[15] As in the edition used in the present essay: Anne Laskaya and Eve Salisbury, *The Middle English Breton Lays* (Kalamazoo: TEAMS, 1995).

[16] Alcuin Blamires, "The Twin Demons of Aristocratic Society in *Sir Gowther*," in Nicola McDonald, ed., *Pulp Fictions of Medieval England: Essays in Popular Romance* (Manchester: Manchester U, 2004), 45-62 (45).

[17] Cohen, 120-41.

[18] Cohen, 124.

[19] Blamires, 53-54; see also E. M. Bradstock, "*Sir Gowther*: Secular Hagiography or Hagiographical Romance or Neither?," AUMLA: *Journal of the Australasian Universities Language and Literature Association* 59 (1983), 26-47 (35); Shirley Marchalonis, "*Sir Gowther*: The Process of a Romance," *Chaucer Review* 6 (1971-72), 14-29 (18).

[20] Blamires, 54.

[21] Henry Vandelinde, "*Sir Gowther*: Saintly Knight and Knightly Saint," *Neophilologus* 80 (1996), 139-47 (141).

[22] That demoniality can be considered a real and damning possibility is explored, in the context of Marlowe' *Doctor Faustus*, by Walter Greg, "The Damnation of Faustus," *Modern Language Review* 41 (1946), 106.7. The thesis that Faustus is irredeemable after having sex with a vision of Helen of Troy which he knows to be a devil in disguise, although widely accepted, has been challenged: Nicholas Kiessling, "Doctor Faustus and the Sin of Demoniality," *Studies in English Literature, 1500-1900* 15:2 (Spring, 1975), 205-11. That demoniality is a sin is not seriously questioned by anyone.

[23] Neil Cartlidge, "'Thereof Seyus Clerkus': Slander, Rape, and *Sir Gowther*," in Corinne Saunders, ed., *Cultural Encounters in the Romances of Medieval England* (Woodbridge: D.S. Brewer, 2005), 135-47; Corinne Saunders, "'Symtyme the Fende': Questions of Rape in *Sir Gowther*," in M.J. Toswell and E.M. Tyler, eds., *Studies in English Language and Literature: 'Doubt Wisely'* (London: Routledge, 1996), 286-303.

[24] Geoffrey of Monmouth, *The History of the Kings of Britain*, ed. Lewis Thorpe (Harmondsworth: Penguin, 1977), 168.

[25] The tradition is summarized in Andrea Hopkins, *The Sinful Knights: A Study of Middle English Penitential Romance* (Oxford: Oxford UP, 1990), 167-8.

[26] Cohen, 127.

[27] Cohen, 121.

[28] Cohen, 130.

[29] Cohen, 129-30.

[30] Hopkins, 174-5.

[31] Dieter Mehl, *The Middle English Romances of the Thirteenth and Fourteenth Centuries* (London: Routledge, 1968), 126-7.

[32] Guthlac was an Anglo-Saxon saint with personal origins in the warrior class; see Jeffrey Jerome Cohen, "The Solitude of Guthlac," in his *Medieval Identity Machines* (Minneapolis: U of Minnesota P, 2003), 116-53.

[33] Brian McFadden, "Fear of Difference, Fear of Death: The *Sigelwara*, Tolkien's Swertings, and Racial Difference," in Jane Chance and Alfred K. Siewers, eds., *Tolkien's Modern Middle Ages* (New York: Palgrave MacMillan, 2005), 155-69 (156).

[34] J.R.R. Tolkien, *The Lord of the Rings* (London: Unwin, 1968), henceforth *LOTR*.

[35] McFadden, 161.

[36] McFadden, 163.

[37] Victoria Gaydosik implies, but does not develop, this same thought in "'Crimes Against the Book?' The Transformation of Tolkien's Arwen from Page to Screen and the Abandonment of the Psyche Archetype," in Janet Brennan Croft, ed., *Tolkien on Film: Peter Jackson's* The Lord of the Rings (Altadena, CA: The Mythopoeic Press, 2004), 215-30.

[38] Cathy Akers-Jordan, "Fairy Princess or Tragic Heroine? The Metamorphosis of Arwen Undomial in Peter Jackson's *The Lord of the Rings* Films," in Croft, 195-213 (201-2).

[39] Akers-Jordan, 208.

[40] Jane Chance, "Tolkien and the Other: Race and Gender in Middle-earth," in Chance and Siewers, 171-86 (173).

[41] Ruth S. Noel, *The Mythology of Middle-Earth* (Boston, Houghton Mifflin, 1977), 101.

[42] T.S. Shippey, *Author of the Century* (London: HarperCollins, 2000), 88.

[43] J.R.R. Tolkien, *The Silmarillion* (London: Unwin, 1979).

[44] McFadden, 165.

[45] T.S. Shippey, "Orcs, Wraiths, Wights: Tolkien's Images of Evil," in George Clark and Daniel Timmons, eds., *J.R.R. Tolkien and His Literary Resonances: Views of Middle-earth* (Westport, CT: Greenwood, 2000), 183-98 (184).

[46] J.R.R. Tolkien, *Morgoth's Ring*, The History of Middle-earth 10 (London: HarperCollins, 1994), 416-22; henceforth *MR*.

[47] Randel Helms, *Tolkien's World* (London: Thames and Hudson, 1994), 77-79.

[48] Helms, 82.

[49] Shippey, "Orcs, Wraiths, Wights," 186.

[50] Colin Manlove, *The Fantasy Literature of England* (New York: St. Martin's, 1999), 136-7.

[51] Terry Pratchett, *Soul Music* (London: Corgi, 1994); *Hogfather* (London: Corgi, 1996); *Thief of Time* (London: Corgi, 2002).

Volume XXI
2006

Back to the Future: Revitalizing Contemporary Society through Medieval Morality in the *Harry Potter* Film Series

Karen Borresen Walsh

As is the case with its literary counterpart, the *Harry Potter* film series is a blockbuster of the highest magnitude. Of course, this is in large part due to the success of the books, which appeal to children in traditional ways while also luring mature audiences by blurring the barriers between children's and adults' books (Dawtrey A2). That those from older generations are as obsessed with *Harry Potter* as Rowling's targeted readership is evidenced in the volume of fan fiction clogging Internet connections around the world: according to Marianne MacDonald, "A conservative estimate would peg the number at over 25,000 stories posted on the Internet, but the real total could be closer to 100,000" (28). With such an overflow of enthusiasm on the part of Rowling's audience, it is no wonder that the films, despite arguable flaws, consistently draw long lines at theaters and capture record-breaking ticket sales. Nonetheless, it is on their own merit that they earn such a high degree of audience appreciation. With an ever-changing list of directors, composers, cinematographers, and producers contributing to the translations of the texts to the big screen, each of the films has its own energy, pace, and focus. They offer familiar yet unique interpretations of the stories—as well as of the events and locales which define the magical world in which Harry travels.

At the same time, viewers often walk out of theaters with divergent perceptions of the film they have just watched. Whereas some see the first two installments, directed by Chris Columbus, as being somewhat sugar-coated, others, such as Raphael Shargel, have starkly contrasting views: "the cinematic version emphasizes dark conflict far more strongly than the original. Columbus somehow transforms a colorful tale into very grim material" (35). Similarly, many would argue that Alfonso Cuarón's translation of *The Prisoner of Azkaban*, the third installment in the series, is significantly darker than Columbus's handling of the first two films. However, the methods by which the directors attempt to focus and intensify their respective films are very different. The former turns his spotlight to the action in Rowling's tales. Nonetheless, as Rachel Johnson points out in her review of *The Chamber of Secrets*, "There is a daring attempt to grapple with 'contemporary' issues of racism, ethnicity and bullying" (80). Columbus is primarily concerned with fitting as much of the texts into the films as possible. In contrast, Cuarón simplifies the development of the third film's story by scrapping "everything that didn't relate to the central theme or didn't keep the plot flying" (Smith 67). Doing so allowed him to increase the emotional intensity and symbolic power of the film through the artistic qualities of cinematography. As he explains, "'The idea was to . . . give the audience a spectacle like they have come to expect, but a new one. We have a different color palette, for instance, from the previous movies, but within that, the same architecture'" (Goldman 98). Nearly nonexistent in the first film, serious questions pertaining to real life emerge in the sequels, and they are reinforced by the cinematography and the set designs. In the case of the second film, there are "many scenes in which the camera pans across the sinister gloom of the forbidden recesses of Hogwarts" (Simmons and Evely 78). The same can be said of the third and fourth installments, although Cuarón's personal touch gives the symbolism of *Azkaban* a stirring, artistic, creepy quality that subtly unsettles the audience.

Despite various magic-related obstacles, all those involved in the production process strive to provide the films with a heavy dose of realism. Because they "tap into the common fantasy of children that another world can coexist [alongside the real world], unseen by adult eyes" (Simmons and Evely 77), it would be easy for them to fail in this effort by allowing themselves to be carried away while depicting the truly fantastic. Doing so—bowing to the hype that involves flashy special effects—would undermine the illusion that is the Harry Potter world of imagined possibilities. To a certain degree, a large part of the responsibility for avoiding this result lies on the shoulders of the animators, whose artistic spirits are no doubt eager to create the next infamous eye-popping action sequence. However, the balance lies on those of the filmmakers, whose duty it is to convey the moral and ideological gravity inherent in the story and character arcs of the series while still offering popcorn entertainment. Their success is, in many ways, due to the fact that, as is the case with the books, each successive film is more mature than its predecessor—visually, dramatically, and, most importantly, thematically. Although the majority of the films' fans may not realize it, those involved in the productions have done a remarkable job of accomplishing far more than imitative translations of Rowling's stories. In the process of portraying the magical realm and Harry's maturation, they have also succeeded at making significant moral statements by drawing on traditional literary themes and commonly understood cinematic motifs.

In addition to rendering yet another mythic tale of an orphan destined for greatness, the producers of the *Harry Potter* film series offer a complex visual study of the society which spawned Rowling and her towering literary achievement. In particular, they manipulate disparate modern views of the Middle Ages into a criticism of contemporary Western culture. They do so by recreating and counter-pointing two of Umberto Eco's "little middle ages," the barbaric and the romantic. The former, defined by its cruelty, brutality, and narrow-mindedness, is most obviously manifested in the attributes which distinguish Muggles and Dark Wizards from "good" magical characters.

Conforming to Eco's description, these two groups, with their dangerously exclusionary idealism, ask others "to celebrate, on this earth," or, as is the case here, in their own realm, "virile, brute force, the glories of a new Aryanism" (Eco 69). In the case of Voldemort and his cronies, this translates into a desire to eradicate Muggles and, first and foremost, purge magical society of mud-blood Wizards. Similarly, the comparatively powerless Dursleys, who represent the Muggle population, wish just as passionately that magic and those who practice it would disappear from the earth. These personifications of the barbaric view are balanced by the portrayal of the romantic "little middle age," which Eco associates with "stormy castles and their ghosts" (Eco 69). It is exemplified by Harry and his cohorts, who embody the chivalric idealism of the romantic vision. Their depictions resurrect our childhood fantasies of fearless knights, selfless heroics, and noble quests, reviving our hope that evil will not prevail.

The producers of the films contrast these two visions of the age by focusing on physical details and descriptions which are, for the most part, *not* found in the books. To develop the magical and Muggle worlds as seemingly contrary reflections of a shared past, the filmmakers contrast them by employing carefully chosen camera angles, lighting, metaphorical imagery, and incisive stereotyping. When used in conjunction with purposefully crafted sets and props, these reveal the similarities between the modern Muggle world and Voldemort's vision for the future while simultaneously exposing the magical realm as the victim of cultural stagnation born out of intellectual and moral apathy.

Despite seemingly associating Muggles with modernity and Wizards with the distant past, the films play a game with time and our perceptions of reality: the non-magical world is the natural consequence of stubbornly clinging to the unlearned, violent, and unjust aspects of the barbaric Middle Ages. Meanwhile, the wizarding realm, despite its initial appearance, is on the brink of a similar collapse. Both the wielders of Dark Magic and the "good" Wizards who adhere to tradition are contributing in different ways to the destruction of magical culture. It is Harry who must lead the wizarding world—not to *recover* the past, but to create a positive future by reviving the medieval ideals of honor, valor, and cultural responsibility.

Establishing visual translations of these interpretations of the Muggle, magical, and Dark Wizard spheres was a complex, multi-tiered process which began with the making of the first film, *Harry Potter and the Sorcerer's Stone*. It was imperative that the producers clearly defined the Muggle world in which Harry had lived for the first eleven years of his life, because all of his subsequent experiences would be interpreted within that context. To accomplish this, they focused almost exclusively on Harry's family. In the books, and even more so in the films, the Muggle realm is exemplified by the Dursleys. We are led to believe their traits characterize the culture to which they belong: Aunt Petunia's devotion to sterile perfection excludes Harry and is therefore unwelcoming to us; Uncle Vernon's rejection of creativity and eccentricity is so irrationally repressive that we imagine the non-magical universe as a world which will not sustain our interest; and Dudley's bullying talents and spoiled nature are more than enough to prevent his cousin from experiencing childhood happiness, causing readers to be glad they are not his classmates. As Simmons and Evely explain, "The Dursleys suffer from sensory deprivation, oblivious to the world of the soul and the leaping, tangential, affective part of the psyche. Instead, the mundane and the material rule in Privet [Drive]" (77). The Muggle world is not one of which we desire to be a part. Of even greater importance is the fact that the possession of these qualities has garnered Harry's relatives what economic success and social standing they enjoy, immediately revealing the corrupt values and base nature of non-magical society. The filmmakers depict these attributes of Harry's extended family—the sole window into the non-magical realm's moral and intellectual character—by employing a variety of visual tools. Ultimately, the methods they use highlight the barbarity of the Muggle world and expose its fallen nature.

One of the most basic devices employed for the critical examination and depiction of non-magical culture is that of stereotyping. While other means are utilized to shed light on the overall condition of the Muggle world, this assists in revealing *why* it is a fallen reflection of the barbaric Middle Ages. The second scene of *The Sorcerer's Stone* promptly insinuates the Dursleys' flaws, which in turn suggest the attitudes and values of Muggles in general. As in the books, Harry is treated like a servant while his cousin, Dudley, is dissatisfied upon receiving thirty-six birthday presents. The fact that Dudley is spoiled rotten (and perhaps quite stupid) is apparent from his first words, when he sees the gifts and demands, "How many are there?" In J.K. Rowling's version, he at least manages to count them himself before throwing a temper-tantrum. This slight change from the original version suggests other character flaws that subsequently surface more prominently in the third film.

It is only in *The Prisoner of Azkaban* that we see the full extent of the Dursleys' negative qualities. Vernon and Petunia's house is practically a shrine to their son, numerous pictures of whom are in almost every camera shot taken at 4 Privet Drive. This immediately tells us their priorities and values are misplaced and skewed. By putting their son on a pedestal, the Dursleys' appreciation of their child goes far beyond that which is reasonable. Rather than valuing intellectual, cultural, or spiritual awareness, their shallow focus is upon a boy whom we soon discover is very undeserving of their adoration. Clearly, they are oblivious regarding his faults: the laziness implied by his growing waistline is only interrupted when he bullies his cousin. Not surprisingly, Dudley is as ignorant of the world as his parents are of his numerous flaws. The filmmakers depict this explicitly in *The Prisoner of Azkaban*'s dinner scene, which portrays him as the epitome of sloth—physically, emotionally, and intellectually. When Aunt Marge comes to visit, Dudley does not even *acknowledge* his doting aunt's arrival. As she greets him with a smothering hug, he continues eating and watching a television program without so much as looking at her. The first time he takes note of anything other than food or TV is when Marge's dog attacks his father, and even then he shows no emotional or cognitive response. It is not until his aunt, who has been accidentally turned into a human balloon by Harry, is floating off the ground that Dudley reacts to the events taking place around him. Then, when given the opportunity, he demonstrates no ability to comprehend or sensibly respond to what is occurring. After one of his aunt's flying blouse buttons hits him in the forehead and knocks him to the ground, he does not think to avoid possible other projectiles: he returns to his initial position and is immediately hit in the forehead by still another button. Yet, in spite of this and his initial shock, by the time his aunt is floating toward the horizon, Dudley has returned to watching television and eating the food that spilled on his bib during the meleé.

That Dudley cares little for those around him could not be more obvious. That he is a reflection of his parents is also quite clear. Just as he mindlessly returns to watching television once the disruption Harry has caused moves outside, his father ultimately shows barely any genuine concern for Marge. As seemingly determined as Vernon initially is to prevent his sister from floating up into the ether, it takes little to convince him to abandon his noble brotherly quest. At first, he grabs Marge's ankles in an attempt to keep her from rising too high and does not seem particularly alarmed when his feet leave the ground. However, when her dog clamps down on his pant leg, he readily accepts the excuse to let go of her. Despite her yelling "Don't you dare!" at him, which strongly suggests she knows his character well enough to realize he will gladly abandon his heroic attempt to save her, he offers a perfunctory "sorry" and releases his grip. Moments later, he is on his knees in the back yard, yelling her name with the most desperately concerned and brotherly voice he can muster. Meanwhile, the music that accompanies the action—a lively, dramatic, and celebratory classical piece written by John Williams and appropriately titled "Aunt Marge's Waltz"—makes a mockery of Vernon's contrived distress. The scene is carefully crafted to inform the audience that Vernon and Petunia, just like Dudley, care little for those other than themselves. Ultimately, they are selfish, petty, and short-sighted; as representatives of Muggle culture, they are excellent proof of its ignoble modern condition.

In addition to revealing Muggles' lack of positive qualities, the dinner scene also highlights discriminatory values which morally and ideologically align them with Dark Wizards. While in the book Aunt Marge offers numerous explanations for Harry being a horrible child, in the third film her *only* explanation is, "It's all got to do with blood—*bad* blood." On the one hand, Voldemort and the Dursleys have different conceptions of what constitutes "bad." The former despises non-magical people, and, indirectly, he also fears them. He and his followers draw on their purportedly pure-blood ancestry for power and influence, and successful half-bloods threaten their ascendancy by undermining the legitimacy and importance of bloodlines. Ironically, the Dursleys feel essentially the same way about Wizards as Voldemort does about "mud-bloods." They scorn and fear them because they are different and, as is often demonstrated, capable of achieving things with magic that are more difficult to accomplish by non-magical means. Although Dark Wizards and Muggles dislike each other for almost identical reasons, they clearly agree that heredity is infinitely more important than character. Not surprisingly, their valuation of genetics is a negative hold-over from the later Middle Ages, when social, political, and economic standing were greatly influenced by heredity. They have taken the beliefs that justified kingship being passed from father to son and twisted them to discriminate against those they fear and do not understand.

The films' producers clearly incorporate traditional stereotypes into the depictions of the Dursleys in an effort to represent negatively Muggle culture. However, they also devise their own, while partially drawing on less familiar icons. Although Rowling effectively describes Harry's relatives as unpleasant people, the films portray them in a visually and aurally unappealing manner which encourages the audience to disdain them and, by extension, Muggles in general.

Everything about Harry is different from that of his adoptive family. Small and scrawny, any similarities he has to Aunt Petunia are merely skin-deep: her looks of disdain are only interrupted by jittery paranoia. Whereas Harry speaks in a rather smooth, middling tone, his cousin's voice blares impetuously. When not angry, Uncle Vernon is very much like his name: he drawls when he speaks and moves in a heavy manner. Meanwhile, all three react to any displays of magic with a madness and fear that would shame any member of the films' audience. Harry, on the other hand, responds in the way we hope we would. In the first film, when his Hogwarts letters are flying down the chimney like a swarm of belligerent birds, the action slows as he leaps excitedly into the air, thrilled by the wildness that is taking place and eager to get his hands on one of the envelopes. "The magic of Harry Potter is a metaphor for unleashing the human spirit, unblocking the mind, believing in ourselves, acting on instinct, [and] taking risks" (Simmons and Evely 77), and Harry is the conduit for the representation of that magic during the scene with the letters. In the background, Vernon flails at them as if they are a swarm of killer bees, and Petunia shrieks while holding her cowering son on her lap. An event that would excite and intrigue many of us—even the *Tom and Jerry* housekeeper, Mammy Two-Shoes, of whom Petunia is so reminiscent—is utterly terrifying to Muggles. There is no openness, no curiosity—only terror and confusion. It is with these depictions that the producers of the films portray what the book cannot: how the fear of going against tradition and "normalcy," so common during the late medieval period, still influences contemporary Muggles; it has had a paralyzing effect on their culture. Unwilling and therefore unable to think creatively, daringly, and eccentrically, they have clung to the social and intellectual rigidity they believe was the bedrock of the earlier era's stability. In so doing, they have fallen—morally, intellectually, and culturally—into a cannibalistic, cultural black hole of their own making.

Although the filmmakers employ various forms of stereotyping to depict the Dursleys and the society they represent in a negative light, they must use other means to relay the interpretation of the Muggle realm in general as one of an uninviting, unpleasant, and distinctly fallen world. The primary tools on which they rely for this purpose are lighting and symbolic coloring, which carefully limit how certain scenes and depictions can be interpreted by audiences. In conjunction with metaphorical imagery, they emphasize the fallen nature of the Muggle world by using colors and shading in a way that contrasts it with the merely teetering magical realm.

The scene that most successfully utilizes all these devices is the introduction to the second film, which presents the dichotomy created by the intertwined yet parallel worlds. As it begins, the camera flies over a sea of clouds toward an orange and pink sunset. Romantically reminiscent of the classic western in which the heroic cowboy rides toward the setting sun, the initial image is exceedingly picturesque. As the opening shot of what is sure to be an exciting film, it is designed to inspire anticipation and optimism. However, the feelings it creates are quickly quashed as the camera abandons the warm sunset and slips below the clouds. The audience is suddenly faced with a stifling sight: the sun sadly hunkers below a hazy horizon, and the pinks and oranges have been replaced by barely distinguishable shades of soot. A sea of streets lined with dull, grey, cookie-cutter houses fans out, like a web of spiders' legs, from the center of the picture. While the objects on the screen have some definition, the cinematography transforms a potentially awe-inspiring view into a nearly solid grey panorama. In one image of suburban monotony, the filmmakers have successfully depicted the bleak, soulless, and sterile nature of non-magical culture. That feelings of freedom and joy cannot exist in the world the Dursleys inhabit is patently obvious. Creativity, individuality, and the vibrancy of life are all expunged by Muggle society.

It should not be surprising, then, that almost no Dursley scenes take place during the daytime. The two primary exceptions are when Vernon warns Harry about doing anything wrong on the trip to the zoo and when Harry sees the delivery owls congregating on the front lawn, both of which take place during the first film prior to his receiving the letter from Hogwarts. Once Harry discovers his true identity, the time of day in which many scenes are set becomes visually symbolic: multiple magical scenes begin at dawn, whereas Muggle scenes are restricted to sunset and night-time. By making this distinction, the filmmakers successfully indicate that the non-magical world is both repressive and fallen and that the magical realm is the only remaining source of hope and opportunity.

Although the opening sunset scene is an example of color combining with powerful symbolic imagery to make an important interpretive statement, other instances of cinematic manipulation are not so complex. One which has less pure symbolism is the sequence in which Harry is dreaming about the Riddle mansion's caretaker at the beginning of the fourth film. Colors dominate the scenes: a cold bluish-grey tone permeates the gothic imagery of the nightmare. When Harry awakes, he does so to Hermione's caring voice and the warm oranges and reds of Ron's candlelit, Quidditch-themed bedroom. The latter image, complete with the familiar and welcome details of a teenage boy's room, contrasts superbly with the preceding dream of lurking death. However, while the set designs have a predictable impact on how the scenes are perceived, the colors used to characterize them are effective at influencing the emotions and perceptions of the audience.

Nonetheless, this sequence gains further import when considered in terms of the first Dursley scene of the film series, in which Harry is awakened inside his prison-like cupboard by his aunt banging on the door and his cousin jumping above him so that sawdust rains down on his head. The progression in the fourth film clearly recalls our first introduction to the Dursley household; in fact, it so closely mirrors the earlier scene that one cannot easily deny the filmmakers' goal of highlighting the difference between the two worlds. Yet it also does much to complicate the notion of the Muggle/Wizard dichotomy. Although color is often used to distinguish the magical and Muggle realms, such as in the sunset scene in the second film, it is also used to differentiate between "good" and "bad" Wizards within the magical realm itself, as is the case in the dream sequence of the fourth film.

The cold bluish-grey tone recurs throughout the third and fourth films, most notably when Voldemort or his henchmen are looming. Thus, it is used primarily as a way of foreshadowing danger and linking Dark Magic to the destruction of the magical realm we have come to know. An example of this is when the Dementors are stalking the Hogwarts grounds in *The Prisoner of*

Azkaban. In one of the most strikingly beautiful and successfully metaphorical uses of cinematography in the entire series, we see a Dementor skimming silently across the school grounds. The blue lighting infuses the shot with a sense of cold that is imposed upon physical reality when the creature passes a flower. As the camera focuses on the bloom, it shrivels and crinkles within a coating of fresh ice. The image confirms that Harry's response to the creatures, whether in the Hogwarts Express or on his broom during the Quidditch match, is entirely justified; Dementors clearly leech the life and warmth out of living things in their vicinity. At the same time, the image foreshadows the Dementors' inherent evil and impending betrayal of the Ministry of Magic. Just as one who has a positive influence on nature can in most cases be assumed to be "good," so can one which has a negative consequence be presumed to be "bad." Meanwhile, the scene's blue tint, particularly in contrast to the warm, crisp, and vibrant coloring of the flower, infuses the audience with an inescapable sense of foreboding.

Artfully constructed cinematography is not the only means by which the producers of the movies illustrate complex meaning while translating the books to film. Although the Muggle world is blighted by a "Dark Ages" lack of individuality and creativity, the production designers depict the magical realm as its polar opposite by subtly—and sometimes *not* so subtly—lacing it with imaginative details. One such example involves the Leaky Cauldron, which is depicted very differently in the first than in the subsequent two films. Much as in Rowling's original description, its depiction in *The Sorcerer's Stone* resembles a dingy Muggle pub. However, were that not the case, the visual impact of the subsequent introduction to Diagon Alley would be far less potent. The Leaky Cauldron of the *third* film, on the other hand, is suffused with numerous magical details: a man is casually stirring his teacup by swirling his finger in the air, chairs stow themselves at the wave of a waiter's hand, and a kettle drifts around the common room, pouring cups of tea. By furnishing the set with inconspicuous magical elements, the production designers imbue the scene with a *realness* that is not generally associated with things "magical."

These subtle details are the necessary foundation for a convincing portrayal of the dynamic magical world. Without them, the popular locales of the wizarding realm would not convince us that they are the stomping grounds of people who can circumvent the laws of nature. Fortunately, the films' producers create a world that is often more luxuriously outlandish than Rowling describes in her books. It is no surprise that Harry is awed when he first looks down the crooked, winding road of Diagon Alley; there is not a single ninety-degree angle to be found within the jumbled morass stretching before him: buildings lean every-which-way and look as if they should have collapsed long before being completed. The same can be said of the Weasley house, and even the

Hogwarts Castle has at least one tower oddly angling out of another. All the places and objects that define the Magical world are conspicuously unique. The Gryffindors' common room, for example, is round, warm, and welcoming, whereas the Slytherins' is linear, cold, and echoing. The distinctiveness of all things in the realm give it the impression of being both more magical *and* more realistic than the non-magical universe in which Harry was raised, calling into question the "realness" of its Muggle counterpart while simultaneously tipping its hat to the periods that preceded the Industrial Revolution.

The inside of Gringotts Bank is the ultimate introduction to both the magnificence and, much more significantly, the potentialities of the magical realm. It offers the first true hint that a world governed by magic is not bounded by stunted imaginations. Reminiscent of pre-Black Friday banks with its shining floors and grand lines of tellers, the building is an impressive salute to aging magical opulence. Shimmering chandeliers hang from the ceiling, marble floors sparkle, and hundreds of candles light the main room. When Harry and Hagrid enter the underground vault area, we discover yet another defining trait of the wizarding universe: with the camera angled down at the mining car in which the two are traveling, we see that the floors of personal vaults seem to extend downward forever. The filmmakers are clearly suggesting the boundless nature of the non-Muggle world, which exists in stark contrast to the repressive domain Vernon Dursley rules. This infinity motif is repeated later in the film, when Harry and his fellow Gryffindors enter the main stairway of Hogwarts. In a seemingly inverted reflection of the Gringotts vault area, the stairs extend for at least fourteen stories and actually seem to rise forever. The natural laws and scientific concepts that regulate the Muggle world do not apply to the magical realm, and, to a certain extent, they do not even exist; physical and dimensional limitations in places such as Gringotts and Hogwarts are theoretical, not binding.

When contrasted with the suffocating representations of the Dursleys' neighborhood, these aspects of magical architecture do more than demonstrate the disparity between the two realms. They also imply Harry has, at least in some sense, entered a different dimension. This interpretation is encouraged by the first travel scene of the fourth film, in which the camera swings to the peak of a hill and finds a port key—an old boot—backlit by the rising sun. When the port is triggered, the actual hilltop appears as a gateway: the boot flings them into the sky before dragging them down into the flashing light that pours from the hill's crest. Although we know Muggles and Wizards co-exist in the same world, several details of the scene indicate Rowling and the film's producers are encouraging the audience to distinguish between the physical realities of their particular realms. The primary one of these is a clear reference to medieval Celtic tradition, which stipulated that passing from our realm into the Otherworld is facilitated by being at border points during transitional times of the day. In the case of Harry and his friends, they are transported from the hilltop—the border point between earth and sky—as night transforms into morning. That the scene's setting seems carefully crafted to draw a parallel between the magical realm and the Otherworld is hard to ignore. As such, it is equally injudicious to disregard the potential meaning that seems implied by the incorporation of this medieval motif into the production of the film.

In many ways, the realm we find in the movies is indeed just that: a truly distinct world which is not only *spatially* separated from its non-magical counterpart but is also physically *different* from it. As the Knight Bus scene of the third film shows, a more complex relationship with nature—and in particular with *time*—defines magical life. A shrunken head hanging in the bus's front window counts the passing seconds as an elderly Muggle pedestrian slowly crosses the street: "...five, four, three, three-and-a-half, two, one and three-quarters...." Meanwhile, the triple-decker shows more life than the Muggle does as it groans and exhales steam. The scene is reminiscent of earlier depictions of the Dursleys who, while not quite as ponderously slow as the pedestrian, are just as necessarily oblivious to their surroundings as she is. It is yet another reminder that Muggles inhabit a world in which action, excitement, and curiosity are sorely lacking. At the same time, the scene does much more to further our understanding of the magical realm Harry has claimed as his home. Although the shrunken head's counting seems intended as a joke, it is also the first hint that time is *literally* relative to Wizards—not subject to the rules that govern modern life, but a tool to be manipulated.

Moments later, when warned of an impending collision with two approaching double-decker busses, the driver pulls several levers. One of these immediately slows to a crawl everything surrounding the bus, and another horizontally squeezes it so that it can slide safely through oncoming traffic while the occupants continue to function at normal speed. Known as "bullet-time" and popularized in the film *The Matrix*, this cinemagraphic tool is often used to highlight and depict subjects' abilities to interact uniquely with the world around them. In Rowling's description of this scene, there are no references to time's pace being altered in any way, nor does the bus at any point shrink in width; objects such as lampposts, trashcans, and double-deckers conveniently jump out of its haphazard path in a more *traditional* magical way. By having the Wizards in this scene manipulate the world around them rather than simply moving it aside, the filmmakers empower them in a way Rowling did not. As such, the scene does more than excite and impress. It also strongly suggests that the magical world is far more complex than at first appears, and that it does not consist solely of wand-waving Wizards and magical creatures.

That the producers wish to communicate this to the audience is confirmed in the very next scene, when the first thing we see is a man absentmindedly "stirring" his tea while reading an apparently old edition of Stephen Hawking's *A Brief History of Time*. This detail is clearly a direct reference to the twisting and manipulation of time and space that permeate the film. In addition, this familiar reference reveals just how pointedly the producers are judging non-magical society. We know from Rowling's books and from the film depictions of Ron's father that it is only due to an abnormal and inexplicable kind of inquisitiveness that Wizards busy themselves with Muggle-related things. Fantastic scientist or not, Hawking is still a Muggle, and therefore we can be almost certain that the reference to him is intended to mock gently non-magical understanding of the natural world. The Wizard's reading of the book is not unlike an avowed atheist's reading of a religious text: curiosity—oftentimes the amused variety—frequently fuels their interest more so than does belief or a desire to learn. Thus, while the shot of the bookish man buttresses the depiction of the complicated relationship Wizards have with the surrounding world, it also lends doubt to how seriously Muggles and their views of the world can be taken.

The entire Knight Bus sequence, from the moment the triple-decker arrives in front of Harry until he is met by the Minister for Magic, is pivotal in differentiating between Muggles and Wizards and their respective cultures and realities. The filmmakers intentionally portray Muggles as oblivious drones who, unlike Witches and Wizards, have no comprehension of, relationship with, or interest in the natural world that sustains them. They are clearly suggesting that, as non-magical people abandoned their belief in the centaurs and other creatures who roam the Forbidden Forest, they also discarded a deep understanding of the universe that has only recently begun to be "recovered" by science greats such as Einstein and Hawking. Nonetheless, the recovery that has begun in the scientific community is cold, intellectual, and spiritually lifeless. The understanding Muggles have is systematic and restrained, lacking the meaning and infusion of life that defines the relationship between magical people and the natural world.

Wizards have a more complete understanding of the universe they inhabit, and, despite its supposedly imaginary magical aspects, their comprehension of the complexity of life gives it a realism not found in the flat Muggle dimension. We find proof of this in the boggart scene of the third film, when the shape-changer is locked in the cabinet and Lupin is introducing his lesson. The opening shot appears to be of a mirrored cabinet reflecting the students, but, as the camera advances, it moves *through* the mirror so that the original reflection of the class becomes a direct view of the students listening to their professor. This subtle but clever use of cinematography demonstrates more clearly than ever that perception and reality in the magical world are interdependent and often closely entwined. Invited to enter the realm, we begin to view nature in a fresh light: as a complex, multi-facetted universe that encourages us to think creatively, not as the inanimate backdrop for Muggle conformity.

Another example of when camera shots are used to distinguish the magical realm's dynamic nature can once again be found in the Knight Bus scene. The sharp camera angles reveal the lively, interactive quality of wizarding life by accentuating the jarring movements of the bus as it careens through London like a mad bull. Whereas most of the travelers seem hardly to notice the erratic swerving and sudden jolts, the way their blasé attitude contrasts our perceptions only heightens our awareness of how different the magical and "real" worlds are and how much more appealing the former is.

Nonetheless, the filmmakers' production choices reveal that the realm Harry has entered is on the brink of following in its counterpart's footsteps. Although Lord Voldemort's destructive interference in wizard culture is certainly not slowing the downward spiral, neither is it the root cause; there is much evidence to suggest that the magical world would be at risk even if he were not a factor. The earlier description of Gringotts Bank being an example of "aging opulence" was carefully worded. Despite its grand appearance, cobwebs hang from the glorious chandeliers and the building shows its age. Later in the first film, we find similar structural decomposition in the abandoned room which houses the Mirror of Erised and in the forbidden third-floor corridor of Hogwarts.

This is not the fully-preserved, romantic medieval vision the books promised. The magical world's physical grandeur is eroding, and Voldemort cannot be blamed for its degeneration: he alone does not have the power to destroy the very infrastructure of their realm otherwise. Although he can blackmail and otherwise lasso Wizards into joining his movement, the majority of the magical population are still relatively true to their moral natures; Voldemort's power is thus significantly limited. The question then becomes, what else could be causing the disintegration of their culture? The answer lies in the very values which define it, for while they encourage individualism, they also discourage experimentation and development. The world is decaying from the inside.

The symptoms of the disease are the contraptions with which the producers ornament the films' sets. Dozens of objects from pre-industrial eras are peppered throughout the locations which define the magical world. One example is Lupin's gramophone. Invented in the 19th century, it is the most "modern" object found in the films. Other things which harken to the past include *The Daily Prophet*, which is printed on parchment in "medieval"-style font, and the library book in which Hermione finds the directions for making Polyjuice Potion—a moldy and tattered manuscript that has been produced by hand. While there is certainly nothing wrong with appreciating arcane objects, one wonders why so many articles not detailed in the books are emphasized in the films.

Although they obviously contribute to the cinematic atmosphere, arcane objects also play a crucial role in revealing Magical society's dangerous fascination with—and futile attempt to preserve—the past. The best example of this is the tent at the World Cup, which at first sight appears incapable of comfortably sleeping more than two occupants. However, once again the "natural" laws do not apply: it has a gigantic, multiple-room interior decked with couches, plants, tables, and even a chandelier. Just as importantly, it resembles the variety of tent we would imagine as belonging to an ancient king camping beside a battlefield; it is eminently comfortable and lavishly decorated with medieval tapestries. Keeping in mind that the Weasleys are poor and Harry was deprived of creature comforts as a child, the tent has an artificially transformative effect on them. Although their backgrounds earmark them for a small, drab tent, magic has allowed them to have one which is far more grand. They suddenly find themselves living like the kings and queens of a noble former era. However, their high status is merely a short-lived illusion. An encounter with those of the magical elite, Lucius and Draco Malfoy, recalls the reality of their position. It pops the bubble of their imagined good fortune and reminds us that their societal status is limited by age-old prejudices and persistently rigid class distinctions. By relying on magic to improve superficially their lives and thereby mask the reality of their place in society, working-class Wizards artificially buttress their self-esteem and contentedness. At the same time, by clinging to the trappings of bygone eras in an attempt to preserve and associate themselves with a glorious past, they delude themselves into believing they are privileged. Their actions are no different than those of poor Muggles who live in squalor while treasuring valuable family heirlooms. The things that remind them of earlier success blind them to their current condition. The mistaken sense of well-being that results from this ultimately encourages them to neglect their duty to themselves and to those who share their lowly position in society. They take pride in the artificial—in the luxurious tent and ancient remnants of opulence that adorn it—and thus inadvertently preserve the medieval ideals that continue to repress them.

However, this approach to life is not solely possessed by the disadvantaged. The community as a whole romanticizes the past to a perilous degree. As is the case with any culture that has already had its Golden Age, it draws its confidence from former rather than current greatness. The consequence of this mind-set is that the modern magical world is only a tattered remnant of its supposedly noble progenitor. Physical evidence of this can be found throughout the films. The school library's ratty old spell-books and the shabby shop signs along Diagon Alley are indicative of the community's decline. There are no completely *new* things—whether conceptual or physical—depicted in the movies. For example, McGonagall, the personification of tradition, almost invariably wears a stereotypical black hat not dissimilar to those worn by Muggle children on Halloween. Meanwhile, her less conservative comrades show their creativity by wearing brimless, oftentimes decorated hats, but age-old tradition is the ultimate guide for how the majority of wizards live their lives. Even the one item which appears to be valued for its newness—the latest quidditch broom model—is really only a better mousetrap: it remains a broom, not a new means of transportation.

The static materialism of the magical realm reflects and ultimately causes intellectual, moral, and social regression. For instance, in none of the films has there been mention of Wizards creating new spells. (That Snape invented new spells as a student appears only in book 6, long after the first movies were made.) The gramophone, although very charming, is certainly not an example of technical advancement. The world has obviously changed very little during the previous few generations. We can deduce that this is a direct result of embracing the past while shying from change and the progress that is instigated by creativity. Of course, it is difficult to preserve only the positive aspects of earlier times. By clinging to the idealized aspects and physical hold-overs from the medieval period, magical culture has also inadvertently allowed its constrictive class system and aversion to unconventionality to survive into the modern era. Despite being purebloods, the Weasleys are incapable of climbing the social or economic ladder; the half-human Hagrid lives in little more than a shack; and many people wrongly suspect Dumbledore, the only ideologically eccentric character, of being a bit mad. By hoarding the *symbols* rather than the *values* of the romantic Middle Ages instead of agitating creatively for the kind of social justice that, if it existed, would unite the community and forge a better future, average Wizards are contributing to the downfall of magical society with a mortal combination of apathy and complacency. Having contrived to convince themselves that all is well so long as physical evidence of their former greatness remains, they successfully preserve its trappings while allowing the values of the earlier era to atrophy. Meanwhile, Voldemort is pressing his advantage. The ideals of the barbaric Middle Ages, apparently supressed by their romantic counterparts, continue nonetheless to exist. As the "good" Wizards struggle to decide between heroism and self-preservation, the Dark Lord is resurrecting and reinforcing those values which define the barbaric view of the Middle Ages: brutality, judgment, conformity, and unwavering social stratification.

It is Harry, having experienced the consequences of those ideals in his childhood, who has the tools and the vision required to spearhead the reawakening of magical society. After sitting in front of the Mirror of Erised in the second film and dwelling on his parents—whom he sees in the mirror and no doubt wishes he could resurrect—Harry turns from his wistful fantasy of an imagined childhood with them. Only in the following film does he turn to the *real* past for strength—even if unintentionally. When the basilisk is hunting him, after he voices loyalty to Dumbledore Fawkes comes to his aid. Later, when dared by Tom Riddle to concede defeat, he refuses and is rewarded with Gryffindor's sword, which he then uses to fight the giant snake. It is by adhering to the romantic ideals—loyalty, honor, bravery, duty to others—of his house's namesake that he earns the phoenix's help and a sword with which he can repel the attacks of Riddle's monster. Faced with a murderous beast that is much larger in the film than it is as described in the book, Harry defiantly clings to the traits that could never allow him to be a Slytherin. As the headmaster says at the end of the film, "Only a true Gryffindor could have pulled [Gryffindor's sword] out of the hat." Not surprisingly, those traits are the defining characteristics of the romanticized medieval hero. Harry is in every way the antithesis of Voldemort and the evil characters who populate the barbaric version of the Middle Ages.

Harry's response to his down-trodden life with the Dursleys is to embrace the mentality and values that they—and Voldemort—despise: essentially, chivalric traits we associate with the romantic medieval period. Yet to have them is one thing; for a teenage boy to apply them so effectively that he can save the magical realm is quite another. Here at last we return to the uniformity, close-mindedness, and lack of imagination that define the barbaric medieval vision embodied in the culture in which Harry was raised. In the book version of the Buckbeak the Hippogriff scene, Harry is not *remotely* excited to fly the half-horse/half-eagle, and, after a short trip around the clearing, is happy to be back on land. The film version, on the other hand, has Harry soaring over the lake on Buckbeak's back, his arms outstretched, exhilarated by feelings of freedom and adventure, treasuring a *oneness* with it as he hollers his joy while the beast skims the surface of the lake. The film Harry has something his literary counterpart does not: enthusiasm for new, exciting, and potentially dangerous and terrifying experiences. He does not cringe when faced with novelties, as do the Dursleys; he is not afraid of injury, death, or others' perceptions of him, as is Voldemort; and, unlike his classmates and the other Wizards in the books and movies, Harry is not afraid to act on behalf of what he knows is right. He does not idealize the magical world's past because it was not his past until he came to Hogwarts. Rather, he sees the possibility of reviving the values and mentality of his house's namesake by embodying them during his quest to defeat the Dark Lord.

The Muggle world fell because it adopted and perpetuated negative medieval values. That it simultaneously lost touch with the magical dimension of a world populated with marvelous animals and governed by possibility only solidified its descent and complicated even the vague possibility of its rebirth. The magical world, on the other hand, is like an imperfect democracy in which the citizens celebrate their glorious history but stay home on voting days. Unlike any other character in the films, Harry embraces not only everything magical but everything *about* the magical world: the impossibly large tent, the mythical beasts, the ability to manipulate time and the world around him—and especially his responsibility to its future. He rejects the surviving strains of barbaric medieval values found in the Dursleys' world and Voldemort's hopes for the future, but he *also* rejects the fanciful apathy and blind idealism of his magical contemporaries. His reactionary openness and willingness to appreciate the unpredictable and unconventional reflects a deeply-rooted ability to apply creatively and transmit his romantic values to others who are willing to fight for the survival of the wizarding realm. When the war is over, magical society will not merely rebuild the world we saw in the first film—rather, it will build an inherently *new* world founded on, and indebted to, the chivalric attitude and values Harry has resurrected from the rubbish-heap of the Middle Ages.

MONTANA STATE UNIVERSITY

WORKS CITED

Dawtrey, Adam. "It's a wand-erful life: Rowling transforms kid lit and embodies Brit grit." Variety 397.2 (Nov 29, 2004): A1-2.
Goldman, Michael. "Fade to Black." Millimeter 34.6 (Jun 2004): 98.
Harry Potter and the Chamber of Secrets. Chris Columbus, David Heyman, Steve Kloves. DVD. Warner Home Video, 2003.
Harry Potter and the Goblet of Fire. Mike Newell, David Heyman, Steve Kloves. DVD. Warner Home Video, 2006.
Harry Potter and the Prisoner of Azkaban. Alfonso Cuarón, David Heyman, Steve Kloves. DVD. Warner Home Video, 2004.
Harry Potter and the Sorcerer's Stone. Chris Columbus, David Heyman, Steve Kloves. DVD. Warner Home Video, 2002.
Johnson, Rachel. "Hogwarts report. (Harry Potter and the Chamber of Secrets)." *Spectator* 290.9094 (Nov 23, 2002): 78-9.
MacDonald, Marianne. "Harry Potter and the fan fiction phenom." *The Gay & Lesbian Review Worldwide* 13.1 (Jan-Feb 2006): 28-31.
Shargel, Raphael. "The triumph of 'Star Wars'." *The New Leader* 85.1 (Jan-Feb 2002): 34-37. Simmons, Garry, and Christine Evely. "Harry Potter and the Chamber of Secrets. (movie production)." *Australian Screen Education* 38 (Spring 2005): 76-84.
Smith, Sean. "Lightning Strikes." *Newsweek* 143.22 (May 31, 2004): 64-9.

Explaining or Excusing?
The Crusades, Historical Objectivity, and the 'War on Terror'

Michael Evans

The Crusades are generally portrayed as a series of holy wars against Islam led by power-mad popes and fought by religious fanatics. They are supposed to have been the epitome of self-righteous intolerance, a black stain on the history of the Catholic Church in particular and Western civilization in general. A breed of proto-imperialists, the Crusaders introduced Western aggression to the peaceful Middle East and then deformed the enlightened Muslim culture, leaving it in ruins.[1]

This is one historian's description of the 1995 BBC television series *Crusades*, but it could also summarise what was once the consensus on the crusades – and largely remains so in the popular imagination. It is, in fact, a modern version of the view formulated by Edmond Gibbon, expressing Enlightenment anti-clericalism and impatience with the role of ignorance and unreason in human history, and concluding that the crusades "checked rather than forwarded the maturity of Europe."[2] The views expressed by Stephen Runciman in 1954 differ little from Gibbon's verdict on the crusades:

> The triumphs of the Crusade were the triumphs of faith. But faith without wisdom is a dangerous thing … In the long sequence of interaction and fusion between Orient and Occident out of which our civilization has grown, the Crusades were a tragic and destructive episode … There was so much courage and so little honour, so much devotion and so little understanding. High ideals were besmirched by cruelty and greed, enterprise and endurance by a blind and narrow self-righteousness; and the Holy War itself was nothing more than a long act of intolerance in the name of God …[3]

This view is no longer popular among academic historians; in the words of Robert Irwin, "[i]n the decades that followed the publication of Runciman's *History*, scores of specialists … have been at work demolishing his compellingly readable saga."[4] Yet Runciman had largely inspired that very generation of historians responsible for the demolition. Jonathan Riley-Smith, Dixie Professor of History at Cambridge University and perhaps the leading authority in the English-speaking world on the Crusades, stated in December 2002 that he was first drawn to the subject as a school student by Runciman's book: "I read it and was gripped by it."[5] In the most recent general history of the subject, Christopher Tyerman has written that "It would be folly and hubris to pretend to compete [with Runciman], to match as it were, my clunking computer keyboard with his pen…"[6]

Furthermore, Runciman's influence is still very much felt at a popular level. His three-volume history, available since 1965 in a cheap paperback edition, has never gone out of print.[7] His verdict on the crusades seems to fit an age when the West and Islam once more appear to be on collision course. Terry Jones and Alan Ereira's entertaining 1995 television series *Crusades* – for which Runciman acted as a consultant and appeared as a 'talking-head' – expounded this view. It paints a picture of an essentially peaceful and enlightened Islam subjected to an unprovoked attack by Christian religious fanatics, creating a legacy of hatred directed against the West by the Muslim world. The result, according to Jones and Ereira, was "the present mess".[8]

It is not the purpose of this essay to explain in detail the shortcomings of such a view.[9] Academic historians over the last three or four decades have more or less laid what I will call the Enlightenment view of the crusades to rest. A new consensus has emerged in modern crusades studies, which can be summarised thus: we should judge the crusaders by the values of their age, not of ours; the crusades cannot be viewed as a colonial venture, as they did not show a profit, and most crusaders went home again after fulfilling their vows; the participants were, for the most part, sincere in their religious beliefs; the violence associated with the crusades was not untypical of the era, and for this reason should not be condemned by the sober-minded, impartial, historian.

This new consensus, which I will term the Revisionist position, has much to recommend it. It puts historical objectivity in place of moralising and ahistorical condemnation; it seeks to understand the crusaders on their own terms, from a sober assessment of documentary evidence; it treats the history of Europe and the Levant in the twelfth and thirteenth centuries on its own merits, not distorted by the lens of modern values and politics. Its advocates stress their own historicism and objectivity, against the ahistorical value-judgements of popular history. For example, American historian Thomas Madden condemns Terry Jones's *Crusades* as "four hours of frivolous tsk-tsking…"[10] Even more damningly, Riley-Smith condemned Ridley Scott's crusade film *Kingdom of Heaven* as "rubbish," "ridiculous," "complete fiction," "dangerous to Arab relations," and "Osama bin Laden's version of history."[11] It is my contention, however, that the Revisionist view is far from free of bias and of the prejudices of our times, and that there is a danger that, under the mask of 'objectivity,' historians may be excusing, rather than explaining, the crusades, and promoting an Islamophobic agenda that fits all too well the values of the American-led "War on Terror." In short, revisionism has gone too far.

When considering the questions of bias and objectivity, it is worth remembering the comments of George Orwell on these issues. In the following excerpt, he was discussing literary taste and criticism, but his words could equally apply to historians:

> [T]he more one is aware of political bias the more one can be independent of it, & the more one claims to be impartial the more one is biased.[12]

In what follows, it is not my intention to argue that the political bias of scholars renders their views on history unacceptable, nor that they are any less honest and conscientious as historians, but rather to follow Orwell in remembering that there may be unspoken political agendas at work behind the 'objective' historian's art.

I will focus first on the work of the revisionists in academic history, and how it reveals a defensiveness about the crusades, before moving on to analyse the contributions of these historians to the popular post-9/11 debate. A key example in academic history where Western historians risk crossing the threshold from explaining to excusing is their treatment of the massacre of Jews and Muslims in Jerusalem by the victorious armies of the First Crusade in July 1099. The Israeli historian Beni Kedar has traced the western historiography of this event, showing how its depiction has changed throughout the centuries.[13] The contemporary Frankish accounts themselves stressed the bloody nature of this event, and the account by Raymond of Aguilers, an eye-witness, that the crusaders "rode in blood to the knees and bridles of their horses"[14] is invariably quoted in modern histories. This reference, an allusion to Revelation 14:20, was intended to impress upon its reader the providential nature of the capture of Jerusalem. Historians in the Enlightenment tradition tended to interpret the descriptions of the massacre literally, as they confirmed their view of the crusaders as barbaric and fanatical, especially when contrasted with the lack of such blood-letting when the Muslims captured Jerusalem in 638 and 1187. However, revisionist historians have cited Raymond's Biblical allusion, and other such topoi in the account, to downplay the extent of the slaughter. This is accompanied by an historicist appeal not to judge medieval men by our own standards. For example, John France (quoted by Kedar) wrote in 1994 that: "however horrible the massacre at Jerusalem, it was not far beyond what common practice of the day meted out to any place which resisted."[15] Some historians have cited an Arab source to place the death toll at "only" 3,000, which, as Kedar points out, "still exceeds that of the victims of 11 September 2001," and that out of an estimated total population of only 20,000 to 30,000. A similar defensiveness can be perceived in an incident in Terry Jones' *Crusades* series, when Jonathan Riley-Smith becomes visibly agitated when defending the behaviour of the First Crusaders who pillaged from their Byzantine allies:

> These men had marched a thousand miles in, in pretty dangerous conditions, some of them over winter, hmm? And the one thing that any army commander of the time cared more about than anything was

provisions. They had to feed their followers. They approach Constantinople thinking that there they are, the emperor is then going to lead them in this great army, and what do they find? They find a man who's, who's, 'Now, I'm not going to give you any supplies unless you immediately get over the Bosphorus and out of my hair'. And of course they react sometimes violently. But what do you expect them to do?

Kedar also warns us not to dismiss the truth of accounts simply because they employ literary topoi or scriptural allusions: "the fact that the image of infants' heads hurled against stones appears in Psalms 137:4 does not render unrealistic the very many accounts about Germans killing Jewish infants in this way during World War II."[16]

While crusades historians are reluctant to accept narrative sources literally, they are arguably too willing to accept other forms of source material at face value. Jonathan Riley-Smith's work on crusaders' charters is a case in point. These charters recorded occasions when crusaders gave land grants to religious foundations before setting out on crusade. Riley-Smith has used the crusaders' hopes and fears as expressed in these documents to throw light on their state of mind. This analysis has done much to re-establish the image of crusaders who were genuinely, if unsophisticatedly, pious, and who acted out of fear for their souls. "Running through many of their charters is a pessimistic piety… the crusaders openly craved forgiveness."[17] This interpretation, however, relies on an unproblematic reading of these charters. They were preserved in monastic cartularies and therefore are mediated through the clerical scribe who recorded them. They expressed the crusader's public reasons for taking the cross, not his private motives. And they are at root property transactions. In the words of Robert Moore, commenting on such a reading of the charters in a recent book by the English crusade historian Thomas Asbridge, "[t]his is like trying to understand the inner dynamics of a modern corporation – or university – by reading its mission statement… these were public documents, couched in public language, designed to express the worthiest possible sentiments in the loftiest possible way, not to expose the personal impulses of the benefactors."[18]

Do these problems of interpretation reflect (albeit perhaps unconsciously) the spirit of the times, in which we are supposedly engaged in a clash of civilisations, making war against Islam respectable again? Can we, for example, read a sinister subtext in the choice of *Victory in the East* as the title for a 1994 history of the First Crusade?[19] Or are they simply part of the process whereby an old scholarly consensus is overturned and replaced by a new one? We may be able to see some clues in the reaction of crusades historians to the 9/11 attacks, which made the question of conflict between the West and Islam an urgent one.

The September 11, 2001 atrocities sparked a renewed public interest in the Crusades. Osama bin Laden's rhetoric made frequent reference to the enemy as "Crusaders and Jews" – an ironic coupling, given the violence inflicted on medieval Jewry by the crusaders. George W. Bush, for his part, notoriously used the expression "crusade" to refer to his "War on Terror." As Thomas Madden put it, "in the space of one horrible day the medieval crusades suddenly became relevant. Hungry for answers, reporters descended on crusades historians, who were not at all accustomed to the attention."[20] Since 2001, two new general crusades histories in English by scholarly authors have appeared, alongside books by popular historians, works by academics for a popular readership, and new editions of histories by Madden and Riley-Smith.[21] But it is the attempts of these two to engage with the issues in the media that I will address. They illustrate more clearly than scholarly writing the question of political bias.

Thomas Madden is a Catholic professor of History at St Louis University, a school with historic links to the Jesuits. He is one of the leading contemporary crusades scholars. I will refer in this paper to two articles by Madden. The first, entitled "Crusade Propaganda: The abuse of Christianity's holy wars," appeared in November 2001 in the conservative magazine the *National Review*. The second comes from the conservative Catholic publication *Crisis: Politics, Culture and the Church*, and appeared in April 2002. Madden's starting point is to attack the Terry Jones 'Enlightenment' view of the crusades histories, which he neatly summarises in the quotation that opened this paper. No serious crusades historian would disagree with him in seeing this as a two-dimensional view of the crusades. Nevertheless, while Madden's starting point is unobjectionable, he uses it as the foundation to construct a revisionist edifice that is equally ludicrous.

In his *National Review* article, Madden makes the following breathtaking statement: "The crusades were in every way a *defensive war* [his emphasis]. They were the West's belated response to the Muslim conquest of fully two-thirds of the Christian world." Belated indeed; the capture of Jerusalem by the First Crusade in 1099 occurred more than four and a half centuries after the city had been taken by the armies of the Caliph 'Umar in 638. On this basis, Britain might invade France in 2006 as a "self-defensive" act to "liberate" Calais, which was captured by the French a mere 448 years previously. Madden takes up the same theme in his *Crisis* article, maintaining again that the crusades "were in every way defensive wars" and "a response to more than four centuries of conquests in which Muslims had captured two-thirds of the old Christian world. At some point, Christianity as a faith and a culture had to defend itself or be subsumed by Islam. The Crusades were that defence." In fact, far from being on the defensive, Christendom at the time of the First Crusade had been expanding for nearly four centuries. Between the Muslim conquest of Spain in

711 and the launch of the First Crusade in 1095, Western (Catholic) Christendom suffered no net losses to Islam and had gained Scandinavia and Central Europe from paganism. The Eastern Church, while continuing to lose ground to Islam in Anatolia, had won Russia and the Slavs of the Balkans. On the frontier between Western Christendom and Islam in the Western Mediterranean, it was Christianity that was on the offensive in Spain and southern Italy. Indeed, Christendom's offensive war in Spain was in many ways the crucible of the crusading idea, as papal indulgences were offered to warriors.

So, where does the idea of the crusades as a defensive struggle come from? Following a crushing victory over the Byzantines at Manzikert in 1071, the Seljuk Turks pressed ever deeper into Anatolia: "The Christian emperor in Constantinople, faced with the loss of half his empire, appealed for help to the rude but energetic Europeans."[22] We might note in passing Madden's rather Victorian vocabulary. "Rude but energetic Europeans" are contrasted with decadent Orientals, who, elsewhere in the article, are referred to as having built an "opulent" empire. Yet, the notion that the Byzantine Empire was on the defensive and appealed to the West for aid is true. However, Madden is disingenuous in arguing that Western Europe's assault was purely defensive. Nearly all historians agree in seeing the First Crusade as the outcome of a number of developments *within* the society and church of Western European. As Moore puts it, "it was no more than the froth, or scum, thrown off by the ferment of the making of Europe."[23] Furthermore, the Sunni Seljuk Turks who were pressuring Byzantium did not hold Jerusalem by the time the crusaders attacked it in 1099; it was held by the Shi'i, Arab, Fatimids of Egypt, who were the Seljuks' enemies. So the conquest of Jerusalem can hardly be seen as a defensive act; rather, it was a religio-ideological one.

Madden is a good, scholarly historian; he must know that much of what he writes here is ahistorical. So why does he do it? The answer is political; he believes that Western Christian civilisation is superior and that the Crusades were a Good Thing. For him, this civilisation's "unique respect for commerce and entrepreneurialism,"[24] its invention of "individualism and capitalism,"[25] and its "respect for women and antipathy toward slavery"[26] make it self-evidently superior to Islam. He openly compares the crusaders to the U.S. military; "[e]ven with smart technology, the United States has killed far more innocents in our wars than the Crusaders ever could. But no one would seriously argue that the purpose of American wars is to kill women and children."[27] While for Madden crusader violence is not representative of Christianity, Muslims are seen in essentialist terms as inherently violent and hostile: "Muslim thought divides the world into two spheres, the Abode of Islam and the Abode of War."[28] This statement is typical of the 'Clash of Civilizations' discourse that is popular among some American conservatives, which stresses only the hostile and warlike aspects of the concept of *jihad*. It ignores those currents in Islamic thought that see the Holy War as only one aspect of *jihad*, which more generally "refers to the obligation incumbent on all Muslims, as individuals and as a community, to exert themselves to realize God's will, to lead virtuous lives, and to extend the Islamic community though preaching, education and so on."[29] In practice, Muslims of the crusade period learned pragmatically to accept the presence of Christian states in the Levant. "Thus an intermediate *Dar al-Sulh* (Territory of Truce) was permitted to exist between the otherwise starkly opposed *Dar al-Islam* (Territory of Islam) and *Dar al-Harb* (Territory of War)."[30]

Jonathan Riley-Smith shares many features with Madden. He is Catholic and conservative, and has appeared in the *National Review* discussing the crusades and 9/11. His views are more sober than Madden's, however. His interview for the *National Review* restates the ideas of an article in *Crusades* journal about the evolution of Arab and Muslim view of the crusades. He argues that the modern Middle-Eastern view of the crusaders as proto-colonialists is a creation of nineteenth- and twentieth-century Arab Nationalism and political Islam, influenced by the Western Enlightenment view of the crusades.[31] This article is a scholarly and highly useful contribution to the debate, but both here and in the *National Review* he betrays something of the 'us vs. them' attitude expressed by Madden. He refers to "Muslims who are studying history to see if they can replicate the destruction of Jerusalem,"[32] when, of course, the Muslims did not 'destroy' Jerusalem in either 638 or 1187, and even the most extreme Al-Qa'ida *mujahid* would not wish to 'destroy' the third holiest city in Islam and putative capital of Palestine. He clearly sees these Muslims as the other side in a war, as he accuses advocates of the Enlightenment view of the crusades of giving succour to radical Islam: "over and over again, in words and in deeds westerners have reinforced Muslim preconceptions."[33] His condemnation, quoted earlier, of Scott's *Kingdom of Heaven* as "Osama bin Laden's version of history" suggests a frame of mind that sees any pro-Muslim sentiment as tantamount to aiding the terrorists. To paraphrase Riley-Smith's own words, this is George W. Bush's version of history.

To conclude, I would not argue that their political views negate these historians' scholarship, nor do I believe that academics should not engage with contemporary politics. Conservative historians from Cambridge have as much right to comment on global affairs as radical linguists from MIT. Indeed, it could even be progressive if popular misconceptions about crusades were undermined. It might challenge the idea of an inevitable "Clash of Civilisations" between Islam and the West, and encourage us to focus on twentieth-century colonialism, rather than on medieval crusading, as the historical source of contemporary Muslim grievances. But the attempt, not to explain, but to excuse the crusades does a disservice to history and reinforces the very misconceptions that fuel terrorism and its Western mirror image, the "War on Terror."

UNIVERSITY OF READING

NOTES

[1] Thomas F. Madden, "Crusades Propaganda: The abuse of Christianity's holy wars," *National Review*, 2 November 2001.

[2] Quoted by Elizabeth Siberry, "Images of the Crusades in the Nineteenth and Twentieth Centuries," in Jonathan Riley Smith (ed.), *The Oxford History of the Crusades* (Oxford: Oxford UP, 1999), 364.

[3] S. Runciman, *A History of the Crusades*, 3 vols. (Harmondsworth: Penguin, 1965), iii, 480.

[4] Robert Irwin, "Lost with the Cross," review of Christopher Tyerman, *God's War: A new history of the Crusades*, *TLS* 8 September 2006.

[5] "From the Crusades to 9/11," interview by Tim Drake with Jonathan Riley-Smith, *National Review*, 27 December 2002.

[6] Christopher Tyerman, *God's War: A new history of the Crusades* (Harmondsworth: Allen Lane, 2006).

[7] First published in 1965, it was reissued in 1971 and 1979, and reprinted in 1990 and 2002).

[8] Terry Jones and Alan Ereira, *The Crusades* (London: BBC Books, 1994), p. 9.

[9] For a critique of Jones and Ereira, see the review of the book by David S. Green, J. M .B. Porter and myself in *Nottingham Medieval Studies*, 39 (1995), 200-2.

[10] Madden. 'Crusades Propaganda'.

[11] Charlotte Edwardes, "Ridley Scott's new Crusades film panders to Osama bin Laden," *Sunday Telegraph*, 18 January 2004.

[12] George Orwell, Letter to Sir Richard Rees, Bt, 28 July 1949, in Sonia Orwell and Ian Angus (eds.), *The Collected Essays, Journalism and Letters of George Orwell*, Vol. 4: *In Front of Your Nose, 1945-50* (London: Secker and Warburg, 1968), pp. 504-5.

[13] B. Z. Kedar, "The Jerusalem massacre of July 1099 in the Western Historiography of the Crusades," *Crusades* 3, 2004 15-75.

[14] Raymond of Aguilers, *Historia Francorum qui cepereunt Iheruslam*, in *Recueil des Historiens des Croisades: Historiens Occidentaux*, 5 Vols. (Paris: Académie des Inscriptions et Belles Lettres, 1844-95) 3, 300.

[15] Ibid., 69.

[16] Ibid., 72.

[17] Jonathan Riley-Smith, *The Crusades: A History*, 2nd edn. (London: Continuum, 2005), p. 14.

[18] R. I. Moore, "First Froth," review of Thomas Asbridge, *The First Crusade: A New History*, *TLS*, 1 October 2004.

[19] John France, *Victory in the East: a military history of the First Crusade* (Cambridge: Cambridge UP, 2004).

[20] Thomas F. Madden, *The New Concise History of the Crusades*, updated student edition (Lanham, MD: Rowman and Littlefield, 2006), p. vii.

[21] Christopher Tyerman, *God's War: A New History of the Crusades* (Harmondsworth: Penguin, 2006); Jonathan Phillips, *The Crusades 1095-1197* (Harlow: Longman, 2002); Madden, ibid.; Riley-Smith, *The Crusades*.

[22] Madden, "Crusade Propaganda."

[23] Moore, "First Froth," 26.

[24] Thomas F. Madden, "The Real History of the Crusades," *Crisis*, 1 April 2002. Online version, www.crisismagazine.com/april2002/cover.htm, accessed 31 March 2004.

[25] Madden, "Crusade Propaganda."

[26] Ibid.

[27] Ibid.

[28] Ibid.

[29] John L. Esposito, *Islam: The Straight Path*, 2nd edn. (Oxford: Oxford UP, 1991), 93.

[30] Robert Irwin, "Islam and the Crusades, 1096-1699," in *Oxford History of the Crusades*, 237.

[31] Jonathan Riley-Smith, "Islam and the Crusades in History and Imagination, 8 November 1898 – 11 September 2001," *Crusades* 2 (2003), 151-167.

[32] Riley-Smith, "From the Crusades to 9/11."

[33] Riley-Smith, "Islam and the Crusades," 167.

Psychedelic Medievalism

Michael A. Cramer

On May 1ˢᵗ 1966, a party was held in the back yard of an old frame house in Berkeley California--a costume party that included dancing, games, and a medieval tournament. This party was the genesis of the world's largest organization of medievalists, the Society for Creative Anachronism. For those readers who've never heard of it, the SCA is (or rather we are: in the interest of full disclosure I should point out that I have been a member of the SCA for 27 years) a group of fantasy medievalists. We are not re-enactors, nor living historians, nor scholars—well, not all of us. There are some such in the society, but most people are there to party and, as Marcellus Wallace would say "get medieval." This is only appropriate, since the SCA started as a party. It was, as long time member Ron Simmons/Duke Ronald Wilmot often says, "a bunch of Berkeley Hippies protesting the 20ᵗʰ Century." Although the SCA has grown into an international organization and has in some ways left behind its counterculture roots, this paper is primarily concerned with the psychedelic medievalism that existed in Berkley in the sixties and it relationship to the SCA.

The game the SCA plays has precedents in the very time period its members are trying to re-create. It was primarily a reference to one source, Sir Walter Scott's *Ivanhoe,* that first led the SCA to have a queen of love and beauty, and one chosen by the winner of a tournament, from which grew the SCA's version of the mock king. Early SCA members did not consciously set out to re-create the king game, but the medieval tropes that they decided to employ in their game led them quite naturally to what Dr. Fred Hollander/Duke Frederick of Holland, one of the SCA's founders, once described as "a fairly good re-creation of a period recreation."[1] Over the 40 years of its existence, the SCA has created an elaborate medieval game with costumed knights and jewel bedecked ladies (and occasionally lady knights). As the world has become more conservative, so has the SCA. As their skill at recreating medieval material culture has increased, so has their distance from the counterculture. But once upon a time, the SCA's peculiar form of medievalism was very closely tied to the counterculture.

With the exception of Tolkien scholars, few people have examined the links between the counterculture and medievalism. In the 1960s, during the upheaval of the free speech movement and Viet Nam war protests, some people looked to Victorian pastoral utopias, to the Middle Ages, and to Tolkien's Middle Earth as places where right and wrong were clearly defined, war could be just, and the enemy, although shadowy, was both knowable and defeatable. Tolkien's *Lord of the Rings,* just recently published in the U.S., found an enthusiastic following in the counterculture and inspired the SCA. Another series written between the wars, T.H. White's *The Once and Future King,* was also influential. During the mid-sixties not only White's book but also a musical and cartoon version were immensely popular: Disney's *The Sword in the Stone,* released in 1963, and *Camelot,* which ran on Broadway from 1960 to 1963 and was produced as a movie in 1967. Of all these popular culture phenomena, it was Tolkien who had the most impact on the counterculture and on the SCA. Lev Grossman, in a 2001 article in *Time,* points out that early SCA members were searching for the romantic ideals of honor, chivalry, and courtesy, which they found lacking in contemporary society.[2] Dianna Paxson/ Countess Dianna Listmaker, who threw the party that became the SCA's first tournament, writes,

> The first Anachronists came from the leading edge of the Baby Boom. We grew up in the fifties, that triumph of plastic suburban culture, and we hated it. For the most part, no matter how hard we tried, or our parents pushed, we could not bring ourselves to truly conform. But in the sixties, the Civil Rights movement and the "New Society" heralded the possibility of change. When we gathered for the first Tournament, a catalytic reaction occurred. The moment was magic, and no one wanted it to end. And suddenly we realized that it did not have to—if we did not like the world we had been born into, we had the power to change it and create one of our own.[3]

Paxson clearly links the SCA's founding in Berkeley to the protest movements that were taking place on campus at the same time.[4]

This strain of counterculture medievalism and escapist fantasy was not limited to the SCA, but it did seem to be centered in the Bay Area. In a recent internet article on the website "Disinformation," one journalist notes that the Church of Satan was officially founded at midnight on the same day as the SCA, just across the bay in San Francisco. The Church of Satan was a non-conformist, anti-Christian group set up in protest of the strictures that existed in American society at the time. Church of Satan founder Anton LeVay said,

> We established a *Church* of Satan—something that would smash all concepts of what a 'church' was supposed to be. This was a temple of indulgence to openly defy the temples of abstinence that had been built up until then. We didn't want it to be an unforgiving, unwelcoming place, but a place where you could go to have fun.[5]

As the article in *Disinformation* points out,

> Though the two groups, at first glance, would seem to be nothing alike, in fact, they share much common ground: A sense of profound alienation from the banality of twentieth-century American culture, the embrace of a romantic alternative ethos held to be more "true" than that adhered to by the vast herd of humanity, and the creation of an alternative space in which this ethos could be translated into real life.[6]

A year earlier, in 1965, another non-conformist group was founded in San Francisco that has a similar social structure to that of the SCA. The International Imperial Court system is a society of drag queens that now has branches all over the world. Their main function is to hold an annual charity ball and coronation in which an elected emperor and empress are crowned. Their court structure, with not only emperors, but princes, dukes, and barons, is very similar to that of the SCA.[7] Another branch of science fiction fandom (which is how early members viewed the SCA) that started about this same time is the Trekkies, fans of the television show "Star Trek" who stage their own type of performative escape by holding conventions where they can trade memorabilia, meet people involved with the production of the show, and even dress up and pretend to be Star Trek characters. All of these groups demonstrate something about the late sixties and early seventies: a desire to escape, resist, and even subvert contemporary society. Umberto Eco suggests a relationship between the new Satanism, Tolkien, Excalibur, the Avalon sagas, Jacques Le Goff, and Star Wars. "Indeed," he says, "it seems that people like the Middle Ages."[8]

What happens when adults play make-believe? The comedian Margaret Cho said in her film *Notorious C.H.O.*, "you ever notice there's this strange relationship between leather sex, Star Trek, and the Renaissance Faire?"[9] The reason is simple—they are all fantasies. They all involve role-playing. In *The Theatre of Life,* Nikolas Evreinov writes that make-believe is a human imperative as important as air and food.[10] To Evreinov, all performance descended not for ritual, but instead from make-believe. He coined the term "Don Quixotism" to describe this type of fantasy role-playing, and certainly this word can be used to describe SCA members, tilting at windmills of the 20th Century.

The SCA's particular brand of incomplete history demonstrates the tension between product and process. SCA members take elements and artifacts of medieval history, movies, books, and fantasies about the Middle Ages, period romances, and Victorian melodramas, and combine them into their own personal performance of medievalism. The SCA was created not from the top down but organically, and participants' performances are based on the knowledge, beliefs, and fantasies they bring with them to the group. In a sense, the SCA is a postmodern construction of a Hollywood version of a Victorian image of a Romantic Middle Ages that never actually existed. In *The Courtesy Book,* a guide for new members of the SCA, the author, under his persona name, Orlando Ambrosius, writes, "The SCA incorporates aspects of living history but remains a rather formless, anarchistic sort of living history, owing more to the Victorian idea of medieval culture than to actual medieval culture."[11]

It is important to note how strongly the SCA was tied to fantasy literature in the sixties and seventies: the confluence of the counterculture and fantasy literature in Berkeley was the genesis of the SCA. Carey Lenehan, in "Postmodern Medievalism," identified what he called a "taste group" centered around science fiction fandom that included role-playing gamers and computer hobbyists, as well as the SCA, as subsets.[12] All four of these groups were concentrated in the Bay Area in the late sixties and through the seventies, the SCA's formative years. Moreover, the SCA could not have existed without the circle of writers in Berkeley that eventually became known as Greyhaven. Greyhaven (a clear reference to Tolkien and the Grey Havens from which the elves set sail when they leave Middle Earth at the end of *The Return of the King*) is the name of Ms. Paxson's house in the Berkeley hills. It is also the name of a literary circle that grew up around Paxson and Marion Zimmer Bradley/Mistress Elfrida of Greenwalls concurrent with the SCA. Bradley, her brother Paul Edwin Zimmer, Poul Anderson, Paxson, and many others who became science fiction and fantasy authors were among the SCA's founders, and it was through science fiction circles that the SCA first spread beyond the Bay Area.

Science fiction and fantasy fandom—particularly to the works of Tolkien— provided a context and inspiration for early SCA events, as well as a community of fans to draw upon for new members, and the early SCA was made up of members of what Tolkien ruefully referred to as his "deplorable cultus."[13] Hollander often lists what he calls "roots literature," meaning literary works that had a great influence on the SCA: Tolkien's trilogy, *Sir Nigel, The Chronicles of Narnia* by C.S. Lewis, *The Once and Future King*, etc.. His list also includes some primary sources such as *Le Morte d'Arthur* and the tales of Sir Parsifal, but it is made up mostly of contemporary sources, and all of them are literary works.[14] It is these works that, according to Hollander, informed the SCA's version of medievalism. To many in the SCA, literature informs history and vice versa. Serious re-enactors both inside and outside the SCA criticize members' use of literary (and filmic) tropes in constructing their SCA performances, but this is also very postmodern. As Linda Hutcheon points out in *A Poetics of Postmodernism*:

> ...[I]t is this very separation of the literary and the historical that is now being challenged in postmodern theory and art, and recent critical readings of both history and fiction have focused more on what the two modes of writing share than on how they differ. They have both been seen to derive their force more from verisimilitude than from any objective truth; they are both identified as linguistic constructs, highly conventionalized in their narrative forms, and not at all transparent either in terms of language or structure; and they appear to be equally intertextual, deploying the texts of the past within their own complex textuality.[15]

This statement applies very well to SCA practice. The SCA uses a fiction (persona, their created world, images from literature and film) in order to explore aspects of the historical Middle Ages, while at the same time employing the texts of historians, fantasists, and medieval authors of both chronicle and romance in the performance of their game.

The SCA provides a social structure that mirrors that of a late medieval or Renaissance court, in which people occupy various positions on a social hierarchy that begins with a king and queen at the top with various dukes, duchesses, knights, peers, and non-armigerous nobles beneath them. Members play the roles of the king and his court, and although many of them study and re-create earlier parts of the Middle Ages or even non-medieval or non-European cultures, donning the garb or armor of a twelfth-century Norman or a tenth-century Viking, or a Mongol warrior, the social structure of the SCA more closely parallels the late medieval courts of the dukes of Burgundy or the Renaissance courts of the Medicis and the Tudors, courts in which power was centralized in an efficient bureaucracy and the nobility was kept close at hand to the prince. Titles and rank are either awarded (rather like merit badges) or earned, in the case of the royal peerages that are given out to those who have reigned as either king/queen or prince/princess of one of the SCA kingdoms or principalities. The awards structure in the SCA is wholly modern but coded as medieval.

Although the official reckoning of the SCA puts its beginning on May 1, 1966, the date of the first SCA event, (in SCA documents it is stated as "Anno Societatis I," meaning the first year of the society. The SCA new year begins on May 1), it actually traces back to about 1960, when two of the SCA's founders, Ken de Maiffe/Duke Fulk de Wyvern and David Thewlis/Duke Siegfried von Höflichkeit, met while attending language school in the military. Both were posted to Germany and began to study and to teach themselves about sword combat. When they returned to the United States, they began experiments in medieval combat, making leather helmets, shields, and wooden swords with which to practice. About this time, they met Paxson, who was studying medieval history.[16] Since Thewlis and deMaiffe were already attempting recreations of medieval combat and practicing in Paxson's backyard, she decided to throw a theme party, "a tournament of chivalry" inspired by the famous "last tournament" at Eglinton, Scotland in 1839. The Eglinton tournament was one of the first organized re-creation events in modern times. Inspired by the novels of Sir Walter Scott, a group of British nobles decided to hold an elaborate tournament of chivalry. They had armor made, procured horses, made costumes, and prepared to joust, just as in *Ivanhoe*. It is primarily remembered as a disaster, because on the opening day it rained, the mud grew thick, and the costumes were ruined; the fact that the tournament was continued successfully two days later when the weather broke is forgotten by most historians.[17]

Paxson's tourney was not so elaborate as the one in 1839. It was announced as a "Tournament of Chivalry," the winner of which was to have the honor of declaring his lady the "fairest." All the fighting was to be done afoot (since they were college students, most of them could not afford a horse). Instead of being announced by invitation, this and other early SCA events were announced by fliers that were posted at college dormitories, as well as along streets such as Telegraph Avenue in Berkeley. Such fliers appeared in the dormitories of San Francisco State University, Mills College, and the San Anselmo and Berkeley Theological Seminaries, as well as all over the city of Berkeley. Guests were encouraged to "wear the dress of some age of Christendom, Outre-Mer, or Faerie in which swords were used."[18] According to Paxson, people came from all over the Bay Area. The day included fighting, dancing, and music, and as it was Berkeley and it was 1966, it ended with a march up Telegraph Avenue protesting the twentieth century.[19]

The fliers that were used to advertise early SCA events are an important way in which the SCA linked itself to the counterculture. They were in public places where members of the counterculture gathered. They had to compete with fliers advertising rock concerts, and often resembled rock and roll poster art. People looking for something to do on the weekend were able to scan the postings on Haight street and decide to go to a Jefferson Airplane concert in the panhandle, see the Grateful Dead at the Fillmore, check out the folk fest at Freight and Salvage, or go to an SCA tourney in San Anselmo. While science fiction fans were the largest segment of SCA members, the crossover with dead-heads and other rock fans should not be ignored. In fact, Hollander, who was attending Claremont College in Southern California, had driven up to Berkeley for a rock concert and ended up going to the first tournament as well.

From the very beginning, the performance of medievalism in the SCA was done in a tongue-in-cheek fashion, combining period elements with a modern sense of irony. The knights and their ladies entered into the lists to a processional from *The Play of Herod* (Paxson doesn't say which play of Herod), and they were blessed by a mock bishop who recited the first sentence from *Winnie the Pooh* in Latin ("Ecce Edvardus Ursus..."). Some people came as medieval knights but others as fantasy characters. There were even a Napoleonic officer, a Roman, and a hobbit.[20]

In a class she taught on SCA culture, Dr. Dana Kramer-Rolls/Viscountess Meythen of Elfhaven (and if that name isn't a Tolkien reference, nothing is) argued that garb in the early SCA did not mark people as being "medieval" so much as it marked them as being not modern and as non-conformists, and therefore members of the counterculture. She notes that in the early days of the SCA a person could walk up Telegraph Avenue in Berkeley in SCA clothes and not be out of place. The dress of the counterculture—poet's shirts, vests, harem pants, t-tunics, caftans, etc.—was the dress of the SCA at the time. However, there were exceptions. Bill Jouris/Count William the Lucky pointedly wore a t-tunic to SCA events over blue jeans with engineer's boots, even when he was king. Not only were his SCA clothes "normal," but they were also pointedly modern. His tunic alone coded him as being at an SCA event. The blue jeans and engineer's boots he wore under it were inconsequential because he was not playing a character other than himself. His tunic was a uniform, not a costume or the clothing of an imaginary medieval person. In this way, Jouris resisted the concept of the SCA as re-enactment and instead re-inscribed the idea of SCA as contemporary counterculture.

The centerpiece of the party was a tournament, which was fought using a variety of weapons. Some people used broadswords or axes made of wood, others used modern fencing gear. The Roman fought with a net and trident. Although Thewlis and deMaiffe had been experimenting with making armor, and some of the participants had built their own reconstructions, the equipment used by early SCA members was very *ad hoc* and often owed more to pop culture or modern athletics than to a study of history. One person fought in a motorcycle helmet and black leather armor. Another fighter competed as a cavalier. The visual image most SCA fighters wanted to project was what they themselves recognized as historical, and this led them to adopt an aesthetic taken from comic books, children's novels, movies, and fantasy art. One early SCA warrior, taking his cue from the sword and sandal epics of the 1950s, fought as a Spartan, wearing simple greaves, a Greek-style helmet, and a loin cloth. Although this was not authentic in the sense of being an accurate representation of history, the tolerance of variety which accepted such an outfit allowed members of the SCA to have experiences that were emotionally authentic, as they employed those faux-medieval (and, in this case, classical) tropes they brought with them. This is also typical of the SCA's organic development. If a single body of authority had formed the SCA, established standards of authenticity, and dictated what areas and time periods were to be studied, these links to popular culture would be much fewer and weaker. Because the SCA was a group of amateurs trying to live out their personal fantasies of the Middle Ages, it became a combination of many different Middle Ages from many sources.

Fencing bouts at the first tourney were scored by modern rules. Fights with medieval weapons were scored by a group of judges plus all other fighters in the lists. When someone was struck, the group had to decide what would have happened if the blade had been real. They decided that a person who was struck on a limb couldn't use that limb any longer. Therefore, a person who was hit in the leg had to continue from his knees or stand on one leg. Likewise, a person hit on the sword arm had to fight with his other hand. A fighter had lost "when he was considered to have been completely chopped up."[21] At the end of the day, David Breen/ David the Herald, who was later known as Ardral Argo ver Kaeysc, was knighted. Several conventions of the SCA were thus established, including the creation of an SCA persona name, the practice of fighting from one's knees if struck on the leg, and the SCA order of knighthood, of which David the Herald is the principal member.

It was supposed to be a one-time costume party, but it wasn't. According to Paxson, the fighters had so much fun they wanted to do it again, and so another tournament was scheduled for the following Midsummer's Eve; then another in the fall, and another that next spring. SCA events in the sixties and seventies in a sense thus resembled Earth Day festivals more than they did medieval tournaments. The name of the group was coined by Bradley. When reserving a city park for the SCA's second tournament that summer, she was asked the name of the group and she just made one up on the spot. The SCA quickly developed into a series of tournaments held on regular dates throughout the year, gatherings in which men (originally only men) fought in a faux-medieval style to honor their ladies. To some, these tournaments were simple fantasy, informed as much by the works of Tolkien as by the chronicles of Froissart. To others, they were an attempt to create a Pre-Raphaelite utopia. Still others, viewing them in the context of the anti-war movement, saw them as exercises in honorable combat, the type of "just war" that many found in Tolkien's *Lord of the Rings*. Early SCA members agreed that they were attempting to recreate a medieval-style tournament culture, but they weren't exactly clear about what that meant, and what they actually created was a culture unique unto itself.

According to Thewlis, two events occurred in 1968 that were pivotal in the transition of the SCA from a collection of theme parties into an international organization of medievalists.[22] The first is the World Conference of Science-fiction and Fantasy that September. The second is the incorporation of the SCA, which took place that October. However, two equally important events from 1968 were the founding of the East Kingdom that July and the establishment of the SCA court structure and the orders of peerage at the SCA's second 12th Night celebration in January of that year.

In 1968, Bradley moved to New York City and founded a new branch of the SCA. That July the New York branch held a tournament on Staten Island to choose its own king. Sir Ardral was present as an emissary from the king in Berkeley. He knighted the victor, Bruce of Cloves, who was then crowned king. From then on, the Berkeley chapter was known as the Kingdom of the West and the New York chapter as the Kingdom of the East. This is yet another bow to Tolkien: the West, name of the first kingdom of the SCA, is also one of the names for the first kingdom of men in *Lord of the Rings*, and Aragorn is often referred to as "The King of the West."

The World Conference of Science-fiction and Fantasy took place that September (1968) at the Claremont Hotel in Berkeley. Several members of the SCA were on the convention organizing committee. The SCA held a tournament as part of the convention and released a book, *A Handbook for the (Current) Middle Ages,* which was included in the convention packet. Several attendees when they went back to their homes founded local SCA chapters based on the handbook and what they had seen at the convention.

Bruce of Cloves, the first King of the East, also attended the Conference. According to those who were there, Bruce of Cloves was convinced that the East needed "guidance," and he reportedly asked the King of the West to take the East under his kingdom's wing. This essentially put the East under the West, and greatly upset the East's founders.[23] This conflict was exacerbated when Paxson and her husband, Don Studebaker/Baron John deClese, incorporated the SCA as a non-profit organization in California, an act seen as a power grab in the East (but, as we will see, it was perceived in the same way by many members of the West).

The third kingdom of the SCA, the Middle Kingdom or Midrealm, was founded around Chicago in 1969 by science fiction fans who had attended WorldCon in Berkeley the previous year. The founding of the Middle Kingdom formed the nucleus of a conflict that was to continue for some years over who exactly was in charge of the SCA. There were actually two SCA groups chartered in Chicago in 1969. The Board of Directors in Berkeley chartered the first, while the East Kingdom, which gave the area the name "The Barony under the Mountain," chartered the second group. All was part of the competition between East and West as to who had the right to charter branches. Writes an early SCA member:

> Berkeley, in the person of Jon DeCles, wanted a centralized operation in Berkeley, while the Easterners, led by Walter and Marion, were looking for a kind of decentralized operation where any kingdom could establish a branch."[24]

This conflict between East and West went on for several years, but the two competing groups in Chicago quickly merged and a crown tournament was held that was won by David Friedman/Duke Cariadoc of the Bow, who was knighted by the King of the West upon his victory.

The power struggle between the kingdoms and the SCA Inc. lasted a long time and, although Easterners cast it as a conflict between East and West, the board of directors soon got into a similar power struggle with the Kingdom of the West as well. The nature of the conflict was that the board, as the legal authority of the SCA Inc., insisted on maintaining control over the group in nearly all matters, including monies. One of the first results of the incorporation of the SCA was that the Kingdom of the West no longer received the subscription fees from the SCA newsletter ($1.50 per person) and consequently had no funds for some time after incorporation.[25] This struggle came to a head in 1971/AS VI during the first reign of Jim Early/Duke James Greyhelm as King of the West. The kingdom newsletter, *The Page*, was at the time edited by Dorothy Heydt/Mistress Dorothea of Caer Myrddin. She had printed an editorial critical of the SCA board of directors, which upset Studebaker, who was still the chairman of the board. At that time, *The Page* was printed on an old hand-cranked mimeograph machine. Studebaker demanded that Heydt be removed from her office and, when that didn't happen, ordered her to hand over the means of production—the mimeograph machine. He was refused. One night, he attempted to seize the means of production by showing up at Dorothea's apartment door in Berkeley and demanding that, since it was SCA property, she must hand over the mimeograph machine. She refused and called the king, who lived across town. James strapped on his sword (the real one, that made of steel), jumped on his motorcycle and raced across town. When he got to Dorothea's apartment, he found her clinging to the mimeograph machine as Studebaker was dragging it and her out the door.

"What are you doing?" demanded the king.

"I'm confiscating this mimeograph machine," replied Studebaker.

"On what authority?"

"I'm the chairman of the SCA. This mimeograph machine is SCA property and I'm taking it."

At this point, King James drew his sword, placed the tip at Studebaker's throat and said, "I'm the king of the West and that's my mimeograph machine!" Studebaker prudently let go of the mimeograph machine and left.[26]

This is one of the most important tales of early SCA history. Not only does it illustrate how the early conflicts between the SCA and the Board developed, but it also illustrates how much the SCA was entwined with people's everyday lives. These three people, dressed in contemporary clothes and arguing over a contemporary piece of technology, were nonetheless acting out their SCA roles, and although Studebaker's role had authority under modern law, James's authority came from two sources: 1) his subjects' (represented by Dorothea) recognition of his authority as king, and 2) his sword. If this story is accurate, then what James did was felony assault with a deadly weapon, but within the context of the SCA he was exercising his authority as King of the West and making sure that Studebaker understood it in the clearest way possible. But such behavior was not that unusual in Berkeley in the sixties, where the police weren't very trusted and the people of the counterculture were trying to find their own more personal sources of authority.

In many ways, the SCA is still a big party. Over the course of the past forty years, the SCA has grown from a backyard party in Berkeley into the largest medievalist organization in the world. One hundred thousand people participate in the SCA in a known world divided into 18 kingdoms, with branches in Canada, Australia, Japan, Korea, New Zealand, all of Europe, and every state in America. Their biggest annual event draws 12,000 people a year to Western Pennsylvania for a two-week war and medieval festival. But it is still in many ways a product of Berkeley in the sixties, a psychedelic era where it didn't seem so strange to imagine a world better than the one that existed at the time, where wars could be just and life could be noble and beautiful. With only their imaginations SCA members turned polyester dresses into velvet gowns and canvass tents into pavilions. They became knights and damsels. They tuned in to Tolkien, turned on to the Middle Ages and, for brief periods of time, dropped out of the 20th Century.

CITY COLLEGE OF NEW YORK

NOTES

[1] Fred Hollander, "SCA Culture," panel discussion at the Society for Creative Anachronism Thirty Year Celebration, June 1996.

[2] Lev Grossman, "Feeding on Fantasy," *Time*, 2 December 2002, 90.

[3] Diana Paxson, "The Seed and the Tree" (accessed 15 December 2003); available from http://www.currentmiddleages.org/3yc/seed.html.

[4] Andrew Rodwell, "Anti-Modern Performance in the Society for Creative Anachronism" (M. A. Thesis, University of Western Ontario, 1998), 38.

[5] Anton Levay, quoted in Blanche Barton, "The Church of Satan: A Brief History" (The Church of Satan, 2003, accessed November 27 2004); available from www.churchofsatan.com.

[6] Ken Mondschein, "The Society for Creative Anachronism" (Disinformation, 2002, accessed February 8 2002); available from http://www.disinfo.com/site/displayarticle2028.html.

[7] Empress Milo, "An Introduction to the ICS" (Imperial Court Internet Services, accessed March 23 2005); available from www.impcourt.org/icis/about/intro.html.

[8] Umberto Eco, "Dreaming of the Middle Ages," in *Travels in Hyperreality* (New York: Harcourt Brace Jovanovich, 1986), 61.

[9] Margaret Cho, *Notorious C.H.O.,* ed. Lorene Machado (Wellspring Media, 2002).

[10] Nikolas Evreinov. *The Theatre in Life.* Translated by Alexander Nazaroff (New York: Brentanos, 1927), 84.

[11] Orlando Ambrosius. *The Courtesy Book*, 3rd ed. (Urbana, IL: Folump Enterprises, 1989), 9.

[12] Carey Lenehan, "Post Modern Medievalism: A Sociological Study of the Society for Creative Anachronism" (BA Honors Thesis, University of Tasmania, 1994), 31.

[13] Grossman, 92.

[14] Fred Hollander, interview by author, 15 February 2004, video recording, Phoenix, AZ.

[15] Linda Hutcheon. *A Poetics of Postmodernism* (New York: Routledge, 1998), 105.

[16] David Thewlis, "A Brief Look at the Past," in *The Known World Handbook*, ed. Hillary Powers. (Milpitas, CA: The Society for Creative Anachronism, 1992), 26-27.

[17] Diana Paxson, "The Last Tournament," in Powers, 24.

[18] Flier for the first SCA event, in William Keyes, "The West Kingdom History Project" (Golden Stag, 2001, accessed February 4 2004); available from http://.history.westkingdom.org.

[19] Paxson, "The Last Tournament," 24-25.

[20] Paxson, 24.

[21] Paxson, 25.

[22] Thewlis, 27.

[23] Keyes.

[24] Stephan de Lorraine quoted in, "The Formation of the SCA Inc," in Keyes.

[25] Sir Robert of Dunharrow, quoted in Keyes.

[26] Dorothy Heydt, "SCA History," panel discussion, Collegium Occidentalis, Kensington, CA, 19 October, 1996. This is the story as Heydt tells it. Early insists that, although he had his sword with him, he only drew it halfway out of the scabbard and never put it to Studebaker's throat.

The Legend of St. Ogg and the Problematics of the Ending in Eliot's *The Mill on the Floss*

Kyoung-Min Han

"'They're such children for the water, mine are,'" cries Maggie's mother, Mrs. Tulliver, "'They'll be brought in dead and drownded someday. I wish that river was far enough'" (166). As if to fulfill Mrs. Tulliver's "prophecy," Maggie, along with her brother Tom, suffers unexpected drowning in a flood of the river Floss at the end of the novel. Unable to find an adequate explanation for the heroine's sudden death and the tale's abrupt ending, many critics argue that it flaws the novel, that Eliot uses an external calamity as a way of extricating her protagonist from a situation that cannot be otherwise resolved within the narrative. Ignês Sodré, for example, believes that the novel's ending is forced and unnatural, and that Eliot "concludes Maggie's story with an external catastrophe, a great flood...to allow the guilty Maggie to die heroically and therefore to be admired, forgiven, and loved" (196). A close look at Maggie's situation right before her death explains why the novel's ending seems so odd. In the middle of the night, Maggie is reading a letter from her lover, Stephen Guest, previously her cousin Lucy's paramour. A few weeks earlier in the narrative, Maggie had supposedly "eloped" with him but at the last moment resisted the "Great Temptation" to consent to his insistent proposal of marriage, returning alone to the town of St. Ogg's. In his letter, Stephen vehemently blames Maggie for her "perverted notion of right which led her to crush all his hopes" (647). Torn between her desires and her moral scruples about loving her cousin's lover, Maggie cries out in agony, "'I will bear it, and bear it till death....But how long it will be before death comes! I am so young, so healthy. How shall I have patience and strength?'" (649). Ironically, at the very moment Maggie laments the prospect of her "long" and "healthy" life, death announces itself as the river bursts in and puts an end to all her moral conflicts.

Although Maggie's death is quite unexpected in terms of plot development, close examination of the narrative function of the town's legend in the novel suggests its conclusion is not only natural but inevitable. There are numerous portents of Maggie's drowning throughout the narrative, not least the legend of St. Ogg. Through these hints, the novel sets up a significant, albeit implicit, connection between Maggie's death and her community's lack of sympathy. Eliot's use of a medieval legend in articulating this is particularly significant because it elucidates her role in the construction of Victorian medievalism.

Even though Eliot's employment of the pastoral tradition has drawn considerable critical attention,[1] her novels have seldom been discussed in relation to Victorian re-envisioning of the past. Antony H. Harrison makes the generalization that most Victorian medievalists "looked back nostalgically upon what they perceived as a period of uniform social and spiritual values, of social integration, of political and cultural stability" (3). Thomas Carlyle's *Past and Present* supplies an apt example of this idealization. In diagnosing and proposing a remedy for the ills of his age, Carlyle turns to the ethical and religious values of the Middle Ages. Carlyle's references to the ideal society represented by Gurth the Swineherd and his master Cedric the Saxon effectively encapsulate his longing for feudal times. Calling Gurth "an exemplar of human felicity" (211), Carlyle claims that the thrall's liberty is less important than his well-being. Carlyle's romanticization of the bonds of loyalty that existed between lord and worker in feudal times is, of course, closely related to his disapproval of the principles of capitalist economy, particularly the Laissez-faire philosophy, and he draws upon the medieval past to criticize his contemporary society.

Although Harrison does not number Eliot among Victorian medievalists, the use of the legend of St. Ogg in *The Mill on the Floss* indicates that Eliot indeed attempted to use the medieval past to understand and evaluate contemporary British society. As Joseph Wiesenfarth points out in *A Writer's Notebook, 1854-1879, and Uncollected Writings*, the legend of St. Ogg bears a striking resemblance to the legend of St. Christopher, which is included in Anna Jameson's *Sacred and Legendary Art* as an example of "the religious parables of the middle ages" (439). Victorian medievalism, however, was not a fixed phenomenon, and Eliot neither blindly accepted the simple idealization of the Middle Ages nor merely copied the legend of St. Christopher in her novel. Instead, she employs the legend of St. Ogg to illuminate the ending of the novel and, in doing so, complicates our understanding of Victorian medievalism.

Before we examine the significance of the legend of St. Ogg in comprehending Maggie's sudden death, one question needs to be addressed: what are we to make of the fact that nature serves as a medium of Maggie's death? Are we to interpret her drowning in the river as nature's justification of the St. Ogg's communal condemnation of Maggie's behavior? Such would seem to contradict the novel's intense critique of the townspeople's lack of sympathy for Maggie, while positing nature as a source of human love. In order to resolve this apparent disjuncture, it is essential to understand Eliot's theory of sympathy, which emphasizes early experience of nature. The importance of childhood memories in the development of sympathetic imagination is best articulated in *The Mill on the Floss*, in the description of Maggie and Tom Tulliver's early years:

> It was one of their happy mornings. They trotted along and sat down together with no thought that life would ever change much for them: they would only get bigger and not go to school, and it would always be like the holidays . . . Life did change for Tom and Maggie; and yet they were not wrong in believing that the thoughts and loves of these first years would always make part of their lives. . . . These familiar flowers,

these well-remembered bird-notes, this sky with its fitful brightness, these furrowed and grassy fields, each with a sort of personality given to it by the capricious hedgerows—such things as these are the mother tongue of our imagination, the language that is laden with all the subtle inextricable associations the fleeting hours of our childhood left behind them. Our delight in the sunshine on the deep bladed grass today, might be no more than the faint perception of wearied souls, if it were not for the sunshine and the grass in the far-off years, which still live in us and transform our perception into love. (93-94)

As children, Maggie and Tom do not have a proper sense of time and what changes its passage will bring to them. As both an adult and a person with narrative hindsight, the narrator knows that "life did change for Tom and Maggie" and that it would certainly not "always be like the holidays"—obviously, adulthood is viewed as a time of suffering and pain. The narrator nevertheless passionately advocates their belief that their childhood memories of love will continue to hold significant power over their minds throughout their lives. The reason is quite clearly stated: such memories are the most fundamental source of love. Though Eliot does not provide a specific definition of love here, the rest of the novel suggests that it includes love of humankind—in other words, sympathy.[2] What is striking about the narrator's description of childhood memories is that they are understood as a language, which emphasizes their role as a medium. Moreover, they are not simply any kind of language, but "the mother tongue of our imagination." This phrase is particularly noteworthy in its implications. First, it draws attention to the role imagination plays in transforming "our perception into love," which implies that our perception might not automatically do so without proper use of imagination. At the same time, by expressing childhood memories of love as the native language of imagination, the novel suggests that our imaginative minds, cultivated in our childhood, are not something that can be easily lost. This, in turn, explains the trope of life used to describe the abiding power of childhood memories—for Eliot, they do not disappear but instead are ingrained in our minds and "still live in us," whether we are conscious of their presence or not. The feeling of familiarity that Tom and Maggie sense in every natural creature is especially vital because it allows them to experience feelings of infinite trust, which can be transformed into more mature sentiments of sympathy in their adulthood.

Eliot's explanation of the transformative power of childhood memories is very similar to Wordsworth's account in *The Prelude* of how his sympathetic mind has developed, especially in that both emphasize the role of nature. For Wordsworth, his love of nature in childhood has led to his love of humankind in his later life. That Tom and Maggie's objects of love are all natural forms of life—flowers, grass, hips and haws on the autumn hedgerows, and redbreasts—reveals that Eliot shares Wordsworth's belief in the value of learning to appreciate and love of nature in childhood. This belief stems from the assumption that children are closer to nature. More protected from the corrupting power of civilization than adults, children are able to take lessons from the natural world without reservation. What differentiates Eliot's view of sympathy from Wordsworth's, however, is that she attaches as much importance to childhood memories of pain and suffering as to those of love. For Eliot, children have their own share of sorrow and suffering, and their pain can be as severe as that of adults. Again, the narrator of *The Mill on the Floss* offers an explanation:

> Every one of those keen moments has left its trace and lives in us still, but such traces have blent themselves irrevocably with the firmer texture of our youth and manhood; and so it comes that we can look on at the troubles of our children with a smiling disbelief in the reality of their pain. Is there any one who can recover the experience of his childhood, not merely with a memory of what he did and what happened to him, of what he liked and disliked when he was in frock and trousers, but with an intimate penetration, a revived consciousness of what he felt then. (122-23)

Adults think lightly of the troubles of children because they think children's sufferings are trifling and unimportant in comparison to theirs. The novel suggests, however, that the sorrows and pain we suffer as children are not only real at the moment, but, like our early experience of nature, they live "in us still" and leave lasting traces, whose presence we forget because "such traces have blent themselves irrevocably with the firmer texture of our youth and manhood." This idea is significant in its implication that childhood memories have power over us in our adulthood in a way of which we are mostly unaware. If we were conscious of the permanent impact of early sorrows, we would probably not be able to "pooh-pooh the griefs of our children" (123). Particularly important, childhood memories produce "a revived consciousness," indicating their power to bring back vivid sensations of pain and bitterness felt in the past and allow them to be experienced again. In short, memories of pain have a life of their own that can be *revived*, if given the opportunity, on a *conscious* level.

What is striking here is that, although Eliot makes a similar point about the enduring power of childhood memories of love nurtured in nature, she does not say that they *blend* themselves permanently with adulthood memories. Instead, by calling them "the mother tongue of imagination," Eliot emphasizes their value as a force that can transform our pain into sympathy. Childhood memories of pain, on the other hand, need to be sublimated into sympathetic feelings. This transformation, however, cannot occur during childhood, because children's experiences of pain and suffering are too direct and thus unavailable for mature reflection. Children do not have "memories of outlived sorrow" (145), and, more importantly, childhood memories of pain can be recovered only on a conscious level, which is irredeemably adult. This explains why Eliot challenges the adult "disbelief in the reality of their [children's] pain" (122). Whether we are aware or not, experiences of pain and sorrow in our childhood leave lasting marks on our minds and therefore need to be processed and transformed in our adulthood, through the operation of childhood memories of love cultivated in nature.

Apparently, Maggie's childhood memories of love in nature successfully perform their function of turning the traces of keen moments of sorrow and pain in her childhood into mature sentiments of sympathy, for she grows up to be a sympathetic person. On the other hand, her brother Tom and most of the other members of her community fail to achieve growth in the sympathetic faculty, as is demonstrated in their responses to Maggie's "violation" of communal ethics. Even though he shares most of Maggie's earlier experiences of nature, Tom, in his adulthood, is a completely different person from Maggie. Extremely practical, narrow-minded, and focused only on restoring his family's reputation, Tom is incapable of forgiving Maggie for the "disgrace" she has brought upon the family and, therefore, says to her, "'You don't belong to me'" (612). The townspeople's reaction to Maggie's transgression is even more ruthless. To the St. Ogg's community, Maggie's inner struggle with or her resistance to temptation is not a matter of concern or interest; instead, "St. Ogg's Passes Judgment"³ according to the fact that Maggie has returned unmarried. Commenting on the deeply hypocritical nature of "public opinion" in St. Ogg's, the narrator points out that it is not her elopement itself but her return "without a *trousseau*, without a husband" (620) that makes her conduct seem detestable and heinous in their eyes. The fact that the absence of a *trousseau* is mentioned even before the absence of a husband reveals the superficiality of the community's moral sense, as well as its obsession with materiality. For the townspeople, marriage is merely a monetary transaction, which is why they focus more on the absence of a *trousseau*. The townspeople's materialistic mindset accounts for their wish to "purge" their community of Maggie's physical presence: "It was to be hoped that she would go out of the neighbourhood—to America, or anywhere—so as to purify the air of St. Ogg's from the taint of her presence" (621). This intimates that Maggie is seen as some kind of infectious disease.

The limitations of Tom and the St. Ogg's community's capacity for sympathy signify that childhood experiences of love in nature do not necessarily guarantee the development of sympathetic minds. It is true that rustic folk are more exposed to nature's influence, but not everyone is able to realize the power of his or her childhood memories of love in nature, of "the mother tongue of [their] imagination," and use them to process childhood memories of pain "blent . . . irrevocably with the firmer texture of his or her youth and manhood." Hence, Eliot does not suggest that rural people are automatically less corrupted and more appreciative of the power of nature than urban people. They might have a better chance of developing love of nature in their childhood, but, as is seen in the case of Tom, it does not mean that they all learn to acknowledge the continuing presence of childhood memories.

That said, Tom's or the St. Ogg's community's lack of sympathy for Maggie is nonetheless not a direct cause of her tragic death, and the question of why nature becomes the instrument of it still remains unanswered. Furthermore, the novel does not provide a clear explanation for how some people succeed in developing the faculty of sympathy while others do not. Instead of explaining how Maggie learns to turn her childhood memories of nature into sympathy, the latter half of the tale focuses on the townspeople's failure to sympathize. By establishing a close connection between the community's disrespectful attitude toward nature and Maggie's death by nature, the novel offers an implicit explanation of how some people come to ignore their childhood memories of love in nature.

As was mentioned earlier, the novel presents many omens of Maggie's drowning, and these suggest, on a symbolic level, that the community is indeed responsible for her death in the flood.[4] The most obvious foreshadowing of death is the prediction frequently and unknowingly made by her mother. Haunted by the fear that Maggie might drown some day, Mrs. Tulliver tells her nine-year-old daughter, "'where's the use o' my telling you to keep away from the water? You'll tumble in and be drownded some day, an' then you'll be sorry you didn't do as mother told you'" (61). In her later life, although not as a conscious response to her mother's warning, Maggie does "keep away from the water," for she stays in her room, wide awake, as the town floods. Nevertheless, the water finds its way to Maggie and mercilessly destroys her along with her brother. Maggie's vulnerability to the destructive power of the river suggests that mere caution would not save her, which in turn underscores the idea that humans are not really in control of nature. Additionally, that it is Mrs. Tulliver who predicts Maggie's drowning implies that one individual's sympathy might not be enough to save Maggie from the fury of nature out of human control. It is true that when Maggie comes back to the town of St. Ogg's "disgraced," Mrs. Tulliver shows unconditional sympathy for Maggie, and the embrace and "one draught of simple human pity" (614) that she gives to Maggie are described as "[m]ore helpful than all wisdom" (614). When it comes to rescuing her daughter from a mortal peril, however, Mrs. Tulliver is still helpless, which draws attention to the seriousness of communal indifference to Maggie's ordeal.

The community's implicit involvement in Maggie's terrible fate is even more powerfully presented through another foreshadowing of Maggie's drowning: the legend of St. Ogg, the patron saint of the town. The legend recounts that Ogg, the son of Beorl, was a boatman, and one day he encountered a young woman with a child in her arms who wanted to be taken across the river Floss.

When no one offered help, Ogg took pity on her and ferried her across the river without asking any questions. Fortuitously, the woman was the disguised Blessed Virgin, who thanked him later that he "didst not question and wrangle with the heart's need but wast smitten with pity and didst straightway relieve the same" (182) and promised that "whoso steps into [his] boat shall be in no peril from the storm, and whenever it puts forth to the rescue it shall save the lives both of men and beasts" (182). Here, the form the Blessed Virgin takes in the legend draws a parallel with Maggie's story: just as Maggie is subject to her community's judgment because of her supposed sexual transgression, a young mother without a husband is bound to suffer people's "question[ing] and wrangl[ing] with the heart's need."[5] However, in contrast with St. Ogg in the legend, the townspeople show no sympathy for Maggie but instead morally condemn her, which intimates that her death by the flood is not unrelated to her community's rejection of the "blessing on the boat" (122) through their unwillingness to take pity on a fellow human being in distress. The narrator's remark that the communal mind of St. Ogg's "inherited a long past without thinking of it, and had no eyes for the spirits that walked the streets" (184) suggests that the discontinuity between the past and the present is largely responsible for "the want of fellowship and sense of mutual responsibility" (625) in St. Ogg's. In other words, the community's neglect and ignorance of its communal past has resulted in the relaxation of sympathetic ties within the community.

The novel's emphasis on the significance of human beings' intimate relationship with nature can be understood in this regard. Unlike humans, who become oblivious to their past too easily, nature's continuities retain the traces of human history, which explains why nature is considered the greatest source of love and sympathy in the novel. For Eliot, collective memory of "suffering, whether of martyr or victim, which belongs to every historical advance of mankind" (363) constitutes the basis of human sympathy through its stress on the universality of the erring nature of human beings. Consequently, nature, which stores collective memory by uniting with the material, cultural landscape of human communities, provides a way to reconnect to the foundation of moral feelings.[6] The description of collective memory lodged in the physical environment of St. Ogg's effectively demonstrates that Eliot finds the reason for the community's failure in connecting to its communal past in its inability to communicate with, and learn from, nature:

> It is one of those old, old towns, which impress one as a continuation and outgrowth of nature as much as the nests of the bower birds or the winding galleries of the white ants: a town which carries the traces of its long growth and history, like a millennial tree, and has sprung up and developed in the same spot between the river and the low hill from the time when the Roman legions turned their backs on it from the camp on

the hill-side, and the long-haired sea-kings came up the river and looked
with fierce, eager eyes at the fatness of the land. It is a town "familiar with
forgotten years." (181)

The most striking characteristic of the town of St. Ogg's is its appearance as
a "continuation and outgrowth of nature," and the town is aptly compared to
a tree that "carries the traces of its long growth and history," pointing to the
enduring presence and power of the communal past. Despite this, the town
is also described as "familiar with forgotten years,"[7] which emphasizes the
contrast between nature and human beings in their relations to human history.
Although the material part of the town is still *familiar* with its past history, its
inhabitants have long *forgotten* its significance and presence in their lives. The
consequence of the townspeople's ignorance of their communal past is clearly
illustrated in the superficiality of their moral sense, as demonstrated in their
treatment of Maggie. Alienated from the place as well as its history, the people
also have lost any sense of "obligation which has its roots in the past" (625).

The question is, then, how do the people of St. Ogg's come to lose contact
with nature? In the passage following the account of the town legend, the
narrator explains:

This legend, one sees, reflects from a far-off time the visitation of the floods,
which even when they left human life untouched, were widely fatal to the
helpless cattle, and swept as sudden death over all smaller living things. But
the town knew worse troubles even than the floods: troubles of the civil
wars when it was a continual fighting place where first puritans thanked
God for the blood of the loyalists and then loyalists thanked God for the
blood of the puritans. (183)

Here, we see that, although nature is an important source of love, at the same
time it has the power to destroy humans, a fact forgotten when the townspeople
encountered "worse troubles than the floods." The two different aspects of the
river Floss illustrate these conflicting powers of nature. On the one hand, it is
represented as a force that "flows for ever onward and links the small pulse
of the old English town in the beatings of the world's mighty heart" (363). On
the other hand, when it is out of control, the river can destroy almost every
living creature. What matters here is that, whether constructive or destructive,
the power of nature to affect human lives should not be underestimated.

That hardly anyone in St. Ogg's pays attention to the town legend and
its message about sympathy and the power of nature emphasizes the gap
between the past and the present. As the narrator suggests, the legend of St.
Ogg and the Blessed Virgin can be seen as a human attempt to understand
the awe-inspiring power of nature, and his comment that people made up a
legend about floods suggests that, at an earlier point in history, people were
able to appreciate it.[8] Even when the floods did not directly affect human life,
the realization of the deadly effects of the floods on "the helpless cattle" and

"all smaller living things"—in other words, sympathy learned from animals' suffering—made humans become aware of the power of nature and thus maintain an intimate relation with it. The appearance of "worse troubles even than the floods," however, turned people's attention away from nature and ultimately led them to undervalue its power. That those troubles were none other than wars among humans suggests a close connection between the loss of sympathetic feelings for fellow human beings and the failure to pay due deference to nature or seek communion with it. The example of puritans and loyalists who thanked the same God for each other's blood further suggests that losing touch with nature can even result in alienation from the focus of religious worship and demonstrates that the historical processes Eliot criticizes for having disrupted the stability of rural communities are not, in fact, limited to industrialization or urbanization in the eighteenth or nineteenth century, but date farther back in human history.

Given the significance of nature, it seems reasonable that the flood causes Maggie's death, because it makes the townspeople's role in it even more obvious. Their ignorance of the power of nature—both constructive and destructive—has led to their lack of sympathy, and nature gives them a warning against their indifference to their fellow member's suffering by killing that member. One might argue that it would be more "logical" to destroy those who lack sympathy. Yet, by allowing St. Ogg's unsympathetic population to continue living without realizing their responsibility for Maggie's death, the novel illustrates even more emphatically the seriousness of the lack of sympathy in rural communities.

The novel's emphasis on the discontinuity between the past and the present is significant in its implication that in the past—that is, in the supposed medieval times—communities were somehow more "natural," with stronger sympathetic relations among people. This assumption about the "naturalness" of St. Ogg's in medieval times seems to correspond with what Harrison describes as the most important characteristic of Victorian medievalism: "they [Victorian medievalists] perceived medieval man and his society as existing in idyllic harmony with nature. Victorian depictions of the medieval world usually emphasize (often with startling simplicity) a life of fulfilling industry, of heroic achievement and endurance, of shared values, of filial devotion, and of integration with nature" (4). A look at the legend of St. Ogg, however, reveals that Eliot's view of the past is a little more complicated. First, except for St. Ogg, no one in the legend shows sympathy for the woman in distress, indicating that Eliot's view of the ancient world is not simply idealistic. Yet, apparently, failure in sympathetic relationships is a much more serious problem in present days than it was in the Middle Ages, for, back then, one individual member's sympathy could save the entire community. In contrast, Mrs. Tulliver's sympathy for Maggie fails to save her. Thus, Eliot's purpose in contrasting the present with the past seems less to emphasize the power of St. Ogg's sympathetic mind but to highlight the serious lack of sympathy in the present. In addition, the detail that even after his death, "Ogg the son of Beorl was always seen with his boat upon the wide-spreading waters" with the Blessed Virgin beside him draws attention to how and why people came to lose the power of the "blessing on the boat," rather than to how things were better in those days. In short, the novel's attention is more to the problems of the present time than to the contrast between the past and the present itself.

It is therefore hard to sense in *The Mill on the Floss* the kind of nostalgic feelings for the past prominent in Carlyle's *Past and Present*. Unlike Carlyle, who wholeheartedly endorses a strict notion of hierarchy that characterizes feudal times, Eliot does not mention any specific values or practices of the Middle Ages as a remedy for the problems of her time. Instead, she emphasizes staying in touch with nature as a way of connecting to the communal history and restoring the moral foundations of human minds—that is, one does not need to go back to medieval times in order to learn to sympathize with others. The parallel between the St. Ogg's community's dismissal of its past and the adult ignorance of the continuing presence of childhood memories of love in nature further illuminates the differences between Eliot and other Victorian medievalists in their uses of the medieval past. While the novel does not clearly explain why or how some people fail to learn from the lesson of nature and nurture sympathy, by implicitly drawing a parallel between the present day community of St. Ogg's and adulthood, the novel intimates that most adults are bound to forget about the abiding existence and power of their childhood memories, and that overcoming this is a challenging task. That is to say, the community's inability to sympathize with Maggie is only a small part of a much bigger, more serious problem that concerns the progress of human history which has alienated humans from nature.

Despite the novel's interest in how the discontinuity between the past and the present came about, it does not point to any specific historical process as a major cause of humanity's loss of respect for nature, implying that alienation from nature is more or less an inevitable consequence of the formation of human society. The modern fragmentation instigated by an industrialized system of production and distribution in the nineteenth century might have facilitated alienation, but it is not a direct cause. Given the parallel between nineteenth-century St. Ogg's and human adulthood, this view of human history indirectly conveys the idea that, just as those who lose touch with their childhood memories of love miss the opportunity to develop sympathy, so is human socialization in general more than likely to disrupt intimate human relation to nature and thus discourage the development of sympathetic minds, because for those in society, "troubles of the civil wars" (183) are worse problems than their fellow members' deaths in natural disasters. For Eliot, then, the medieval past exists primarily as a literary device for her critique of present society rather than as a locus of nostalgic longing.

THE OHIO STATE UNIVERSITY

NOTES

[1] Unlike the traditional criticism that interprets Eliot's use of the pastoral tradition as a socially empty "mythologizing" of rustic people, recent analysis attempts to "redeem" Eliot's fictional reconstruction of the historical past in her novels. For example, comparing Thomas Macaulay's and Eliot's representations of the rural past, Eleni Coundouriotis argues that, even though Eliot's portrayal of the pastoral world captures a nostalgia that idealizes the eighteenth century, it at the same time "critically examines the way in which her own period misremembers the past" (286). Focusing on characters who destabilize the myth about the pastoral world by transgressing against social norms, Mary Jean Corbett also emphasizes that Eliot never uncritically accepts "the myth of the rural past" (288).

[2] Numerous references to Percy Bysshe Shelley in *Middlemarch* suggest that Eliot read Shelley, and his definition of love as "the bond and the sanction which connects not only man with man, but with every thing which exists" in his essay "On Love" seems quite relevant to Eliot's definition of sympathy in this passage.

[3] This phrase is the title of Chapter 2 of Book 7.

[4] Given that Tom dies with Maggie, it is hard to talk about his responsibility for Maggie's death. For this reason, I will focus on Eliot's criticism of the community's sense of morality in the rest of the argument.

[5] Not coincidentally, the image of a young woman with a child is quite reminiscent of Hetty Sorrel with her baby in *Adam Bede*.

[6] This is why Eliot attaches so much importance to childhood experiences of nature—children can have more immediate communion with nature than adults.

[7] This phrase is originally from William Wordsworth's *The Excursion*.

[8] Kimberly VanEsveld Adams' remark on Eliot's view of the legends or stories of the past seems quite relevant the novel's criticism of the townspeople's indifference to the legend of St Ogg. According to Adams, Eliot, along with Anna Jameson and Margaret Fuller, "looked back at the legends, liturgies, and sacred images of the past to find what [she] called the living spirit within the ancient beliefs and forms" (3). In *The Mill on the Floss*, the townspeople's inability to find "the living spirit" in their town legend is presented as the most significant reason for the failure of their growth in sympathetic ability.

WORKS CITED

Adams, Kimberly VanEsveld. *Our Lady of Victorian Feminism: The Madonna in the Work of Anna Jameson, Margaret Fuller, and George Eliot*. Athens, OH: Ohio UP, 2001.
Carlyle, Thomas. *Past and Present*. 1843. Ed. Richard D. Altick. Boston: Houghton Mifflin, 1965.

Corbett, Mary Jean. "Representing the Rural: The Critique of Loamshire in *Adam Bede*." *Studies in the Novel* 20.3 (1988 Fall): 288-301.

Coundouriotis, Eleni. "Hetty and History: The Political Consciousness of *Adam Bede*." *Dickens Studies Annual: Essays on Victorian Fiction* 30 (2001): 285-307.

Eliot, George. *The Mill on the Floss*. 1880. London: Penguin, 1985.

_____. *A Writer's Notebook, 1854-1879, and Uncollected Writings*. Ed. Joseph Wiesenfarth. Charlottesville: UP of Virginia, 1981.

Harrison, Antony H. *Swinburne's Medievalism: A Study in Victorian Love Poetry*. Baton Rouge: Louisiana State UP, 1988.

Jameson, Anna. *Sacred and Legendary Art*. 1896. New York: AMS Press, 1970.

Shelley, Percy Bysshe. "On Love." *Essays, Letters from Abroad, Translation and Fragments, by Percy Bysshe Shelley*. Ed. Mrs. Shelley. London: Edward Moxon, 1840.

Sodré, Ignês. "Maggie and Dorothea: Reparation and Working Through in George Eliot's Novels." *The American Journal of Psychoanalysis* 59.3 (1999): 195-208.

Wordsworth, William. *The Prelude 1799, 1805, 1850*. Eds. Jonathan Edwards, M.H. Abrams, and Stephen Gill. Norton: London, 1979.

Time and Influence in Illustrations of Dante's *Divine Comedy*[1]

Karl Fugelso

In the past five years, I have written four articles on the ways in which *Commedia* miniatures may have influenced modern illustrations of Dante's text. I have noted parallels to the miniatures in the compositional arrangement, narrative timing, and/or mood of late eighteenth-century *Commedia* drawings by Henry Fuseli and John Flaxman, as well as mid-nineteenth-century *Commedia* engravings by Gustave Doré.[2] I have proposed that some of the *Commedia* prints designed by Joseph Anton Koch in the early nineteenth century derive their iconography and style from the miniatures.[3] I have claimed that Robert Rauschenberg built his *Commedia* collages of the late 1950s and early 1960s around pictorial conventions found in the miniatures.[4] And I have argued that his *Commedia* illustrations--as well as those of Renato Guttuso, Rico Lebrun, and Leonard Baskin--often invoke the extraordinary expressionism of the miniatures.[5] That is to say, for the past five years I have treated artistic influence among *Commedia* images as univectoral, as unfolding solely from past to present.

Recently, however, some scholars have proposed that not only may the past shape the present but, in fact, the present may also shape the past. Noting that time is the only dimension treated as asymmetrical by Einstein and his immediate followers, numerous scientists and philosophers have proposed that causation may not be a one-way street, that influence may not flow solely from past to present. They have suggested that outside of dimensions dependant on human perception, the arrow of time may travel in reverse, that backward causation may be a possibility.[6]

Of course, this hypothesis flies in the face of traditional scholarship and has been subject to a great deal of ridicule and abuse.[7] But given the growing number and sincerity of its supporters, as well as its association with the theory of relativity and other pillars of modern science, I think it deserves careful consideration. I therefore propose to reverse course from my previous studies of *Commedia* images and to take this hypothesis seriously, to investigate the possibility that modern illustrations of Dante's text influenced pre-modern miniatures of it.

Unfortunately, most modern illustrations of the *Commedia* are poor candidates for such a study, as their parallels to the miniatures can be explained by the likelihood that the artists of those modern images almost certainly had access to the miniatures and/or images heavily affected by the miniatures. Indeed, the miniatures were influencing other illustrations as early as the 1480s, when Botticelli derived his unfinished *Commedia* drawings, as well as his designs for *Commedia* engravings by Baccio Baldini, from a lost cycle of early fourteenth-century miniatures by Pacino di Bonaguida's workshop.[8] Whether Botticelli was acquainted with those miniatures directly or via some of their many other offshoots is not clear. However, there is no doubt that his drawings and his designs for Baldini's engravings often parallel those other offshoots. For example, his drawing of *Inferno* 8, like Baldini's engraving of that canto, joins the early fourteenth-century manuscript Biblioteca Laurenziana Strozziani 152 in portraying the Pilgrim's entry to Dis as a continuous narrative.[9] Indeed, like the anonymous Strozziani artist, Botticelli assigns the Styx to the middle of the scene, the first watchtower to the left of that river, and the second watchtower to the right of it. That is to say, Botticelli invokes not only the narrative format of the Strozziani miniature but also the latter's compositional arrangement.

In thus borrowing from the miniatures, Botticelli greatly expanded their influence, for his designs apparently served as prototypes for many subsequent images of the *Commedia*. His drawing of *Inferno* XII, for example, seems to have been the model for that canto in a cycle of Venetian woodcuts issued in 1544 and reprinted in 1564.[10] Like Botticelli, the Venetian master designed the episode as a continuous narrative in which Dante and Virgil meet the Minotaur in the upper right corner of the illustration, descend a steep slope at right, and encounter Nessus and the other centaurs at its base, just above the tyrants immersed in blood. In fact, the Venetian artist even has some of the figures in the woodcut, such as the centaurs at lower left, strike the same poses as do their counterparts in Botticelli's illustration. That is to say, he joins many other sixteenth-century illustrators in demonstrating the power and influence of Botticelli's designs, and, by extension, of their medieval sources.

Of course, that impact waned from the early seventeenth to mid-eighteenth century, as Dante's text temporarily faded in popularity and as many early prints of the *Commedia* were damaged or destroyed.[11] But it never completely disappeared, for works distantly derived from Botticelli's designs, or from the miniatures themselves, continued to exert at least some influence throughout the Baroque period. For example, the engraving of *Inferno* IV from a Venetian cycle published in 1757 evidently descends from Guglielmo Giraldi's illustration of *Inferno* IV in the late fifteenth-century manuscript Biblioteca Apostolica Vaticana Urbinati latini 365, or from an image closely related to that miniature, for both the Venetian print and Giraldi's illustration depict Virgil and Dante meeting a small group of virtuous pagans in front of a landscape that stretches back to a seven-wall castle at the upper right.[12] Admittedly, the Venetian artist reverses the position of the protagonists relative to that of the pagans, and the landscape in the engraving is far lusher than that in the miniature, but these differences are relatively minor in comparison to the similarities in the subject matter, format, and composition of the two images, for many other illustrations of this scene are horizontal, ignore Dante's meeting with the pagans, show that encounter unfolding in a walled courtyard, and/or depict it from a great distance. It would therefore seem that, although the Venetian artist almost certainly could not have seen the Vatican manuscript in person, as it was already in the Apostolic collection by the mid-eighteenth century, he may have gained inspiration for his engraving from a lost copy of Giraldi's image.[13]

Of course, had the Venetian artist lived another hundred years, he may have had a much easier time seeing Giraldi's image and many of the other miniatures, for, by the mid-nineteenth century, new methods of transportation were rapidly reducing travel times to manuscript collections, private libraries were increasingly being absorbed by their public counterparts, rising literacy rates and waning class distinctions were encouraging libraries to expand visiting privileges, and a surge in funding was enabling them to do so. Moreover, improvements in the mass reproduction of images were beginning to greatly enhance the quality with which the miniatures could be copied and the degree to which those reproductions could be disseminated. In the 1850s and 60s, for example, the growing commercialization of lithography enabled wealthy Italophiles, such as Lord George Vernon, to publish some of the most striking and/or renowned miniatures. In the 1870s and 80s, the advent of photography opened the door to copying and disseminating the rest of the miniatures. And in the late twentieth and early twenty-first centuries, the Internet eliminated almost all remaining barriers to circulating those copies. Thus, like many Renaissance and Baroque artists, most and perhaps all mid-nineteenth- to early twenty-first-century illustrators have had a wide range of *Commedia* miniatures to which they could look for inspiration.

They therefore stand in stark contrast to their late eighteenth- and early nineteenth-century predecessors, for *Commedia* illustrators working during that period probably had an extraordinarily difficult time finding pre-modern models for their work. As implied above, almost none of the miniatures had yet been published, few of them or their immediate offshoots were in public libraries, transportation to and from the libraries was slow and inefficient, the libraries often lacked the resources to stay open long hours or to facilitate large numbers of visitors, and the libraries concomitantly screened visitors to a great degree. Moreover, many of the illustrators faced great personal difficulties in consulting the manuscripts. Some, such as Sofia Giacomelli, were located far from most of the miniatures and apparently from many of their early offshoots.[14] Others, such as Giovan Giacomo Macchiavelli, apparently lacked the financial resources and/or time to consult extensively the miniatures or Renaissance engravings of them.[15] Finally, particularly given the tremendous proliferation of commissions for *Commedia* illustrations, and in light of the accompanying wane in viewer sophistication, many artists probably lacked incentive to research thoroughly early images of Dante's text.

However, perhaps no other late eighteenth- or early nineteenth-century *Commedia* illustrator faced as many obstacles to consulting the miniatures and their early offshoots as did William Blake. Not the least of these obstacles was the fact that few pre-modern or early modern images of Dante's text were in England during his lifetime.[16] Moreover, fewer still were in English collections that would have been accessible to him,[17] and, as far as we know, he never left England.[18] Indeed, by 1824, when John Linnell commissioned Blake's 102 *Commedia* illustrations, the artist had only three years left to live, rarely traveled, and was sometimes bed-ridden for weeks or months on end.[19]

Of course, visitors may have brought copies of the miniatures and/or their early offshoots to him. As a student in 1777, he could hardly have missed one of the most famous works in the Royal Academy show that year—Joshua Reynolds' depiction of the Ugolino episode from *Inferno* 33.[20] Moreover, given Blake's great esteem for Michelangelo, he almost certainly saw at least one of the many, widely circulated engravings of the Sistine *Last Judgment*, which has several allusions to the *Commedia*.[21] And there can be little doubt that Blake knew the six *Commedia* drawings by his neighbor Henry Fuseli, as well as the 110 *Commedia* drawings by their mutual friend, John Flaxman.[22]

But Blake's *Commedia* illustrations show little sign of having been directly influenced by these or any other post-medieval images of Dante's text, for although he could conceivably have seen copies or early offshoots of the miniatures while working on his illustrations, three factors militate against that possibility. First, he did not receive many guests during that period (though not for lack of effort on the part of Linnell and some of Blake's other devotees).[23] Second, as one of those visitors noted, Blake worked primarily from Henry Francis Cary's unillustrated translation of Dante's text.[24] And third, Blake left a great deal of evidence in the images themselves that he was reacting directly to the *Commedia*.

Perhaps the clearest testimony to the directness of his responses is to be found in the inscriptions on some of the 96 unfinished illustrations, for in those remarks Blake addresses issues in the *Commedia* that were of particular concern to him, issues that are rarely, if ever, discussed in precisely the same way by other commentators. For example, in the first of two illustrations for *Inferno* 4, Blake complains: "Every thing in Dante's Comedia shews That for Tyrannical Purposes he has made This World the Foundation of All & the Goddess Nature & not the Holy Ghost."[25] On a diagram of Hell that may represent Virgil's *Inferno* 11 description of the underworld, Blake wrote at lower left, "It seems as if Dante's supreme Good was something Superior to the Father or Jesus; for if he gives his rain to the Evil & the Good, & his Sun to the Just & the Unjust, He could never have Built Dante's Hell, nor the Hell of the Bible neither, in the way our Parsons explain it--It must have been originally Formed by the devil Himself; & So I understand it to have been."[26] And in the lower right corner of that same illustration, he claims, "Whatever Book is for Vengeance for Sin & Whatever Book is Against the Forgiveness of Sins is not of the Father, but of

Satan the Accuser & Father of Hell."[27] Thus, rather than rely solely on a third party for insights on Dante's text, Blake seems to have reacted directly to the *Commedia* itself.

In fact, his illustrations often have a slightly different focus than that of earlier *Commedia* images. For example, Blake sometimes omits subjects covered by many or all of the illuminators, such as Dante's encounter with Brunetto Latini in *Inferno* 15, Dante and Virgil emerging from Hell in *Inferno* 34, Dante's encounter with the excommunicated in *Purgatorio* 3, the purgation of sin in *Purgatorio* 14 through 26, Dante's encounter with Matilda in *Purgatorio* 28, his arrival at Eunoe in *Purgatorio* 33, his ascent from the Earthly Paradise in *Paradiso* 1, and all but a handful of his other experiences in that last cantica. At other times, Blake depicts textual episodes that are not addressed by many, if any, of the illuminators, scenes such as Virgil and Dante entering the woods in *Inferno* 2, their escape from the demons in *Inferno* 23, their "laborious passage" in *Inferno* 24, Ugolino's narrative in *Inferno* 33, Virgil girding Dante's brow in *Purgatorio* 1, Lucy carrying Dante in *Purgatorio* 9, Virgil inviting Dante to enter the flames in *Purgatorio* 27, and the spiral stairway in *Paradiso* 10.[28] And, on occasion, Blake even invents subjects, as in supplementing the account of the thieves in *Inferno* 24 and 25 with an image of seven women attacked by serpents, and in having a wilting man at the beginning of *Inferno* 14 represent Dante's forlorn love of his native land. That is to say, Blake often departs from the standard subjects of the miniatures and sometimes even from the text to which he and the illuminators were supposedly responding.

Moreover, even on those occasions when Blake does fundamentally adhere to the *Commedia* and does depict the same subjects as do many of the illuminators, he often departs from the rhythm of the miniatures. For instance, while most of his pre-modern predecessors devote no more than two illustrations per canto to Dante's encounter with the peculators in *Inferno* 21 and 22, Blake expands in this case from two images per canto to four. In doing so, he slows the left-to-right momentum of his narrative by dwelling to an extraordinary degree on these sinners and their predicament. Indeed, he sometimes also slows the pace within this sequence of scenes by sprinkling distant views of the bolgia as a whole among close views of Dante's encounters with individual sinners or demons. And he occasionally slows the pace within a single scene by introducing right-to-left vectors, as in portraying a devil pulling Ciampolo's arm from the right while that sinner leans to the left in the second image of canto 22, and in depicting two demons flying directly towards each other from the lateral edges of the third image for canto 22. Thus, even when Blake illustrates the same general subjects as do the illuminators, he often departs so thoroughly and so idiosyncratically from their narrative timing—not to mention that of his other predecessors—as to suggest that, rather than look to them for a model, he relied on his own interpretation of Dante's text.

That reliance on the *Commedia* itself is also suggested by the unique contexts in which Blake sometimes locates his subjects. In the third illustration of *Inferno* 3, for example, he shows Charon in the tattered remains of an outfit that recalls those of early nineteenth-century British sailors, which departs from the letter of Dante's text but, in rendering this ferryman more familiar to Blake's early viewers, accords with Dante's implication that Charon awaits all sinners. In the second illustration of *Inferno* 5, Blake defines the swirl of the lustful with a thick black border that diminishes the three-dimensionality of the image but reinforces the relentlessness of these sinners' momentum and, in harmony with Dante's penal inversion of sin, separates those guilty of excessive intimacy from all of the other figures in the image. In the only illustration for *Inferno* 10, Blake depicts the sarcophagi of the arch-heretics not as vaults above ground but as subterranean chambers, as embedded tombs that suggest these sinners are particularly far from the possibility of redemption. In the second image of *Inferno* 21, Blake constructs the arch over the Lucchese peculators from giant human fragments that thereby embody the petrification of imagination, the ossification of a facility that Blake closely associates in his writing with all human hope for divine redemption.[29] In the first image of *Inferno* 33, Blake depicts Count Ugolino and Bishop Ruggieri in a small cave that departs from all preceding images of this scene but echoes the close confines of the tower in which, according to Dante, Ruggieri supposedly imprisoned Ugolino. And in the only illustrations for *Paradiso* 24 and 25, Blake departs from the miniatures by foregrounding Saints Peter and James against large color swirls that recall the cloak framing God in Michelangelo's *Creation of Adam*, that join Dante in honoring these holy figures to an extraordinary degree.

Yet, even when Blake locates his figures in contexts almost identical to those of the miniatures, he often distinguishes his compositions from those of the illuminators by presenting his scenes from a viewpoint that radically departs from theirs. For example, he shows Charon sailing towards, rather than parallel to, the foreground in the third illustration for *Inferno* 3; he shows Homer turned towards the viewer, rather than towards the side, in the first illustration for *Inferno* 4; he shows the rest of the pagans from a great distance, rather than close-up, in the second illustration for *Inferno* 4; he shows Virgil and Dante preparing to sail away from, rather than towards or lateral to, the viewer as they approach Dis in the fourth illustration for *Inferno* 7; he shows the Divine Messenger from the back, rather than from the side, as that figure opens the gate of Dis in the only illustration for *Inferno* 9; he shows the river of blood from between embankments, rather than from an unencumbered platform, in the second illustration for *Inferno* 12; he shows Jacopo Rusticucci and his companions swirling laterally, rather than into depth, in the only illustration for *Inferno* 16; he shows the hypocrites turning across Caiaphas, rather than marching solely towards or away from the viewer, as they approach from the left middle ground and depart in the left foreground of the second illustration for *Inferno* 23; he shows Vanni Fucci from the front, rather than from the side, in the first illustration for *Inferno* 25; he shows the primeval giants from the back, rather than from the front or side, in the first illustration for *Inferno* 31; he shows Virgil and Dante climbing away from, rather than perpendicular to, the viewer as they ascend to purgatory in the first illustration for *Purgatorio* 4; he shows the backs, rather than the front or sides, of Virgil, Dante, and Sordello as they gaze upon the valley of the negligent rulers in the only illustration for *Purgatorio* 8; he shows Virgil and Dante climbing away from, rather than lateral to, the viewer as they ascend in the second illustration for *Purgatorio* 10 and the first illustration for *Purgatorio* 27; and he shows the backs, rather than the sides, of Virgil and Dante as they gaze across the Lethe at Beatrice and Paradise in the first illustration for *Purgatorio* 30. Indeed, Blake departs so often from the viewpoints of the miniatures that he seems to have envisioned the *Commedia* from a very different imaginary as well as optical perspective than those of the illuminators.

Of course, that difference may at least to some degree have been deliberate—an intentional rejection or emendation of the illuminators' viewpoint(s). But the sheer number of Blake's departures from the perspective(s) of the miniatures militates against that possibility, as does the apparent irrelevance of many of those departures. Although the approach of Blake's Charon towards the viewer may be justified by Dante's implication that this ferryman comes for all whose sins have yet to be redeemed, there does not seem to be much textual basis for Blake's depiction of the pagans from a great distance in *Inferno* 4, his portrayal of the bloody river in *Inferno* 12 through a narrow gorge, or his depiction of the sodomites from the side in *Inferno* 16. Indeed, some of Blake's scenes would seem to be much farther removed from the spirit of Dante's text than are those of the illuminators. For instance, Blake's distant view of Virgil and Dante standing on a cliff in *Inferno* 4 and looking down from a great height on the virtuous pagans is much less passionate than either Dante's account of this episode or the many miniatures that show the pagans rushing towards their reunion with Virgil. And as the sides of Blake's gorge in *Inferno* 12 frame and seem to partially block the view of the river beyond them, they establish a sharp contrast to the immediacy of this scene in the text and in the many miniatures that depict the river from a close, unobstructed vantage point. Thus, at least some of Blake's illustrations suggest that he not only overlooked rather obvious aspects of Dante's text but was also ignorant of the many miniatures that capture those aspects, which were apparently more faithful than he to Dante's text.

Yet, on occasion, Blake's illustrations do, in fact, seem to echo pre-modern and/or early modern images of the *Commedia*. For example, the faces and proportions of the leopard, lion, and wolf in Blake's illustration of *Inferno* I are exaggerated in some of the same ways as are those of their counterparts in one or more of the miniatures. That is to say, Blake's wolf has the same extremely pointy snout as the wolf in Biblioteca Civica Gambalunga MS 4.I.II.25, Bodleian MS Canoniciani italiani 109, Biblioteca Nacional MS Vitrina 23.1, Budapest Universitätsbibliothek MS Ital. I, and Biblioteca Riccardiana MS 1035, as well as the same grotesquely pendulous breasts as the wolf in Musée Condé MS 597, British Library MS Egerton 943, Bodleian MS Holkham Miscellanae 48, Vatican MS Barberiniani latini 4112, Laurenziana MS Strozziani 148, Biblioteca Angelica MS 1102, Biblioteca Nazionale Centrale MS Palatini 320, and Bibliothèque Nationale MS italien 2017; Blake's lion joins the Musée Condé, Holkham, Angelica, Strozziani 148, Vitrina, and Riccardiana examples, as well as those in Laurenziana MS Plutei 40.3, Bodmer Library MS 247, British Library MS Additional 19587, Bibliothèque Nationale MS italien 78, and British Library MS Yates Thompson 36, in having a muzzle as short as that of a housecat, and joins the lion of Musée Condé MS 597, Plutei 40.3, and Bibliothèque Nationale MS italien 78 in having a smile as cute as a Disney character; and all three of Blake's beasts have the same unnaturally large, round eyes as do their counterparts in Angelica MS 1102 and Laurenziana MS Conventi Soppressi 204. Moreover, Blake's Cerberus in *Inferno* 6 has such thoroughly canine features as to recall the manner in which many illuminators depart from depicting that beast as a traditional demon; Blake's zoomorphic Geryon in *Inferno* 17 has the same parts, proportions, and texture as its counterpart in many of the miniatures; and Blake's Lucifer in *Inferno* 34 has the same configuration for his three heads as he does in most miniatures of that canto.

Nonetheless, as medieval as the faces and proportions of Blake's monsters are, they may not invoke the miniatures as thoroughly, or as often, as do the poses and locations of his figures. Like the leopard, lion, and wolf in the opening Gambalunga illustration for the *Inferno* and in the opening images for many of the other extant *Commedia* manuscripts, the three beasts who greet Dante in Blake's illustration of *Inferno* 1 are stacked on a sunny hillside at right. Like the figure of Dante in most of those miniatures, Blake's figure of the poet flees at left and to the left from the three beasts. Like Virgil in the first Musée Condé illustration of the *Inferno*, Blake's *Inferno* 1 figure of him awaits Dante at left with open arms. Like Virgil and Dante in the Biblioteca Trivulziana MS 2263 illustration of *Inferno* 5, Blake's protagonists approach a frontal, seated figure of Minos from the left. Like Virgil and Dante in the Strozziani 152 illustration of *Inferno* 17, Blake's protagonists approach three seated usurers from the left. Like Virgil and Dante in the Biblioteca Nazionale Centrale MS Palatini 313 illustration of *Inferno* 28, Blake's protagonists gaze from the left on a phalanx of instigators displaying their wounds. Like Satan in the Musée Condé illustration of *Inferno* 34, Blake's Lucifer turns his torso and middle head towards the viewer while looking to the left and right, respectively, with his flanking heads. Like Dante in the Yates Thompson illustration of *Purgatorio* 9, Blake's protagonist kneels in front of the angel guarding Purgatory. Like the envious in the additional illustration of *Purgatorio* 13, Blake's figures of them form a phalanx. And like the Queen of Heaven in the Holkham and Yates Thompson illustrations of *Paradiso* 31 and 32, Blake's figure of her appears in the upper petal of a rose tilted towards the viewer.

Yet despite the close proximity and great number of Blake's parallels to the miniatures, all of those apparent echoes can be ascribed to common denominators in the circumstances from which the images emerged rather than to imitation. With regard to the illustration of *Inferno* 1, for example, Blake and the illuminators bring somewhat overlapping backgrounds in Western cultural traditions to an extraordinarily detailed passage in the *Commedia*. Dante specifies that the Pilgrim comes from a forest to the foot of a hill whose shoulders are "clad in the rays of the planet that leads men aright by every path" (*Inf.* 1.17-18) and on which the Pilgrim encounters three beasts in the same order as they are depicted from bottom to top in Blake's illustration and in many of the miniatures. The third of these three animals, a she-wolf, then drives the Pilgrim back to the valley at the base of the hill, where he runs into Virgil. Indeed, that is the moment shown by Blake and many of the illuminators: Dante, having advanced from left to right in accord with the reading habits of Western viewers, now flees from the beasts towards the figure of Virgil, who awaits him on the left side of the illustration.[30] Of course, the Pilgrim's deep strides in Blake's image and in many of the miniatures depart from Dante's description of his protagonist's retreat as unfolding "little by little" (*Inf.* 1.59), but it embodies the fear and despair that were supposedly so great as to outweigh the Pilgrim's exceptional eagerness to advance up the hill. Likewise, though the smile on Blake's lion and the general resemblance of his three beasts to stuffed toys may seem incongruous with the Pilgrim's reaction to these creatures, their features, like the overtly naïve features of the three beasts in some of the miniatures, may be an attempt to distinguish the comparatively benign leopard, lion, and wolf from the far more infernal monsters to come. Thus, Blake's parallels to the miniatures may be explained to a great degree by the fact that he and the illuminators brought many parallels and continuities in cultural context to the same text.

Of course, some of the similarities between Blake's work and the miniatures may also be sheer coincidence. But even when Dante does not give enough detail to ensure identical responses from all *Commedia* illustrators, he often restricts the range of reasonable variations so severely as to foster multiple points of contact between the artists, and he sometimes privileges one option to such a degree that he virtually guarantees most illustrators will pursue it over all others. For example, Dante does not explicitly call Cerberus a dog, and he assigns rather generic features to this beast, such as red eyes and a greasy beard (*Inf.* 6.16). Nonetheless, at the same time he also indirectly foregrounds Cerberus's traditional identity as a hell hound, for he notes that the monster barks "doglike" (*Inf.* 6.14) over the gluttonous, and, in describing the reaction of Cerberus to the clods of earth that Virgil throws down the monster's throats, he compares him to a dog that "barking craves, and then grows quiet when he snaps up his food" (*Inf.* 6.28-29). Indeed, Dante even invokes dogs in discussing the souls under Cerberus's dominion, for he notes that the rain falling on the gluttonous makes them "howl like dogs" (*Inf.* 6.19). Thus, despite the fact that Dante refers to Cerberus as a "demon" (*Inf.* 6.32), it is hardly surprising that Blake and many of the illuminators depict the "foul faces" (*Inf.* 6.31) of this beast as those of a dog rather than those of a conventional devil.

Nor should it be surprising that Blake's Geryon shares its particular zoomorphism with many images of this monster in the miniatures, for Dante specifies that this beast had "the face of a just man, so benign was its outward aspect, and all his trunk was that of a serpent; he had two paws, hairy to the armpits" (*Inf.* 17.10-13), while "his back and breast and both his sides were painted with knots and circlets" (*Inf.* 17.14-15), and he had a tail with a venomous fork that had the point "armed like a scorpion's" (*Inf.* 17.27). What is surprising, however, is the consistency with which Blake and many of the illuminators interpret the unmentioned details and proportions of those parts. Blake ignores the forked aspect of the tail but joins the Musée Condé artist and many of the other miniaturists in depicting the beast's head as that of a youth with long hair. Moreover, like the Angelica illuminator and some of the other miniaturists, Blake depicts Geryon with a ridge of bumps resembling vertebrae, and, like the artist of Vatican MS Vaticani latini 4776 and some of the other illuminators, he gives Geryon's body a small, atextual coil.

Of course, many of these parallels are indirectly invited by the parts of animals to which Dante compares Geryon's components. As suggested by the selectivity of the pre-modern examples to which I compared the components of Blake's Geryon, as well as by my qualifiers in discussing those examples, few of the miniatures invoke every major aspect of Blake's image, for Dante does not provide enough detail to ensure that all artists will produce identical images of Geryon. But the poet does provide enough specificity in his description of that beast to limit reasonable extrapolation from his account and to concomitantly foster many parallels that might otherwise be ascribed to imitation or coincidence.

Those same constraints, as well as the sheer number of illuminators who addressed Dante's text, may also explain why Blake's portrayal of Lucifer's head(s) parallels that in many miniatures of *Inferno* 34. Though some of the illuminators, like some modern *Commedia* artists, depict the Devil with three faces joined on one orb, Dante specifies that, despite the heads being fused "at the crown" (*Inf.* 34.42) and "just over the middle of each shoulder" (*Inf.*

34.41), the faces were independent, for he claims that the Devil had six eyes, three chins, and three mouths (*Inf.* 34.53-57). In fact, he even specifies that those six eyes were weeping (*Inf.* 6.53), those three chins dripped "tears and bloody foam" (*Inf.* 34. 54), and those three mouths each chewed a sinner "as with a heckle" (*Inf.* 34.56). Thus, it should not be surprising that Blake came to the same configuration for the Devil's head as did most of the illuminators.

Far less likely, based on Dante's text alone, are the parallels in portraying Lucifer's pose and location. Though the *Commedia* specifies that the Devil is immersed in ice to mid-breast (*Inf.* 34.29), that the narrator "in size compare(s) better with a giant than giants with (Lucifer's) arms" (*Inf.* 34.30-31), and that the Devil has shaggy flanks (*Inf.* 34.73) as well as six bat-like wings (*Inf.* 34.46-50), Dante does not explicitly describe Lucifer's position relative to the narrator/viewer. That is to say, he does not provide grounds on which to explain the frontality and centering of the Devil in both Blake's illustration and 7 of the 17 extant miniatures for *Inferno* 34. But, of course, these properties are in full agreement with the conventions of Western art during both Blake's era and that of the illuminators. In fact, they are in agreement with widespread conventions for art as a whole. As Rudolph Arnheim has noted, "the power of the center" dominates works by even the most remote cultures.[31] Too, as many other scholars have observed, isolated figures of great power are often turned directly towards the viewer. Thus, it would seem that Blake and many of the illuminators were led to similar compositions in this instance by parallels in the modes of perception that they brought to Dante's text, by cultural or anthropological common denominators that conditioned these iconic depictions of the Devil.

Indeed, those common denominators and others similar to them seem to have steered Blake and the illuminators towards many of the other compositional parallels mentioned above. For example, in depicting Minos seated on an elevated throne, Blake and some of the illuminators invoke conventions that depart from Dante's description of Minos as standing (*Inf.* 5.4) but accord with the author's privileging of Minos as a messenger of punishments for the other sinners. Although Dante does not describe the position of the usurers beyond noting that they were seated on the ground (*Inf.* 17.45), presumably Western tendencies to depict narratives unfolding from left to right like a line of text and the nearly universal tendency to center the main subject of an image led both Blake and many of the illuminators to depict these sinners in the middle of the image, arranged from left to right in the same order as that described by Dante, and being approached from the left by the protagonists. Of course, in the first of Blake's two images of the instigators, he may seem to depart from his tendency to center the main subject of a scene, as he locates Virgil and Dante, rather than the instigators, in the middle of the illustration. Yet, in this case the horror of the Pilgrim is central to the spirit and theme of a canto in which the sinners graphically display their wounds (*Inf.* 28.22-142), and in the rest of Blake's illustrations the protagonists almost invariably return to the left side of the image and cede its center to other figures.

In fact, as *Purgatorio* and *Paradiso* unfold, artistic conventions play an increasingly important role in Blake's illustrations and in the miniatures, for Dante's text becomes ever more ambiguous. By gradually shifting from detailed descriptions of familiar subjects towards generalizations about, and elusive metaphors for, ever more abstract and hypothetical ideas, Dante increasingly forces illustrators to seek inspiration outside of the *Commedia* itself. Some of the illuminators, therefore, base their illustrations to an ever greater degree on earlier miniatures of his text. Yet, like Blake, many of the illuminators seem to have increasingly sought help, not from specific images but from general workshop practices and broad artistic conventions. For example, they translate the Pilgrim's myriad experiences with the rather abstract spirits of *Paradiso* into a series of figural encounters along the same left-to-right vector which dominates many other pre-modern images. Moreover, they tend to reserve each illustration of *Purgatorio* and *Paradiso* for just one episode. And, within each image of the last two cantiche, they almost always center the souls encountered by the Pilgrim. Thus, *Purgatorio* and *Paradiso* are reduced to a pictorial formula that favors clarity over originality, that privileges legibility over transcription.

Of course, in these attempts to maximize viewer comprehension of the images, Blake and the illuminators approach each other more completely and, relative to the narrative, more enduringly than they do in their illustrations of the *Inferno*. Even so, in the very breadth of these parallels, Blake and the illuminators simultaneously underscore the probability that, at least in these instances, they were not borrowing from each other's work, but that these parallels originated in similar responses to similar circumstances. Moreover, as these broad parallels wax in synchronicity with the growing ambiguity of Dante's text, and in an inverse relationship to the wane of specific parallels between Blake's work and that of the illuminators, they underscore the likelihood that those earlier parallels derive directly from the comparatively greater detail in the *Inferno* and at the start of *Purgatorio*. Thus, all of the similarities between Blake's work and that of the miniaturists would seem to originate in shared contexts of production, in either Dante's text or the experiences and demands that the artists brought to it.

Blake's *Commedia* illustrations, therefore, do not support the possibility that the present can influence the past. Indeed, given the pictorial and historical evidence that he was not directly acquainted with any of the *Commedia* miniatures or their early offshoots, his drawings and engravings do not even join other illustrations in suggesting that those miniatures and their early offshoots influenced modern *Commedia* images. Yet, even as Blake's illustrations resist the possibility that they arose from direct artistic influence between his work and that of the illuminators, they embody another form of timelessness, for in their common denominators with the miniatures, they throw a bridge across the centuries. They rise above the relentless flow of time and demonstrate the potential durability of at least some artistic conventions, perceptual habits, and human tendencies.

TOWSON UNIVERSITY

NOTES

[1] An earlier version of this paper was delivered at the Twentieth Annual International Conference on Medievalism, October 14, 2005 at Towson University in Towson, Maryland.

[2] "*Commedia* Images in the Neo-Gothic Age(s)," *Studies in Medievalism* XIV (2005), 175-99.

[3] "Defining Medievalism in Nineteenth-Century *Commedia* Illustrations," *Medievalism: The Year's Work for 2004* XIX (forthcoming).

[4] "Robert Rauschenberg's *Inferno* Illuminations," *Studies in Medievalism* XIII (2004), 47-66.

[5] "Modern Artistic Responses to Pre-Modern Miniatures of the *Divine Comedy*," *Medievalism: The Year's Work for 2001* XVI (2002), 85-106.

[6] For more on time and its "arrow," begin with *The Philosophy of Time*, ed. R. Le Poidevin and M. Macbeath (Oxford: Oxford UP, 1993); S. F. Savitt, ed., *Time's Arrow Today* (Cambridge: Cambridge UP, 1995); and Brian Greene, *The Fabric of the Cosmos: Space, Time, and the Texture of Reality* (New York: Random House, 2004), esp. chap. 6: "Chance and the Arrow: Does Time Have a Direction," 143-76. For more on backward causation in particular, begin with Savitt; Michael Dummett, "Can an Effect Precede its Cause?" and "Bringing about the Past" in his *Truth and Other Enigmas* (Cambridge, MA: Harvard UP, 1978); and M. Chown, "Unwrite This," *New Scientist CLIV* (November 27, 1999), 11. For related discussions about reversing the arrow of time, see the following studies on time travel: P. Horwich, *Asymmetries in Time* (Cambridge, MA: MIT Press, 1987); J. Richard Gott III, *Time Travel in Einstein's Universe: The Physical Possibilities of Travel through Time* (Boston and New York: Houghton Mifflin, 2002), esp. 192-99; and Jenny Randles, *Breaking the Time Barrier: The Race to Build the First Time Machine* (New York: Simon and Schuster, 2005), esp. 213-23.

[7] Among the most well-known and perhaps least condescending rebuttals is Stephen Hawking's discussion of the arrow of time on pages 149 to 157 of *A Brief History of Time* (New York: Bantam, 1988; rev. ed. 1996).

[8] For more on Botticelli's sources and the relationship between his drawings and the designs for Baldini's engravings, see Barbara J. Watts, "Sandro Botticelli's Illustrations for *Inferno* VIII and IX: Narrative Revision and the Role of Manuscript Tradition," *Word & Image* XI (April-June, 1995), 149-73.

[9] For reproductions of Botticelli's drawing, Baldini's engraving, and the Strozziani miniature, see Watts. For the most recent reproductions of all of Botticelli's *Commedia*

drawings and the most recent general introduction to them, see H. Schulze Altcappenberg, *Sandro Botticelli: The Drawings for Dante's "Divine Comedy"* (London: Royal Academy of Arts, 2000). See also Kenneth Clark's dated but still useful introduction to *The Drawings by Sandro Botticelli for Dante's "Divine Comedy"* (New York: Harper and Row, 1976). For another reproduction of the Strozziani miniature and, unless otherwise noted, for reproductions of all the other miniatures mentioned in my paper, see volume two of *Illuminated Manuscripts of the "Divine Comedy"*, ed. Peter Brieger, Millard Meiss, and Charles Singleton, 2 vols. (Princeton: Princeton UP, 1969). Also note that unless otherwise stated, all of my attributions for the miniatures derive from the catalogue by Brieger and Meiss in *Illuminated Manuscripts of the "Divine Comedy"*, I, 209-339. For a catalogue of almost all known *Commedia* manuscripts, see Marcella Roddewig, *Dante Alighieri, "Die göttliche Komödie": Vergleichende Bestandsaufnahme der "Commedia"-Handschriften* (Stuttgart: A. Hiersemann, 1984).

[10] These 87 woodcuts were initially published in Venice by Francesco Marcolini and were reprinted there by G. Marchio Sessa e fratelli. For a selection of them, see Eugene Paul Nassar, *Illustrations to Dante's "Inferno"* (Rutherford, NJ: Fairleigh Dickinson UP, 1994; and London and Toronto: Associated University Presses, 1994). For the woodcut of *Inferno* XII in particular, see page 162 of Nassar.

[11] For more on the post-Renaissance popularity of the *Commedia*, see Nassar's introduction, esp. p. 17; Dino Mattalìa, "Dante Alighieri," in *I classici italiani nell storia della critica*, ed. Walter Binni, 3 vols. (Florence: L. S. Olschki, 1954), I, 3-93; Siro A. Chimenz, "Dante," in *Letteratura italiana*, I Maggiori (Milan: Carlo Marzorati, 1956), 70-103; and Michael Caesar, ed., *Dante: The Critical Heritage 1314 (?)-1870* (New York and London: Routledge, 1989).

[12] For a reproduction of Giraldi's illustration, see Brieger and Meiss, II, pl. 78 or Nassar, p. 79. For a reproduction of the Venetian print, see Nassar, p. 82.

[13] For more on the Vatican manuscript and its provenance, see Luigi Michelini Tocci, *Il Dante urbinate della Biblioteca vatican*, 2 vols., Codices e Vaticanis selecti phototypice espressi XXIX (Vatican City: Biblioteca Apostolica Vaticana, 1965).

[14] Note that "Sofia Giacomelli" was the pseudonym for Madame Chomel, whose illustrations were reproduced in 1813 by the Parisian publisher Salmon.

[15] For Macchiavelli's reproductions see the *Commedia* published in 1819-21 by the Bolognese firm Gamberini & Parmeggiani.

[16] For the location and provenance of all known *Commedia* manuscripts, including those currently or once in England, see Roddewig.

[17] Ibid.

[18] For a slightly dated but highly accessible introduction to Blake and the vast literature on his life, particularly as it relates to his art, see Kathleen Raine's *William Blake* (London: Thames and Hudson, 1970; repr. 1988).

[19] Ibid. For more detail on the commissioning and execution of Blake's *Commedia* illustrations, see *Blake e Dante*, ed. Corrado Gizzi (Milan: G. Mazzotta, 1983); David Fuller, "Blake and Dante," *Art History* XI (1983); and the introductions to the following: A. S. Roe, *Blake's Illustrations to the "Divine Comedy"* (Princeton: Princeton UP, 1953); Ursula Hoff, *William Blake's Illustrations to Dante's "Divine Comedy"* (Victoria, Australia: National Gallery of Victoria, 1961); Milton Klonsky, *Blake's Dante* (New York: Harmony Books, 1980); and David Bindman, *"The Divine Comedy": William Blake* (Paris: Bibliothèque

de l'Image, 2000). For the clearest and most accessible color reproductions of Blake's illustrations, see Bindman.

[20] As noted by Roe (p. 30), who is building on observations by Paget Toynbee in "The Earliest English Illustrators of Dante," *Quarterly Review* CCXI (1909), 399-409; and in "Dante in English Art," *38ᵗʰ Annual Report of the Dante Society* (Cambridge, MA: Dante Society of America, 1919), 2-3.

[21] For more on the *Commedia* aspects of Michelangelo's *Last Judgment*, see Charles de Tolnay, *Michelangelo: V. The Final Period* (Princeton: Princeton UP, 1960), esp. 28, 42, 104-108; Leo Steinberg, "A Corner of the *Last Judgment*," *Daedalus* CIX (1980), 207-73; and Bernadine Barnes, "Metaphorical Painting: Michelangelo, Dante, and the *Last Judgment*," *The Art Bulletin* LXXVII (1995), 64-81.

[22] For more on Flaxman's illustrations begin with Kenneth MacKenzie's introduction to *The Divine Comedy* (London: Folio Society, 1979); Corrado Gizzi's *Flaxman e Dante* (Milan: Mazzotta, 1986); and Francesca Salvadori's discussion in *The Illustrations for Dante's "Divine Comedy"* (London: Royal Academy of Arts, and New York: Harry N. Abrams, 2005), which was translated in that year from *Dante: la "Divina commedia" illustrata da Flaxman* (Milan: Electa, 2004). For more on Fuseli's illustrations, begin with Corrado Gizzi's exhibition catalogue *Füssli e Dante* (Milan: Mazzotta, 1985); and Luke Herrmann's *Nineteenth-Century British Painting* (London: Giles de la Mare, 2000)

[23] For the most detailed account of Blake's social life while he worked on the *Commedia* illustrations, see Roe's introduction, esp. 3-4.

[24] The visitor was Henry Crabb Robinson, and the visits during which he noted Blake's use of Cary's translation are described in entries for Saturday, December 17, 1825 and Friday, February 2, 1827 in the *Diary, Reminiscences, and Correspondence of Henry Crabb Robinson*, ed. Thomas Sadler, 2 vols. (Boston: Fields, Osgood, 1869; 3ʳᵈ ed. repr. New York: AMS Press, 1967), II, 28-30, 74, respectively.

[25] Figure 7, page 33 in Bindman.

[26] Figure 22, page 63 in Bindman.

[27] Ibid.

[28] All quotations of the *Commedia* are from Charles Singleton's three-volume translation (Princeton: Princeton UP, 1970-75) of Giorgio Petrocchi's four-volume edition from 1966-68 (Milan: Mondadori).

[29] This interpretation of the human fragments is grounded in Roe's discussion (90) of a similar bridge in one of Blake's illustrations for *Inferno* 18.

[30] On the correlation between Western reading habits and the tendency for Western artists, especially illuminators, to portray narratives unfolding from left to right, see Meyer Schapiro's classic essay "On Some Problems in the Semiotics of Visual Art: Field and Vehicle in Image-Signs," *Semiotica* I (1969), 223-42.

[31] See Arnheim's *The Power of the Center: A Study of Composition in the Visual Arts* (Berkeley: U. of California P, 1982).